HAMMOND

ODYSSEY WORLD ATLAS

Contents

Revised 2002 Edition

LIBRARY OF CONGRESS
CATALOGING-IN-PUBLICATION DATA

Hammond World Atlas Corporation.
  Hammond odyssey world atlas
    p. cm.
  Rev. ed. of Hammond odyssey atlas of the world/
Hammond Incorporated
    Includes indexes.
    ISBN 0–8437–1477–0 (pbk.)
    1. Atlases. I. Hammond Incorporated.
Hammond odyssey atlas of the world.
II Title. III.Title: Odyssey world atlas
  Odyssey atlas of the world.
  G1021.H27447   1999   <G&M>
  912—dc21   99–34155
                              CIP
                         MAPS

Map Projections

Simply stated, the map-maker's challenge is to project the earth's curved surface onto a flat plane. To achieve this elusive goal, cartographers have developed map projections — equations which govern this conversion of geographic data.

This section explores some of the most widely used projections. It also introduces a new projection, the Hammond Optimal Conformal.

GENERAL PRINCIPLES AND TERMS

The earth rotates around its axis once a day. Its end points are the North and South poles; the line circling the earth midway between the poles is the equator. The arc from the equator to either pole is divided into 90 degrees of latitude. The equator represents 0° latitude. Circles of equal latitude, called parallels, are traditionally shown at every fifth or tenth degree.

The equator is divided into 360 degrees. Lines circling the globe from pole to pole through the degree points on the equator are called meridians, or great circles. All meridians are equal in length, but by international agreement the meridian passing through the Greenwich Observatory near London has been chosen as the prime meridian or 0° longitude. The distance in degrees from the prime meridian to any point east or west is its longitude.

While meridians are all equal in length, parallels become shorter as they approach the poles. Whereas one degree of latitude represents approximately 69 miles (112 km.) anywhere on the globe, a degree of longitude varies from 69 miles (112 km.) at the equator to zero at the poles. Each degree of latitude and longitude is divided into 60 minutes. One minute of latitude equals one nautical mile (1.15 land miles or 1.85 km.).

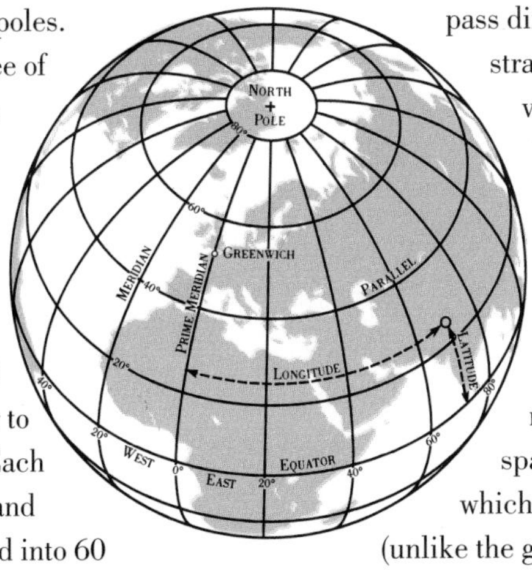

HOW TO FLATTEN A SPHERE: THE ART OF CONTROLLING DISTORTION

There is only one way to represent a sphere with absolute precision: on a globe. All attempts to project our planet's surface onto a plane unevenly stretch or tear the sphere as it flattens, inevitably distorting shapes, distances, area (sizes appear larger or smaller than actual size), angles or direction.

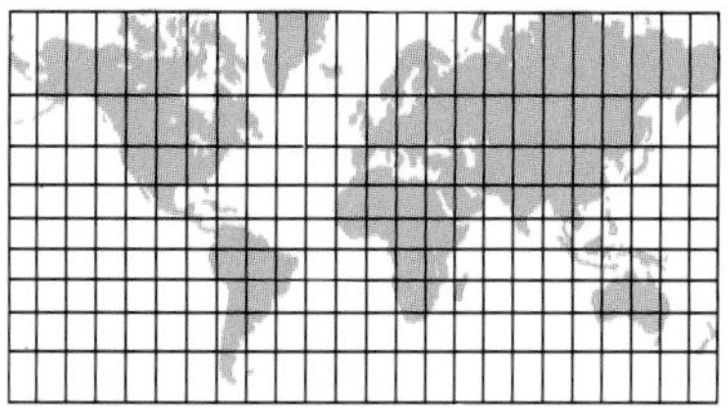

Since representing a sphere on a flat plane always creates distortion, only the parallels or the meridians (or some other set of

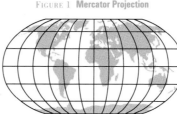

FIGURE 1 Mercator Projection

FIGURE 2 Robinson Projection

lines) can maintain the same length as on a globe of corresponding scale. All other lines must be either too long or too short. Accordingly, the scale on a flat map cannot be true everywhere; there will always be different scales in different parts of a map. On world maps or very large areas, variations in scale may be extreme. Most maps seek to preserve either true area relationships (equal area projections) or true angles and shapes (conformal projections); some attempt to achieve overall balance.

PROJECTIONS: SELECTED EXAMPLES

Mercator (Fig. 1): This projection is especially useful because all compass directions appear as straight lines, making it a valuable navigational tool. Moreover, every small region conforms to its shape on a globe — hence the name conformal. But because its meridians are evenly-spaced vertical lines which never converge (unlike the globe), the horizontal parallels must be drawn farther and farther apart at higher latitudes to maintain a correct relationship.

Only the equator is true to scale, and the size of areas in the higher latitudes is dramatically distorted.

Robinson (Fig. 2): To create the two-page world map in the Maps of the World section, the Robinson projection was used. It combines elements of both conformal and equal area projections to show the whole earth with relatively true shapes and reasonably equal areas.

Conic (Fig. 3): This projection has been used frequently for air navigation charts and to create most of the national and regional maps in this atlas. (See text in margin at right).

HAMMOND OPTIMAL CONFORMAL

As its name implies, this new conformal projection (Fig. 4) presents the optimal view of an area by reducing shifts in scale over an entire region to the minimum degree possible. While conformal maps generally preserve all small shapes, large shapes can become very distorted because of varying scales, causing considerable inaccuracy in distance measurements. The concept underlying the Optimal Conformal is that for any region on the globe, there is an ideal projection for which scale variation can be made as small as possible. Consequently, unlike other projections, the Optimal Conformal does not use one standard formula to construct a map. Each map is a unique projection — the optimal projection for that particular area.

After a cartographer defines the subject area, a sophisticated computer program evaluates the size and shape of the region, projecting the most distortion-free map possible. All of the continent maps in this atlas, except Antarctica, have been drawn using the Optimal projection.

FIGURE 3
Conic Projection

The original idea of a conic projection is to cap the globe with a cone, and then project onto the cone from the planet's center the lines of latitude and longitude (the parallels and meridians). To produce a working map, the cone is simply cut open and laid flat. The conic projection used here is a modification of this idea. A cone can be made tangent to any standard parallel you choose. One popular version of a conic projection, the Lambert Conformal Conic, uses two standard parallels near the top and bottom of the map to further reduce errors of scale.

FIGURE 4
Hammond Optimal Conformal Projection

Like all conformal maps, the Optimal projection preserves angles exactly and minimizes distortion in shapes. This projection is more successful than any previous projection at spreading curvature across the entire map, producing the most distortion-free map possible.

Using This Atlas

How to Locate Information Quickly

This atlas is organized by continent. If you're looking for a major region of the world, consult the Contents on page two.

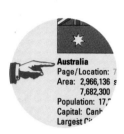

Australia
Page/Location: 7
Area: 2,966,136 s
        7,682,300
Population: 17,7
Capital: Canb
Largest C'

World Reference Guide

This concise guide lists the countries of the world alphabetically. If you're looking for the largest scale map of any country, you'll find a page and alpha-numeric reference at a glance, as well as information about each country, including its flag.

Anguilla (isl.), U.
/D6 **Ankara** (cap.), Turk
55/G3 **Ann** (cape), Ma,US
40/G1 **Annaba**, Alg.
32/C3 **An Nafūd** (des.), SAr.
32/D2 **An Najaf**, Iraq
35/J4 **Annamitique** (mts.),
        Laos, Viet.
54/E4 **Annapolis** (cap.),
        Md,US
34/D2 **Annapurna** (mtn.),
        Nepal
        Ann Arbor, Mi.US

Master Index

When you're looking for a specific place or physical feature, your quickest route is the Master Index. This 7,000-entry alphabetical index lists both the page number and alpha-numeric reference for major places and features in the world.

T his new atlas is created from a unique digital database, and its computer-generated maps represent a new phase in map-making technology.

How Computer-Generated Maps Are Made

To build a digital database capable of generating this world atlas, the latitude and longitude of every significant town, river, coastline, boundary, transportation network and peak elevation was researched and digitized. Hundreds of millions of data points describing every important geographic feature are organized into thousands of different map feature codes.

There are no maps in this unique system. Rather, it consists entirely of coded points, lines and polygons. To create a map, cartographers simply determine what specific information they wish to show, based upon considerations of scale, size, density and importance of different features.

New technology developed by Hammond describes and re-configures coastlines, borders and other linework to fit a variety of map scales and projections. A computerized type placement program allows thousands of map labels to be placed accurately in minutes.

This atlas has been designed to be both easy and enjoyable to use. Familiarizing yourself with its organization will help you to benefit fully from its use.

World Flags and Reference Guide

This colorful section portrays each nation of the world, its flag, important geographical data, such as size, population and capital, and its location in the atlas.

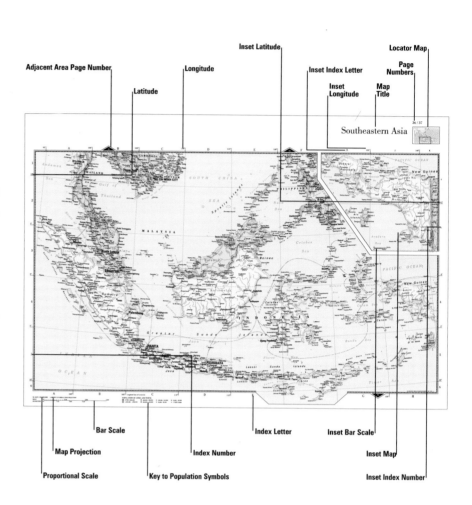

Adjacent Area Page Number · Inset Latitude · Longitude · Inset Index Letter · Locator Map · Page Numbers · Latitude · Inset Longitude · Map Title · Southeastern Asia

Bar Scale · Index Letter · Inset Bar Scale · Map Projection · Index Number · Inset Map · Proportional Scale · Key to Population Symbols · Inset Index Number

Symbols Used on Maps of the World

—·—··— First Order (National) Boundary	City and Urban Area Limits	*Rome* First Order (National) Capital
—··—··— First Order Water Boundary	Demilitarized Zone	*Belfast* Second Order (Internal) Capital
— — — First Order Disputed Boundary	National Park/Preserve/Scenic Area	*Hull* Third Order (Internal) Capital
—·—·— Second Order (Internal) Boundary	National Forest/Forest Reserve	□ Neighborhood
——·—— Second Order Water Boundary	National Wilderness/Grassland	⤝ Pass
———— Third Order (Internal) Boundary	National Recreation Area/Monument	Ruins
·········· Undefined Boundary	National Seashore/Lakeshore	Falls
———— International Date Line	National Wildlife/Wilderness Area	✳ Rapids
———— Shoreline, River	Native Reservation/Reserve	● Dam
———— Intermittent River	Military/Government Reservation	▲ Point Elevation
········· Canal/Aqueduct	Lake, Reservoir	⚘ Park
·········· Continental Divide	Intermittent Lake	✗ Wildlife Area
———— Highways	Dry Lake	■ Point of Interest
———— Roads	Salt Pan	⚲ Well
———— Railroads	Desert/Sand Area	✈ International Airport
········· Ferries	Swamp	✛ Other Airport
········· Tunnels (Road, Railroad)	Lava Flow	⊗ Air Base
▯▯▯▯ Ancient Walls	Glacier	⊘ Naval Base

Point of Interest

National Park

Mountain Peak

Air Base

Desert / Sand Area

Dry Lake

Lake

Dam

River

National Recreation Area

Intermittent River

International Airport

Other Airport

City / Urban Area

2nd Order (Internal) Boundary

1st Order (National) Boundary

Railroad

Principal Highway

PHYSICAL MAPS

The topography (relief) as well as the linework, colors and type for the continents and ocean floors is computer-generated and presents the relationships of land and sea forms with startling realism.

MAPS OF THE WORLD

These detailed regional maps are arranged by continent and introduced by physical and political maps of that continent which utilize Hammond's new Optimal Conformal projection.

On the regional maps, individual colors for each country highlight political divisions. A country's color remains the same on all regional maps. These maps also provide considerable information by locating numerous political and physical geographic features.

MASTER INDEX

This is an A-Z listing of names found on the political maps. It also has its own abbreviation list which, along with other Index keys, appears on page 65.

MAP SCALES

A map's scale is the relationship of any length on the map to an identical length on the earth's surface. A scale of 1:3,000,000 means that one inch on the map represents 3,000,000 inches (47 miles, 76 km.) on the earth's surface. A 1:1,000,000 scale (1/1) is larger than a 1:3,000,000 scale (1/3).

In this atlas, regional maps in Europe and North America are shown at scales of 1:7,000,000 and 1:10,500,000; Asia 1:10,500,000; South America 1:15,000,000; Africa 1:17,500,000; Australia 1:19,400,000.

In addition to these fractional scales, each map is accompanied by a linear scale for measuring distances (in miles and kilometers) on the map.

Boundary Policies
This atlas observes the boundary policies of the U.S. Department of State. Boundary disputes are customarily handled with a special symbol treatment, but de facto boundaries are favored if they seem to have any degree of permanence, in the belief that boundaries should reflect current geographic and political realities. The portrayal of independent nations in the atlas follows their recognition by the United Nations and/or the United States government.

Hammond also uses accepted conventional names for certain major foreign places. Usually, space permits the inclusion of the local form in parentheses. To make the maps more readily understandable to English-speaking readers, many foreign physical features are translated into more recognizable English forms.

A Word About Names
Our source for all foreign names and physical names in the United States is the decision lists of the U.S. Board of Geographic Names, which contain hundreds of thousands of place names. If a place is not listed, the Atlas follows the name form appearing on official foreign maps or in official gazetteers of the country concerned. For rendering domestic city, town and village names, this atlas follows the forms and spelling of the U.S. Postal Service.

PRINCIPAL MAP ABBREVIATIONS

ABOR. RSV.	ABORIGINAL RESERVE	IND. RES.	INDIAN RESERVATION	NWR	NATIONAL WILDLIFE RESERVE
ADMIN.	ADMINISTRATION	INT'L	INTERNATIONAL		
AFB	AIR FORCE BASE	IR	INDIAN RESERVATION	OBL.	OBLAST
AMM. DEP.	AMMUNITION DEPOT	ISTH.	ISTHMUS	OCC.	OCCUPIED
ARCH.	ARCHIPELAGO	JCT.	JUNCTION	OKR.	OKRUG
ARPT.	AIRPORT	L.	LAKE	PAR.	PARISH
AUT.	AUTONOMOUS	LAG.	LAGOON	PASSG.	PASSAGE
B.	BAY	LAKESH.	LAKESHORE	PEN.	PENINSULA
BFLD.	BATTLEFIELD	MEM.	MEMORIAL	PK.	PEAK
BK.	BROOK	MIL.	MILITARY	PLAT.	PLATEAU
BOR.	BOROUGH	MISS.	MISSILE	PN	PARK NATIONAL
BR.	BRANCH	MON.	MONUMENT	PREF.	PREFECTURE
C.	CAPE	MT.	MOUNT	PROM.	PROMONTORY
CAN.	CANAL	MTN.	MOUNTAIN	PROV.	PROVINCE
CAP.	CAPITAL	MTS.	MOUNTAINS	PRSV.	PRESERVE
C.G.	COAST GUARD	NAT.	NATURAL	PT.	POINT
CHAN.	CHANNEL	NAT'L	NATIONAL	R.	RIVER
CO.	COUNTY	NAV.	NAVAL	RA	RECREATION AREA
CR.	CREEK	NB	NATIONAL BATTLEFIELD	RA.	RANGE
CTR.	CENTER			REC.	RECREATION(AL)
DEP.	DEPOT	NBP	NATIONAL BATTLEFIELD PARK	REF.	REFUGE
DEPR.	DEPRESSION			REG.	REGION
DEPT.	DEPARTMENT	NBS	NATIONAL BATTLEFIELD SITE	REP.	REPUBLIC
DES.	DESERT			RES.	RESERVOIR, RESERVATION
DIST.	DISTRICT	NHP	NATIONAL HISTORICAL PARK		
DMZ	DEMILITARIZED ZONE			RVWY.	RIVERWAY
DPCY.	DEPENDENCY	NHPP	NATIONAL HISTORICAL PARK AND PRESERVE	SA.	SIERRA
ENG.	ENGINEERING			SD.	SOUND
EST.	ESTUARY	NHS	NATIONAL HISTORIC SITE	SEASH.	SEASHORE
FD.	FIORD, FJORD			So.	SOUTHERN
FED.	FEDERAL	NL	NATIONAL LAKESHORE	SP	STATE PARK
FK.	FORK	NM	NATIONAL MONUMENT	SPR., SPRS.	SPRING, SPRINGS
FLD.	FIELD	NMEMP	NATIONAL MEMORIAL PARK	ST.	STATE
FOR.	FOREST			STA.	STATION
FT.	FORT	NMILP	NATIONAL MILITARY PARK	STM.	STREAM
G.	GULF			STR.	STRAIT
GOV.	GOVERNOR	No.	NORTHERN	TERR.	TERRITORY
GOVT.	GOVERNMENT	NP	NATIONAL PARK	TUN.	TUNNEL
GD.	GRAND	NPP	NATIONAL PARK AND PRESERVE	TWP.	TOWNSHIP
GT.	GREAT			VAL.	VALLEY
HAR.	HARBOR	NPRSV	NATIONAL PRESERVE	VILL.	VILLAGE
HD.	HEAD	NRA	NATIONAL RECREATION AREA	VOL.	VOLCANO
HIST.	HISTORIC(AL)			WILD.	WILDLIFE, WILDERNESS
HTS.	HEIGHTS	NRSV	NATIONAL RESERVE		
I., IS.	ISLAND(S)	NS	NATIONAL SEASHORE	WTR.	WATER

World Flags and Reference Guide

Afghanistan
Page/Location: 33/H2
Area: 250,775 sq. mi.
    649,507 sq. km.
Population: 27,755,775
Capital: Kabul
Largest City: Kabul
Highest Point: Noshaq
Monetary Unit: afghani

Albania
Page/Location: 21/H3
Area: 11,100 sq. mi.
    28,749 sq. km.
Population: 3,544,841
Capital: Tiranë
Largest City: Tiranë
Highest Point: Korab
Monetary Unit: lek

Algeria
Page/Location: 40/F2
Area: 919,591 sq. mi.
    2,381,740 sq. km.
Population: 32,277,942
Capital: Algiers
Largest City: Algiers
Highest Point: Tahat
Monetary Unit: Algerian dinar

Andorra
Page/Location: 20/D3
Area: 174 sq. mi.
    450 sq. km.
Population: 68,403
Capital: Andorra la Vella
Largest City: Andorra la Vella
Highest Point: Coma Pedrosa
Monetary Unit: euro

Angola
Page/Location: 42/C3
Area: 481,351 sq. mi.
    1,246,700 sq. km.
Population: 10,593,171
Capital: Luanda
Largest City: Luanda
Highest Point: Morro de Môco
Monetary Unit: kwanza

Antigua and Barbuda
Page/Location: 59/J4
Area: 171 sq. mi.
    443 sq. km.
Population: 67,448
Capital: St. John's
Largest City: St. John's
Highest Point: Boggy Peak
Monetary Unit: East Caribbean dollar

Argentina
Page/Location: 64/C4
Area: 1,068,296 sq. mi.
    2,766,890 sq. km.
Population: 37,812,817
Capital: Buenos Aires
Largest City: Buenos Aires
Highest Point: Cerro Aconcagua
Monetary Unit: peso argentino

Armenia
Page/Location: 23/F5
Area: 11,506 sq. mi.
    29,800 sq. km.
Population: 3,330,099
Capital: Yerevan
Largest City: Yerevan
Highest Point: Alagez
Monetary Unit: dram

Australia
Page/Location: 45
Area: 2,966,136 sq. mi.
    7,682,300 sq. km.
Population: 19,546,792
Capital: Canberra
Largest City: Sydney
Highest Point: Mt. Kosciusko
Monetary Unit: Australian dollar

Austria
Page/Location: 21/G2
Area: 32,375 sq. mi.
    83,851 sq. km.
Population: 8,169,929
Capital: Vienna
Largest City: Vienna
Highest Point: Grossglockner
Monetary Unit: euro

Azerbaijan
Page/Location: 23/G5
Area: 33,436 sq. mi.
    86,600 sq. km.
Population: 7,798,497
Capital: Baku
Largest City: Baku
Highest Point: Bazardyuzyu
Monetary Unit: manat

Bahamas
Page/Location: 59/F2
Area: 5,382 sq. mi.
    13,939 sq. km.
Population: 300,529
Capital: Nassau
Largest City: Nassau
Highest Point: Mt. Alvernia
Monetary Unit: Bahamian dollar

Bahrain
Page/Location: 32/F3
Area: 240 sq. mi.
    622 sq. km.
Population: 656,397
Capital: Manama
Largest City: Manama
Highest Point: Jabal Dukhān
Monetary Unit: Bahraini dinar

Bangladesh
Page/Location: 34/E3
Area: 55,598 sq. mi.
    144,000 sq. km.
Population: 133,376,684
Capital: Dhākā
Largest City: Dhākā
Highest Point: Keokradong
Monetary Unit: taka

Barbados
Page/Location: 59/J5
Area: 166 sq. mi.
    430 sq. km.
Population: 276,607
Capital: Bridgetown
Largest City: Bridgetown
Highest Point: Mt. Hillaby
Monetary Unit: Barbadian dollar

Belarus
Page/Location: 19/L3
Area: 80,154 sq. mi.
    207,600 sq. km.
Population: 10,335,382
Capital: Minsk
Largest City: Minsk
Highest Point: Dzyarzhynskaya
Monetary Unit: Belarusian ruble

Belgium
Page/Location: 18/E4
Area: 11,781 sq. mi.
    30,513 sq. km.
Population: 10,274,595
Capital: Brussels
Largest City: Brussels
Highest Point: Botrange
Monetary Unit: euro

Belize
Page/Location: 58/D4
Area: 8,867 sq. mi.
    22,966 sq. km.
Population: 262,999
Capital: Belmopan
Largest City: Belize City
Highest Point: Victoria Peak
Monetary Unit: Belize dollar

Benin
Page/Location: 40/F5
Area: 43,483 sq. mi.
    112,620 sq. km.
Population: 6,787,625
Capital: Porto-Novo
Largest City: Cotonou
Highest Point: Sokbaro
Monetary Unit: CFA franc

Bhutan
Page/Location: 34/E2
Area: 18,147 sq. mi.
    47,000 sq. km.
Population: 2,094,176
Capital: Thimphu
Largest City: Thimphu
Highest Point: Kula Kangri
Monetary Unit: ngultrum

Bolivia
Page/Location: 62/F7
Area: 424,163 sq. mi.
    1,098,582 sq. km.
Population: 8,445,134
Capital: La Paz; Sucre
Largest City: La Paz
Highest Point: Nevado Sajama
Monetary Unit: boliviano

Bosnia and Herzegovina
Page/Location: 21/H2
Area: 19,940 sq. mi.
    51,645 sq. km.
Population: 3,964,388
Capital: Sarajevo
Largest City: Sarajevo
Highest Point: Maglić
Monetary Unit: marka

Botswana
Page/Location: 42/D5
Area: 231,803 sq. mi.
    600,370 sq. km.
Population: 1,591,232
Capital: Gaborone
Largest City: Gaborone
Highest Point: Tsodilo Hills
Monetary Unit: pula

Brazil
Page/Location: 61/D3
Area: 3,286,470 sq. mi.
    8,511,965 sq. km.
Population: 176,029,560
Capital: Brasília
Largest City: São Paulo
Highest Point: Pico da Neblina
Monetary Unit: real

Brunei
Page/Location: 36/D2
Area: 2,226 sq. mi.
    5,765 sq. km.
Population: 350,898
Capital: Bandar Seri Begawan
Largest City: Bandar Seri Begawan
Highest Point: Bukit Pagon
Monetary Unit: Brunei dollar

Bulgaria
Page/Location: 21/K3
Area: 42,823 sq. mi.
    110,912 sq. km.
Population: 7,621,337
Capital: Sofia
Largest City: Sofia
Highest Point: Musala
Monetary Unit: lev

Burkina Faso
Page/Location: 40/E5
Area: 105,869 sq. mi.
    274,200 sq. km.
Population: 12,603,185
Capital: Ouagadougou
Largest City: Ouagadougou
Highest Point: Tena Kourou
Monetary Unit: CFA franc

Burundi
Page/Location: 42/E1
Area: 10,747 sq. mi.
    27,835 sq. km.
Population: 6,373,002
Capital: Bujumbura
Largest City: Bujumbura
Highest Point: Mt. Heha
Monetary Unit: Burundi franc

Cambodia
Page/Location: 35/H5
Area: 69,898 sq. mi.
    181,036 sq. km.
Population: 12,775,324
Capital: Phnom Penh
Largest City: Phnom Penh
Highest Point: Phnum Aoral
Monetary Unit: riel

Cameroon
Page/Location: 40/H7
Area: 183,568 sq. mi.
    475,441 sq. km.
Population: 16,184,748
Capital: Yaoundé
Largest City: Douala
Highest Point: Mt. Fako
Monetary Unit: CFA franc

Canada
Page/Location: 49/G4
Area: 3,851,787 sq. mi.
9,976,139 sq. km.
Population: 31,902,268
Capital: Ottawa
Largest City: Toronto
Highest Point: Mt. Trudeau
Monetary Unit: Canadian dollar

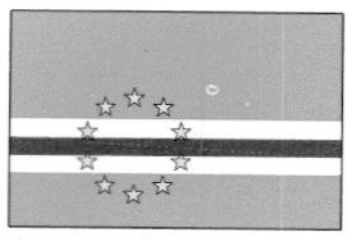

Cape Verde
Page/Location: 14/H5
Area: 1,557 sq. mi.
4,033 sq. km.
Population: 408,760
Capital: Praia
Largest City: Praia
Highest Point: Mt. Fogo
Monetary Unit: Cape Verde escudo

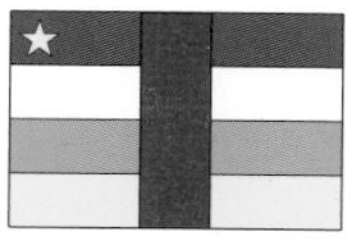

Central African Republic
Page/Location: 41/J6
Area: 240,533 sq. mi.
622,980 sq. km.
Population: 3,642,739
Capital: Bangui
Largest City: Bangui
Highest Point: Mt. Ngaoui
Monetary Unit: CFA franc

Chad
Page/Location: 41/J4
Area: 495,752 sq. mi.
1,283,998 sq. km.
Population: 8,997,237
Capital: N'Djamena
Largest City: N'Djamena
Highest Point: Emi Koussi
Monetary Unit: CFA franc

Chile
Page/Location: 64/B3
Area: 292,257 sq. mi.
756,946 sq. km.
Population: 15,498,930
Capital: Santiago
Largest City: Santiago
Highest Point: Nevado Ojos del Salado
Monetary Unit: Chilean peso

China
Page/Location: 27/J6
Area: 3,705,386 sq. mi.
9,596,960 sq. km.
Population: 1,284,303,705
Capital: Beijing
Largest City: Shanghai
Highest Point: Mt. Everest
Monetary Unit: yuan

Colombia
Page/Location: 62/D3
Area: 439,513 sq. mi.
1,138,339 sq. km.
Population: 41,008,227
Capital: Bogotá
Largest City: Bogotá
Highest Point: Pico Cristóbal Colón
Monetary Unit: Colombian peso

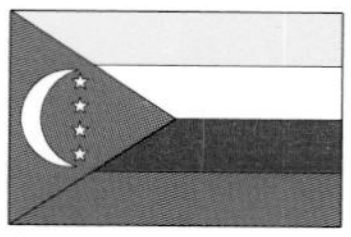

Comoros
Page/Location: 39/G6
Area: 838 sq. mi.
2,170 sq. km.
Population: 614,382
Capital: Moroni
Largest City: Moroni
Highest Point: Karthala
Monetary Unit: Comorian franc

Congo, Dem. Rep. of the
Page/Location: 39/E5
Area: 905,563 sq. mi.
2,345,410 sq. km.
Population: 55,225,478
Capital: Kinshasa
Largest City: Kinshasa
Highest Point: Margherita Peak
Monetary Unit: Congolese franc

Congo, Rep. of the
Page/Location: 39/D4
Area: 132,046 sq. mi.
342,000 sq. km.
Population: 2,958,448
Capital: Brazzaville
Largest City: Brazzaville
Highest Point: Mt. Berongou
Monetary Unit: CFA franc

Costa Rica
Page/Location: 58/E5
Area: 19,730 sq. mi.
51,100 sq. km.
Population: 3,834,934
Capital: San José
Largest City: San José
Highest Point: Cerro Chirripó Grande
Monetary Unit: Costa Rican colón

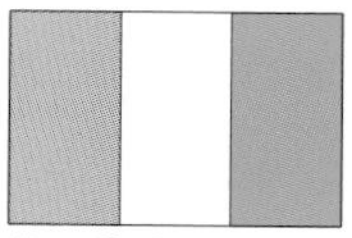

Côte d'Ivoire
Page/Location: 40/D6
Area: 124,504 sq. mi.
322,465 sq. km.
Population: 16,804,784
Capital: Yamoussoukro
Largest City: Abidjan
Highest Point: Mt. Nimba
Monetary Unit: CFA franc

Croatia
Page/Location: 21/G2
Area: 22,050 sq. mi.
57,110 sq. km.
Population: 4,390,751
Capital: Zagreb
Largest City: Zagreb
Highest Point: Dinara
Monetary Unit: Croatian kuna

Cuba
Page/Location: 59/F3
Area: 42,803 sq. mi.
110,860 sq. km.
Population: 11,224,321
Capital: Havana
Largest City: Havana
Highest Point: Pico Turquino
Monetary Unit: Cuban peso

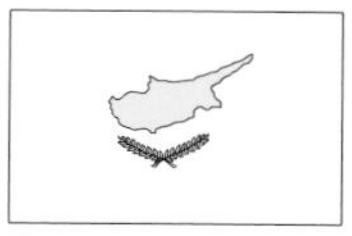

Cyprus
Page/Location: 32/B1
Area: 3,571 sq. mi.
9,250 sq. km.
Population: 767,314
Capital: Nicosia
Largest City: Nicosia
Highest Point: Olympus
Monetary Unit: Cypriot pound

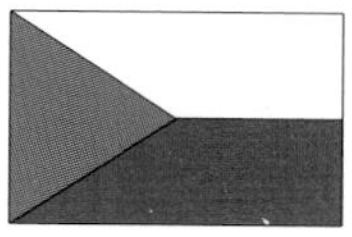

Czech Republic
Page/Location: 19/H4
Area: 30,387 sq. mi.
78,703 sq. km.
Population: 10,256,760
Capital: Prague
Largest City: Prague
Highest Point: Sněžka
Monetary Unit: Czech koruna

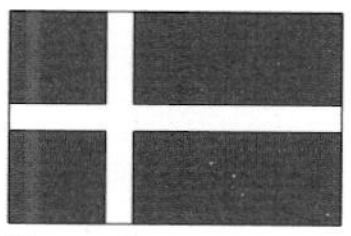

Denmark
Page/Location: 18/G3
Area: 16,629 sq. mi.
43,069 sq. km.
Population: 5,368,854
Capital: Copenhagen
Largest City: Copenhagen
Highest Point: Yding Skovhøj
Monetary Unit: Danish krone

Djibouti
Page/Location: 41/P5
Area: 8,494 sq. mi.
22,000 sq. km.
Population: 472,810
Capital: Djibouti
Largest City: Djibouti
Highest Point: Moussa Ali
Monetary Unit: Djibouti franc

Dominica
Page/Location: 59/J4
Area: 290 sq. mi.
751 sq. km.
Population: 70,158
Capital: Roseau
Largest City: Roseau
Highest Point: Morne Diablotin
Monetary Unit: EC dollar

Dominican Republic
Page/Location: 59/H4
Area: 18,815 sq. mi.
48,730 sq. km.
Population: 8,721,594
Capital: Santo Domingo
Largest City: Santo Domingo
Highest Point: Pico Duarte
Monetary Unit: Dominican peso

East Timor
Page/Location: 37/G5
Area: 5,743 sq. mi.
14,874 sq. km.
Population: 839,719
Capital: Dili
Largest City: Dili
Highest Point: Teta Mailau
Monetary Unit: rupiah

Ecuador
Page/Location: 62/C4
Area: 109,483 sq. mi.
283,561 sq. km.
Population: 13,447,494
Capital: Quito
Largest City: Guayaquil
Highest Point: Chimborazo
Monetary Unit: U.S. dollar

Egypt
Page/Location: 41/L2
Area: 386,659 sq. mi.
1,001,447 sq. km.
Population: 70,712,345
Capital: Cairo
Largest City: Cairo
Highest Point: Mt. Catherine
Monetary Unit: Egyptian pound

El Salvador
Page/Location: 58/C5
Area: 8,124 sq. mi.
21,040 sq. km.
Population: 6,353,681
Capital: San Salvador
Largest City: San Salvador
Highest Point: El Pital
Monetary Unit: Salvadoran colc

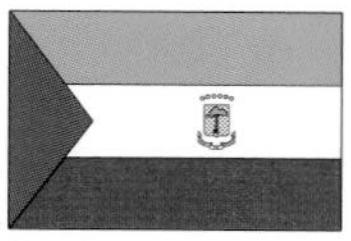

Equatorial Guinea
Page/Location: 40/G7
Area: 10,831 sq. mi.
28,052 sq. km.
Population: 498,144
Capital: Malabo
Largest City: Malabo
Highest Point: Basile
Monetary Unit: CFA franc

Eritrea
Page/Location: 41/N5
Area: 46,842 sq. mi.
121,320 sq. km.
Population: 4,465,651
Capital: Asmara
Largest City: Asmara
Highest Point: Soira
Monetary Unit: nafka

Estonia
Page/Location: 19/L2
Area: 17,413 sq. mi.
45,100 sq. km.
Population: 1,415,681
Capital: Tallinn
Largest City: Tallinn
Highest Point: Munamägi
Monetary Unit: kroon

Ethiopia
Page/Location: 41/N5
Area: 435,184 sq. mi.
1,127,127 sq. km.
Population: 67,673,031
Capital: Addis Ababa
Largest City: Addis Ababa
Highest Point: Ras Dashen Terara
Monetary Unit: birr

Fiji
Page/Location: 46/G6
Area: 7,055 sq. mi.
18,272 sq. km.
Population: 856,346
Capital: Suva
Largest City: Suva
Highest Point: Tomaniivi
Monetary Unit: Fijian dollar

Finland
Page/Location: 22/H2
Area: 130,128 sq. mi.
337,032 sq. km.
Population: 5,183,545
Capital: Helsinki
Largest City: Helsinki
Highest Point: Haltia
Monetary Unit: euro

France
Page/Location: 20/D2
Area: 211,208 sq. mi.
547,030 sq. km.
Population: 59,765,983
Capital: Paris
Largest City: Paris
Highest Point: Mont Blanc
Monetary Unit: euro

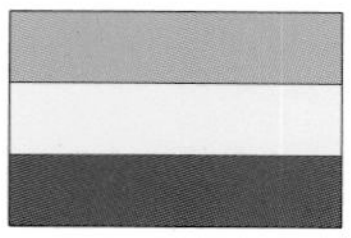

Gabon
Page/Location: 40/H7
Area: 103,346 sq. mi.
267,666 sq. km.
Population: 1,233,353
Capital: Libreville
Largest City: Libreville
Highest Point: Mt. Iboundji
Monetary Unit: CFA franc

Gambia, The
Page/Location: 40/B5
Area: 4,363 sq. mi.
11,300 sq. km.
Population: 1,455,842
Capital: Banjul
Largest City: Banjul
Highest Point: 174 ft. (53 m)
Monetary Unit: dalasi

Georgia
Page/Location: 23/F5
Area: 26,911 sq. mi.
69,700 sq. km.
Population: 4,960,951
Capital: T'bilisi
Largest City: T'bilisi
Highest Point: Kazbek
Monetary Unit: lari

Germany
Page/Location: 18/G4
Area: 137,803 sq. mi.
356,910 sq. km.
Population: 83,251,851
Capital: Berlin
Largest City: Berlin
Highest Point: Zugspitze
Monetary Unit: euro

Ghana
Page/Location: 40/E6
Area: 92,099 sq. mi.
238,536 sq. km.
Population: 20,244,154
Capital: Accra
Largest City: Accra
Highest Point: Afadjato
Monetary Unit: cedi

World Flags and Reference Guide

Greece
Page/Location: 21/J4
Area: 50,944 sq. mi.
131,945 sq. km.
Population: 10,645,343
Capital: Athens
Largest City: Athens
Highest Point: Mt. Olympus
Monetary Unit: euro

Grenada
Page/Location: 59/J5
Area: 133 sq. mi.
344 sq. km.
Population: 89,211
Capital: St. George's
Largest City: St. George's
Highest Point: Mt. St. Catherine
Monetary Unit: East Caribbean dollar

Guatemala
Page/Location: 58/C4
Area: 42,042 sq. mi.
108,889 sq. km.
Population: 13,314,079
Capital: Guatemala
Largest City: Guatemala
Highest Point: Tajumulco
Monetary Unit: quetzal

Guinea
Page/Location: 40/C5
Area: 94,925 sq. mi.
245,856 sq. km.
Population: 7,775,065
Capital: Conakry
Largest City: Conakry
Highest Point: Mt. Nimba
Monetary Unit: Guinea franc

Guinea-Bissau
Page/Location: 40/B5
Area: 13,948 sq. mi.
36,125 sq. km.
Population: 1,345,479
Capital: Bissau
Largest City: Bissau
Highest Point: 984 ft. (300 m)
Monetary Unit: Guinea-Bissau peso

Guyana
Page/Location: 62/G3
Area: 83,000 sq. mi.
214,970 sq. km.
Population: 698,209
Capital: Georgetown
Largest City: Georgetown
Highest Point: Mt. Roraima
Monetary Unit: Guyana dollar

Haiti
Page/Location: 59/G4
Area: 10,694 sq. mi.
27,697 sq. km.
Population: 7,063,722
Capital: Port-au-Prince
Largest City: Port-au-Prince
Highest Point: Pic la Selle
Monetary Unit: gourde

Honduras
Page/Location: 58/D4
Area: 43,277 sq. mi.
112,087 sq. km.
Population: 6,560,608
Capital: Tegucigalpa
Largest City: Tegucigalpa
Highest Point: Cerro de las Minas
Monetary Unit: lempira

Hungary
Page/Location: 21/H2
Area: 35,919 sq. mi.
93,030 sq. km.
Population: 10,075,034
Capital: Budapest
Largest City: Budapest
Highest Point: Kékes
Monetary Unit: forint

Iceland
Page/Location: 22/N7
Area: 39,768 sq. mi.
103,000 sq. km.
Population: 279,384
Capital: Reykjavík
Largest City: Reykjavík
Highest Point: Hvannadalshnúkur
Monetary Unit: króna

India
Page/Location: 34/C3
Area: 1,269,339 sq. mi.
3,287,588 sq. km.
Population: 1,045,845,226
Capital: New Delhi
Largest City: Mumbai
Highest Point: Kånchenjunga
Monetary Unit: Indian rupee

Indonesia
Page/Location: 37/E4
Area: 741,096 sq. mi.
1,919,440 sq. km.
Population: 232,073,071
Capital: Jakarta
Largest City: Jakarta
Highest Point: Puncak Jaya
Monetary Unit: rupiah

Iran
Page/Location: 32/F2
Area: 636,293 sq. mi.
1,648,000 sq. km.
Population: 66,622,704
Capital: Tehràn
Largest City: Tehràn
Highest Point: Qolleh-ye Damávand
Monetary Unit: Iranian rial

Iraq
Page/Location: 32/D2
Area: 168,753 sq. mi.
437,072 sq. km.
Population: 24,001,816
Capital: Baghdad
Largest City: Baghdad
Highest Point: Haji Ibrahim
Monetary Unit: Iraqi dinar

Ireland
Page/Location: 18/B3
Area: 27,136 sq. mi.
70,282 sq. km.
Population: 3,883,159
Capital: Dublin
Largest City: Dublin
Highest Point: Carrantuohill
Monetary Unit: Irish pound

Israel
Page/Location: 32/B2
Area: 8,019 sq. mi.
20,770 sq. km.
Population: 6,029,529
Capital: Jerusalem
Largest City: Tel Aviv-Yafo
Highest Point: Har Meron
Monetary Unit: new Israeli shekel

Italy
Page/Location: 21/F3
Area: 116,303 sq. mi.
301,225 sq. km.
Population: 57,715,625
Capital: Rome
Largest City: Rome
Highest Point: Monte Bianco
Monetary Unit: euro

Jamaica
Page/Location: 59/F4
Area: 4,243 sq. mi.
10,990 sq. km.
Population: 2,680,029
Capital: Kingston
Largest City: Kingston
Highest Point: Blue Mountain Pk.
Monetary Unit: Jamaican dollar

Japan
Page/Location: 29/M4
Area: 145,882 sq. mi.
377,835 sq. km.
Population: 126,974,628
Capital: Tokyo
Largest City: Tokyo
Highest Point: Fujiyama
Monetary Unit: yen

Jordan
Page/Location: 32/C2
Area: 34,445 sq. mi.
89,213 sq. km.
Population: 5,307,470
Capital: Ammän
Largest City: Ammän
Highest Point: Jabal Ramm
Monetary Unit: Jordanian dinar

Kazakhstan
Page/Location: 24/G5
Area: 1,049,150 sq. mi.
2,717,300 sq. km.
Population: 16,741,519
Capital: Astana
Largest City: Almaty
Highest Point: Khan-Tengri
Monetary Unit: Kazakstani tenge

Kenya
Page/Location: 41/N7
Area: 224,960 sq. mi.
582,646 sq. km.
Population: 31,138,735
Capital: Nairobi
Largest City: Nairobi
Highest Point: Mt. Kenya
Monetary Unit: Kenya shilling

Kiribati
Page/Location: 46/H5
Area: 277 sq. mi.
717 sq. km.
Population: 96,335
Capital: Tarawa
Largest City: —
Highest Point: Banaba Island
Monetary Unit: Australian dollar

Korea, North
Page/Location: 29/K3
Area: 46,540 sq. mi.
120,539 sq. km.
Population: 22,224,195
Capital: P'yóngyang
Largest City: P'yóngyang
Highest Point: Paektu-san
Monetary Unit: North Korean won

Korea, South
Page/Location: 29/K4
Area: 38,023 sq. mi.
98,480 sq. km.
Population: 48,324,000
Capital: Seoul
Largest City: Seoul
Highest Point: Halla-san
Monetary Unit: South Korean won

Kuwait
Page/Location: 32/E3
Area: 6,880 sq. mi.
17,820 sq. km.
Population: 2,111,561
Capital: Kuwait
Largest City: Kuwait
Highest Point: 1,003 ft. (306 m)
Monetary Unit: Kuwaiti dinar

Kyrgyzstan
Page/Location: 31/B3
Area: 76,641 sq. mi.
198,500 sq. km.
Population: 5,777,180
Capital: Bishkek
Largest City: Bishkek
Highest Point: Pik Pobedy
Monetary Unit: som

Laos
Page/Location: 35/H3
Area: 91,428 sq. mi.
236,800 sq. km.
Population: 5,777,180
Capital: Vientiane
Largest City: Vientiane
Highest Point: Phou Bia
Monetary Unit: kip

Latvia
Page/Location: 19/L2
Area: 24,749 sq. mi.
64,100 sq. km.
Population: 2,366,515
Capital: Riga
Largest City: Riga
Highest Point: Gaizina Kalns
Monetary Unit: Latvian let

Lebanon
Page/Location: 32/C2
Area: 4,015 sq. mi.
10,399 sq. km.
Population: 3,677,780
Capital: Beirut
Largest City: Beirut
Highest Point: Qurnat as Sawdá'
Monetary Unit: Lebanese pound

Lesotho
Page/Location: 42/E6
Area: 11,720 sq. mi.
30,355 sq. km.
Population: 2,207,954
Capital: Maseru
Largest City: Maseru
Highest Point: Thabana-Ntlenyana
Monetary Unit: loti

Liberia
Page/Location: 40/D6
Area: 43,000 sq. mi.
111,370 sq. km.
Population: 3,288,198
Capital: Monrovia
Largest City: Monrovia
Highest Point: Mt. Wuteve
Monetary Unit: Liberian dollar

Libya
Page/Location: 41/J2
Area: 679,358 sq. mi.
1,759,537 sq. km.
Population: 5,368,585
Capital: Tripoli
Largest City: Tripoli
Highest Point: Picco Bette
Monetary Unit: Libyan dinar

Liechtenstein
Page/Location: 18/G5
Area: 61 sq. mi.
158 sq. km.
Population: 32,842
Capital: Vaduz
Largest City: Vaduz
Highest Point: Grauspitz
Monetary Unit: Swiss franc

Lithuania
Page/Location: 19/K3
Area: 25,174 sq. mi.
65,200 sq. km.
Population: 3,601,138
Capital: Vilnius
Largest City: Vilnius
Highest Point: Juozapines
Monetary Unit: litas

Luxembourg
Page/Location: 18/F4
Area: 999 sq. mi.
2,587 sq. km.
Population: 448,569
Capital: Luxembourg
Largest City: Luxembourg
Highest Point: Buurgplaatz
Monetary Unit: euro

Macedonia (F.Y.R.O.M.)
Page/Location: 21/J3
Area: 9,781 sq. mi.
25,333 sq. km.
Population: 2,054,800
Capital: Skopje
Largest City: Skopje
Highest Point: Korab
Monetary Unit: denar

Madagascar
Page/Location: 42/K10
Area: 226,657 sq. mi.
587,041 sq. km.
Population: 16,473,477
Capital: Antananarivo
Largest City: Antananarivo
Highest Point: Maromokotro
Monetary Unit: Malagasy franc

Malawi
Page/Location: 42/F3
Area: 45,747 sq. mi.
118, 485 sq. km.
Population: 10,701,824
Capital: Lilongwe
Largest City: Blantyre
Highest Point: Sapitwa
Monetary Unit: Malawi kwacha

Malaysia
Page/Location: 36/C2
Area: 127,316 sq. mi.
329,750 sq. km.
Population: 22,662,365
Capital: Kuala Lumpur
Largest City: Kuala Lumpur
Highest Point: Gunung Kinabalu
Monetary Unit: ringgit

Maldives
Page/Location: 27/G9
Area: 115 sq. mi.
298 sq. km.
Population: 320,165
Capital: Male
Largest City: Male
Highest Point: 8 ft. (2.4 m)
Monetary Unit: rufiyaa

Mali
Page/Location: 40/E4
Area: 478,764 sq. mi.
1,240,000 sq. km.
Population: 11,340,480
Capital: Bamako
Largest City: Bamako
Highest Point: Hombori Tondo
Monetary Unit: CFA franc

Malta
Page/Location: 21/G5
Area: 122 sq. mi.
316 sq. km.
Population: 397,499
Capital: Valletta
Largest City: Sliema
Highest Point: Ta'Dmejrek
Monetary Unit: Maltese lira

Marshall Islands
Page/Location: 46/G3
Area: 70 sq. mi.
181 sq. km.
Population: 73,630
Capital: Majuro
Largest City: —
Highest Point: 33 ft. (10 m)
Monetary Unit: U.S. dollar

Mauritania
Page/Location: 40/C4
Area: 397,953 sq. mi.
1,030,700 sq. km.
Population: 2,828,858
Capital: Nouakchott
Largest City: Nouakchott
Highest Point: Kediet Ijill
Monetary Unit: ouguiya

Mauritius
Page/Location: 15/M7
Area: 718 sq. mi.
1,860 sq. km.
Population: 1,200,206
Capital: Port Louis
Largest City: Port Louis
Highest Point: Mont Piton
Monetary Unit: Mauritian rupee

Mexico
Page/Location: 58/A3
Area: 761,601 sq. mi.
1,972,546 sq. km.
Population: 103,400,165
Capital: Mexico
Largest City: Mexico
Highest Point: Citlaltépetl
Monetary Unit: Mexican peso

Micronesia
Page/Location: 46/D4
Area: 271 sq. mi.
702 sq. km.
Population: 135,869
Capital: Palikir
Largest City: Kolonia
Highest Point: Totolom
Monetary Unit: U.S. dollar

Moldova
Page/Location: 19/L5
Area: 13,012 sq. mi.
33,700 sq. km.
Population: 4,434,547
Capital: Chişinău
Largest City: Chişinău
Highest Point: Dealul Balanesti
Monetary Unit: leu

Monaco
Page/Location: 20/E3
Area: 0.7 sq. mi.
1.9 sq. km.
Population: 31,987
Capital: Monaco
Largest City: —
Highest Point: Mont Agel
Monetary Unit: euro

Mongolia
Page/Location: 28/D2
Area: 606,163 sq. mi.
1,569, 962 sq. km.
Population: 2,694,432
Capital: Ulaanbaatar
Largest City: Ulaanbaatar
Highest Point: Tavan Bogd Uul
Monetary Unit: tughrik

Morocco
Page/Location: 40/C1
Area: 172,414 sq. mi.
446,550 sq. km.
Population: 31,167,783
Capital: Rabat
Largest City: Casablanca
Highest Point: Jebel Toubkal
Monetary Unit: Moroccan dirham

Mozambique
Page/Location: 42/G4
Area: 309,494 sq. mi.
801,590 sq. km.
Population: 19,607,519
Capital: Maputo
Largest City: Maputo
Highest Point: Monte Binga
Monetary Unit: metical

Myanmar (Burma)
Page/Location: 35/G3
Area: 261,969 sq. mi.
678,500 sq. km.
Population: 42,238,224
Capital: Rangoon
Largest City: Rangoon
Highest Point: Hkakabo Razi
Monetary Unit: kyat

Namibia
Page/Location: 42/C5
Area: 318,694 sq. mi.
825,418 sq. km.
Population: 1,820,916
Capital: Windhoek
Largest City: Windhoek
Highest Point: Brandberg
Monetary Unit: Namibian dollar

Nauru
Page/Location: 46/F5
Area: 7.7 sq. mi.
20 sq. km.
Population: 12,329
Capital: Yaren (district)
Largest City: —
Highest Point: 200 ft. (61 m)
Monetary Unit: Australian dollar

Nepal
Page/Location: 34/D2
Area: 54,663 sq. mi.
141,577 sq. km.
Population: 25,873,917
Capital: Kāthmāndu
Largest City: Kāthmāndu
Highest Point: Mt. Everest
Monetary Unit: Nepalese rupee

Netherlands
Page/Location: 18/F3
Area: 14,413 sq. mi.
37,330 sq. km.
Population: 16,067,754
Capital: The Hague; Amsterdam
Largest City: Amsterdam
Highest Point: Vaalserberg
Monetary Unit: euro

New Zealand
Page/Location: 45/H6
Area: 103,736 sq. mi.
268,676 sq. km.
Population: 3,908,037
Capital: Wellington
Largest City: Auckland
Highest Point: Mt. Cook
Monetary Unit: New Zealand dollar

Nicaragua
Page/Location: 58/D5
Area: 49,998 sq. mi.
129,494 sq. km.
Population: 5,023,818
Capital: Managua
Largest City: Managua
Highest Point: Pico Mogotón
Monetary Unit: gold cordoba

Niger
Page/Location: 40/G4
Area: 489,189 sq. mi.
1,267,000 sq. km.
Population: 10,639,744
Capital: Niamey
Largest City: Niamey
Highest Point: Greboun
Monetary Unit: CFA franc

Nigeria
Page/Location: 40/G6
Area: 356,668 sq. mi.
923,770 sq. km.
Population: 129,934,911
Capital: Abuja
Largest City: Lagos
Highest Point: Chappal Waddi
Monetary Unit: naira

Norway
Page/Location: 22/C3
Area: 125,053 sq. mi.
323,887 sq. km.
Population: 4,525,116
Capital: Oslo
Largest City: Oslo
Highest Point: Galdhøppigen
Monetary Unit: Norwegian krone

Oman
Page/Location: 33/G4
Area: 82,031 sq. mi.
212,460 sq. km.
Population: 2,713,462
Capital: Muscat
Largest City: Muscat
Highest Point: Jabal ash Shām
Monetary Unit: Omani rial

Pakistan
Page/Location: 33/H3
Area: 310,403 sq. mi.
803,944 sq. km.
Population: 147,663,429
Capital: Islāmābād
Largest City: Karāchi
Highest Point: K2 (Godwin Austen)
Monetary Unit: Pakistani rupee

Palau
Page/Location: 46/C4
Area: 177 sq. mi.
458 sq. km.
Population: 19,409
Capital: Koror
Largest City: Koror
Highest Point: Mt. Ngerchelchauus
Monetary Unit: U.S. dollar

World Flags and Reference Guide

Panama
Page/Location: 58/E6
Area: 30,193 sq. mi.
78,200 sq. km.
Population: 2,882,329
Capital: Panamá
Largest City: Panamá
Highest Point: Barú
Monetary Unit: balboa

Papua New Guinea
Page/Location: 46/D5
Area: 178,259 sq. mi.
461,690 sq. km.
Population: 5,172,033
Capital: Port Moresby
Largest City: Port Moresby
Highest Point: Mt. Wilhelm
Monetary Unit: kina

Paraguay
Page/Location: 61/D5
Area: 157,047 sq. mi.
406,752 sq. km.
Population: 5,884,491;
Capital: Asunción
Largest City: Asunción
Highest Point: Cero Pero
Monetary Unit: guaraní

Peru
Page/Location: 62/C5
Area: 496,222 sq. mi.
1,285,215 sq. km.
Population: 27,949,639
Capital: Lima
Largest City: Lima
Highest Point: Nevado Huascarán
Monetary Unit: nuevo sol

Philippines
Page/Location: 30/D5
Area: 115,830 sq. mi.
300,000 sq. km.
Population: 84,525,639
Capital: Manila
Largest City: Manila
Highest Point: Mt. Apo
Monetary Unit: Philippine peso

Poland
Page/Location: 19/J3
Area: 120,725 sq. mi.
312,678 sq. km.
Population: 38,625,478
Capital: Warsaw
Largest City: Warsaw
Highest Point: Rysy
Monetary Unit: zloty

Portugal
Page/Location: 20/A4
Area: 35,549 sq. mi.
92,072 sq. km.
Population: 10,084,245
Capital: Lisbon
Largest City: Lisbon
Highest Point: Serra da Estrela
Monetary Unit: euro

Qatar
Page/Location: 32/F3
Area: 4,247 sq. mi.
11,000 sq. km.
Population: 793,341
Capital: Doha
Largest City: Doha
Highest Point: Qurayn Abø al Bawl
Monetary Unit: Qatari riyal

Romania
Page/Location: 21/J2
Area: 91,699 sq. mi.
237,500 sq. km.
Population: 22,317,730
Capital: Bucharest
Largest City: Bucharest
Highest Point: Moldoveanul
Monetary Unit: leu

Russia
Page/Location: 24/H3
Area: 6,592,812 sq. mi.
17,075,400 sq. km.
Population: 144,978,573
Capital: Moscow
Largest City: Moscow
Highest Point: El'brus
Monetary Unit: Russian ruble

Rwanda
Page/Location: 42/E1
Area: 10,169 sq. mi.
26,337 sq. km.
Population: 7,398,074
Capital: Kigali
Largest City: Kigali
Highest Point: Karisimbi
Monetary Unit: Rwanda franc

Saint Kitts and Nevis
Page/Location: 59/J4
Area: 104 sq. mi.
269 sq. km.
Population: 38,736
Capital: Basseterre
Largest City: Basseterre
Highest Point: Mt. Liamuiga
Monetary Unit: East Caribbean dollar

Saint Lucia
Page/Location: 59/J5
Area: 238 sq. mi.
616 sq. km.
Population: 160,145
Capital: Castries
Largest City: Castries
Highest Point: Mt. Gimie
Monetary Unit: East Caribbean dollar

Saint Vincent and the Grenadines
Page/Location: 59/J5
Area: 131 sq. mi.
340 sq. km.
Population: 116,394
Capital: Kingstown
Largest City: Kingstown
Highest Point: Soufrière
Monetary Unit: East Caribbean dollar

Samoa
Page/Location: 47/H6
Area: 1,104 sq. mi.
2,860 sq. km.
Population: 178,631
Capital: Apia
Largest City: Apia
Highest Point: Mt. Silisili
Monetary Unit: tala

San Marino
Page/Location: 21/G3
Area: 23.4 sq. mi.
60.6 sq. km.
Population: 27,730
Capital: San Marino
Largest City: San Marino
Highest Point: Monte Titano
Monetary Unit: euro

São Tomé and Príncipe
Page/Location: 40/F7
Area: 371 sq. mi.
960 sq. km.
Population: 170,372
Capital: São Tomé
Largest City: São Tomé
Highest Point: Pico de São Tomé
Monetary Unit: dobra

Saudi Arabia
Page/Location: 32/D4
Area: 756,981 sq. mi.
1,960,582 sq. km.
Population: 23,513,330
Capital: Riyadh
Largest City: Riyadh
Highest Point: Jabal Sawdä'
Monetary Unit: Saudi riyal

Senegal
Page/Location: 40/B5
Area: 75,954 sq. mi.
196,720 sq. km.
Population: 10,589,571
Capital: Dakar
Largest City: Dakar
Highest Point: 1,906 ft. (581 m)
Monetary Unit: CFA franc

Seychelles
Page/Location: 15/M6
Area: 176 sq. mi.
455 sq. km.
Population: 80,098
Capital: Victoria
Largest City: Victoria
Highest Point: Morne Seychellois
Monetary Unit: Seychelles rupee

Sierra Leone
Page/Location: 40/C6
Area: 27,699 sq. mi.
71,740 sq. km.
Population: 5,614,743
Capital: Freetown
Largest City: Freetown
Highest Point: Loma Mansa
Monetary Unit: leone

Singapore
Page/Location: 36/B3
Area: 244 sq. mi.
632.6 sq. km.
Population: 4,452,732
Capital: Singapore
Largest City: Singapore
Highest Point: Bukit Timah
Monetary Unit: Singapore dollar

Slovakia
Page/Location: 19/J4
Area: 18,924 sq. mi.
49,013 sq. km.
Population: 5,422,366
Capital: Bratislava
Largest City: Bratislava
Highest Point: Gerlachovský Štít
Monetary Unit: Slovak koruna

Slovenia
Page/Location: 21/G2
Area: 7,898 sq. mi.
20,456 sq. km.
Population: 1,932,917
Capital: Ljubljana
Largest City: Ljubljana
Highest Point: Triglav
Monetary Unit: tolar

Solomon Islands
Page/Location: 46/E6
Area: 11,500 sq. mi.
29,785 sq. km.
Population: 494,786
Capital: Honiara
Largest City: Honiara
Highest Point: Mt. Makarakomburu
Monetary Unit: Solomon Islands dollar

Somalia
Page/Location: 41/Q6
Area: 246,200 sq. mi.
637,658 sq. km.
Population: 7,753,310
Capital: Mogadishu
Largest City: Mogadishu
Highest Point: Shimber Berris
Monetary Unit: Somali shilling

South Africa
Page/Location: 42/D6
Area: 471,008 sq. mi.
1,219,912 sq. km.
Population: 43,647,658
Capital: Cape Town; Pretoria
Largest City: Johannesburg
Highest Point: Injasuti
Monetary Unit: rand

Spain
Page/Location: 20/B3
Area: 194,881 sq. mi.
504,742 sq. km.
Population: 40,077,100
Capital: Madrid
Largest City: Madrid
Highest Point: Pico de Teide
Monetary Unit: euro

Sri Lanka
Page/Location: 34/D6
Area: 25,332 sq. mi.
65,610 sq. km.
Population: 19,576,783
Capital: Colombo
Largest City: Colombo
Highest Point: Pidurutalagala
Monetary Unit: Sri Lanka rupee

Sudan
Page/Location: 41/L5
Area: 967,494 sq. mi.
2,505,809 sq. km.
Population: 37,090,298
Capital: Khartoum
Largest City: Omdurman
Highest Point: Kinyeti
Monetary Unit: Sudanese dinar

Suriname
Page/Location: 63/G3
Area: 63,039 sq. mi.
163,270 sq. km.
Population: 436,494
Capital: Paramaribo
Largest City: Paramaribo
Highest Point: Juliana Top
Monetary Unit: Suriname guilder

Swaziland
Page/Location: 42/F6
Area: 6,705 sq. mi.
17,366 sq. km.
Population: 1,123,605
Capital: Mbabane; Lobamba
Largest City: Mbabane
Highest Point: Emlembe
Monetary Unit: lilangeni

Sweden
Page/Location: 22/E3
Area: 173,665 sq. mi.
449,792 sq. km.
Population: 8,876,744
Capital: Stockholm
Largest City: Stockholm
Highest Point: Kebnekaise
Monetary Unit: krona

Switzerland
Page/Location: 20/E2
Area: 15,943 sq. mi.
41,292 sq. km.
Population: 7,301,994
Capital: Bern
Largest City: Zürich
Highest Point: Dufourspitze
Monetary Unit: Swiss franc

Syria
Page/Location: 32/C1
Area: 71,498 sq. mi.
185,180 sq. km.
Population: 17,155,814
Capital: Damascus
Largest City: Damascus
Highest Point: Jabal ash Shaykh
Monetary Unit: Syrian pound

Taiwan
Page/Location: 30/D3
Area: 13,971 sq. mi.
36,185 sq. km.
Population: 22,548,009
Capital: T'aipei
Largest City: T'aipei
Highest Point: Yü Shan
Monetary Unit: new Taiwan dollar

Tajikistan
Page/Location: 24/H6
Area: 55,251 sq. mi.
143,100 sq. km.
Population: 6,719,567
Capital: Dushanbe
Largest City: Dushanbe
Highest Point: Pik Imeni Ismail Samani
Monetary Unit: somoni

Tanzania
Page/Location: 42/F2
Area: 364,699 sq. mi.
945,090 sq. km.
Population: 37,187,939
Capital: Dar es Salaam
Largest City: Dar es Salaam
Highest Point: Kilimanjaro
Monetary Unit: Tanzanian shilling

Thailand
Page/Location: 35/H4
Area: 198,455 sq. mi.
513,998 sq. km.
Population: 62,354,402
Capital: Bangkok
Largest City: Bangkok
Highest Point: Doi Inthanon
Monetary Unit: baht

Togo
Page/Location: 40/F6
Area: 21,927 sq. mi.
56,790 sq. km.
Population: 5,285,501
Capital: Lomé
Largest City: Lomé
Highest Point: Mt. Agou
Monetary Unit: CFA franc

Tonga
Page/Location: 47/H7
Area: 289 sq. mi.
748 sq. km.
Population: 106,137
Capital: Nuku'alofa
Largest City: Nuku'alofa
Highest Point: Kao Island
Monetary Unit: pa'anga

Trinidad and Tobago
Page/Location: 59/J5
Area: 1,980 sq. mi.
5,128 sq. km.
Population: 1,163,724
Capital: Port-of-Spain
Largest City: Port-of-Spain
Highest Point: El Cerro del Aripo
Monetary Unit: Trin. & Tobago dolla

Tunisia
Page/Location: 40/G1
Area: 63,170 sq. mi.
163,610 sq. km.
Population: 9,815,644
Capital: Tünis
Largest City: Tünis
Highest Point: Jabal ash Sha'nabī
Monetary Unit: Tunisian dinar

Turkey
Page/Location: 23/D6
Area: 301,382 sq. mi.
780,580 sq. km.
Population: 67,308,928
Capital: Ankara
Largest City: Istanbul
Highest Point: Mt. Ararat
Monetary Unit: Turkish lira

Turkmenistan
Page/Location: 24/F6
Area: 188,455 sq. mi.
488,100 sq. km.
Population: 4,688,963
Capital: Ashgabat
Largest City: Ashgabat
Highest Point: Ayrybaba
Monetary Unit: manat

Tuvalu
Page/Location: 46/G5
Area: 9.78 sq. mi.
25.33 sq. km.
Population: 11,146
Capital: Funafuti
Largest City: —
Highest Point: 16 ft. (5 m)
Monetary Unit: Australian dollar

Uganda
Page/Location: 41/M7
Area: 91,076 sq. mi.
235,887 sq. km.
Population: 24,699,073
Capital: Kampala
Largest City: Kampala
Highest Point: Margherita Peak
Monetary Unit: Ugandan shilling

Ukraine
Page/Location: 23/C4
Area: 233,089 sq. mi.
603,700 sq. km.
Population: 48,396,470
Capital: Kiev
Largest City: Kiev
Highest Point: Goverla
Monetary Unit: hryvnia

United Arab Emirates
Page/Location: 32/F4
Area: 29,182 sq. mi.
75,581 sq. km.
Population: 2,445,989
Capital: Abu Dhabi
Largest City: Dubayy
Highest Point: Jabal Yibir
Monetary Unit: Emirian dirham

United Kingdom
Page/Location: 18/C3
Area: 94,399 sq. mi.
244,493 sq. km.
Population: 59,778,002
Capital: London
Largest City: London
Highest Point: Ben Nevis
Monetary Unit: pound sterling

United States
Page/Location: 49/G5
Area: 3,618,765 sq. mi.
9,372,610 sq. km.
Population: 280,562,489
Capital: Washington, D.C.
Largest City: New York
Highest Point: Mt. McKinley
Monetary Unit: U.S. dollar

Uruguay
Page/Location: 64/E3
Area: 68,039 sq. mi.
176,220 sq. km.
Population: 3,386,575
Capital: Montevideo
Largest City: Montevideo
Highest Point: Cerro Catedral
Monetary Unit: Uruguayan peso

Uzbekistan
Page/Location: 24/G5
Area: 172,741 sq. mi.
447,400 sq. km.
Population: 25,563,441
Capital: Tashkent
Largest City: Tashkent
Highest Point: Adelunga Toghi
Monetary Unit: sum

Vanuatu
Page/Location: 46/F6
Area: 5,700 sq. mi.
14,763 sq. km.
Population: 196,178
Capital: Port-Vila
Largest City: Port-Vila
Highest Point: Tabwemasana
Monetary Unit: vatu

Vatican City
Page/Location: 21/F3
Area: 0.17 sq. mi.
0.44 sq. km.
Population: 890
Capital: —
Largest City: —
Highest Point: 246 ft. (75 m)
Monetary Unit: euro

Venezuela
Page/Location: 62/E2
Area: 352,143 sq. mi.
912,050 sq. km.
Population: 24,287,670
Capital: Caracas
Largest City: Caracas
Highest Point: Pico Bolivar
Monetary Unit: bolivar

Vietnam
Page/Location: 35/J5
Area: 127,243 sq. mi.
329,560 sq. km.
Population: 81,098,416
Capital: Hanoi
Largest City: Ho Chi Minh City
Highest Point: Fan Si Pan
Monetary Unit: dong

Yemen
Page/Location: 32/E5
Area: 203,849 sq. mi.
527,970 sq. km.
Population: 18,701,257
Capital: Sanaa
Largest City: Aden
Highest Point: Nabī Shu'ayb
Monetary Unit: Yemeni rial

Yugoslavia
Page/Location: 21/J3
Area: 39,517 sq. mi.
102,350 sq. km.
Population: 9,979,752
Capital: Belgrade
Largest City: Belgrade
Highest Point: Daravica
Monetary Unit: Yugoslav new dinar

Zambia
Page/Location: 42/E3
Area: 290,586 sq. mi.
752,618 sq. km.
Population: 9,959,037
Capital: Lusaka
Largest City: Lusaka
Highest Point: Mafinga Hills
Monetary Unit: Zambian kwacha

Zimbabwe
Page/Location: 42/E4
Area: 150,803 sq. mi.
390,580 sq. km.
Population: 11,376,676
Capital: Harare
Largest City: Harare
Highest Point: Inyangani
Monetary Unit: Zimbabwe dollar

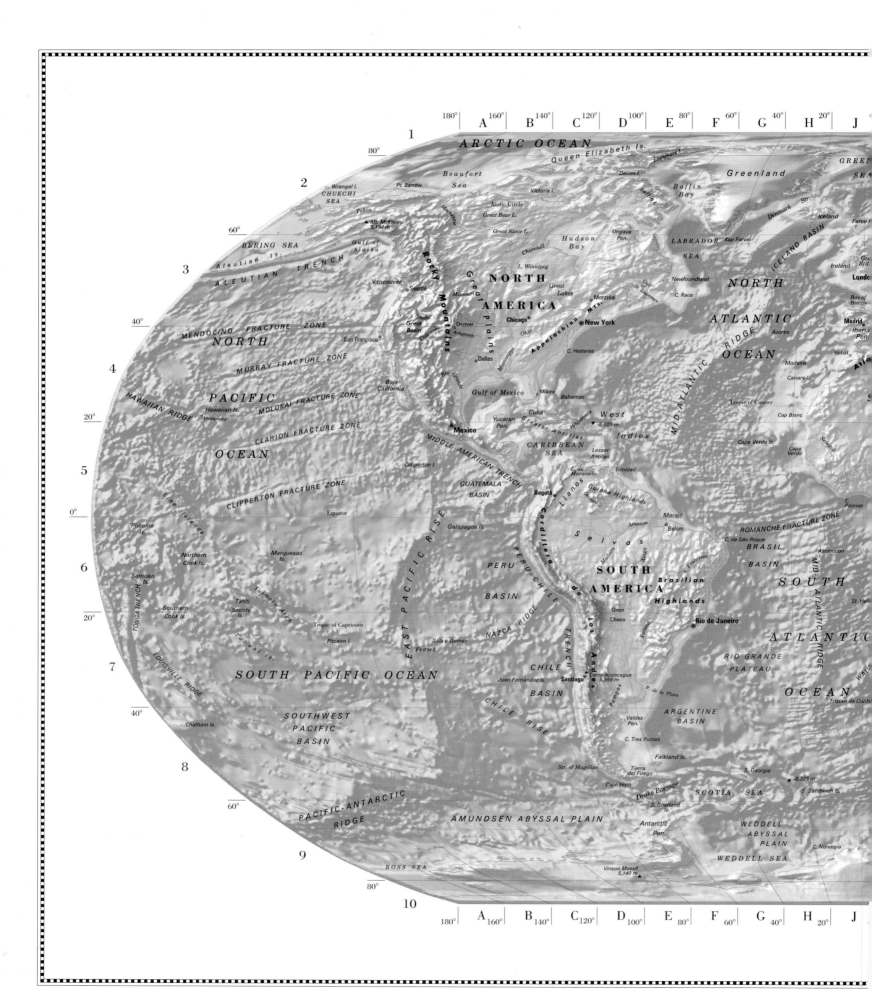

ARCTIC OCEAN

Queen Elizabeth Is.

Ellesmere I.

Greenland

GREEN
SEA

Beaufort Sea

Devon I.

80°

Wrangel I.
Pt. Barrow

Victoria I.

Baffin Bay

Baffin I.

Str.

Denmark

Iceland

Faroe I.

CHUKCHI SEA

Arctic Circle

2

Yukon

Great Bear L.

60°

Mt. McKinley
6.194 m

Mackenzie

Great Slave L.

Ungava Pen.

LABRADOR SEA

Kap Farvel

Gr. Brit.

Ireland

Londo

BERING SEA

Gulf of Alaska

Churchill

Hudson Bay

Newfoundland

NORTH

ICELAND BASIN

3

Aleutian Is.

ALEUTIAN TRENCH

L. Winnipeg

Gulf of St. Lawrence

C. Race

Bay of Biscay

40°

Vancouver

Rocky Mountains

Missouri

Great Lakes

Montréal

ATLANTIC

Madrid

Iberia

Seattle

Great Plains

Chicago

Ohio

New York

Azores

Pen.

MENDOCINO FRACTURE ZONE

Snake

Denver

Appalachian Mts.

OCEAN

Rabat

NORTH

Great Basin

Arkansas

Colorado

Dallas

C. Hatteras

Madeira

4

San Francisco

MURRAY FRACTURE ZONE

Mississippi

Canary Is.

20°

PACIFIC

Baja California

Rio Grande

Gulf of Mexico

Miami

Bahamas

Tropic of Cancer

Cap Blanc

HAWAIIAN RIDGE

Hawaiian Is.

MOLOKAI FRACTURE ZONE

Yucatan Pen.

Cuba

MID-ATLANTIC

Honolulu

Mexico

Greater Antilles

Hispaniola
-8.605 m

West Indies

Cape Verde Is.

Cape Verde

CLARION FRACTURE ZONE

CARIBBEAN SEA

Lesser Antilles

RIDGE

5

OCEAN

Clipperton I.

MIDDLE AMERICAN TRENCH

L. de Maracaibo

Trinidad

CLIPPERTON FRACTURE ZONE

GUATEMALA BASIN

Bogotá

Llanos

Guiana Highlands

C. Palmas

0°

Line Islands

Equator

Galápagos Is.

Cordillera

Amazon

Marajó

ROMANCHE FRACTURE ZONE

Phoenix Is.

de

Selvas

Belém

C. de São Roque

BRASIL BASIN

Ascension

6

Northern Cook Is.

Marquesas Is.

PERU BASIN

Madeira

SOUTH

Xingu

MID-ATLANTIC

Samoan Is.

Tahiti Society Is.

PERU-CHILE

los

AMERICA

Brazilian Highlands

S. Francisco

SOUTH

St. Hel

20°

TONGA TRENCH

Southern Cook Is.

Tubuai Arch.

Tropic of Capricorn

NAZCA RIDGE

Andes

Gran Chaco

Paraná

Rio de Janeiro

RIDGE

7

LOUISVILLE RIDGE

Tubuai Is.

Pitcairn I.

Sala y Gomez

Easter I.

TRENCH

CHILE

Juan Fernández Is.

Santiago

Cerro Aconcagua
6.959 m

R. de la Plata

RIO GRANDE PLATEAU

ATLANTIC

SOUTH PACIFIC OCEAN

BASIN

CHILE RISE

Pampas

ARGENTINE BASIN

OCEAN

Tristan da Cunh

40°

Chatham Is.

SOUTHWEST PACIFIC BASIN

Valdez Pen.

Watl

8

C. Tres Puntas

Falkland Is.

Str. of Magellan

Tierra del Fuego

S. Georgia
-8.325 m

Cape Horn

Drake Passage

SCOTIA SEA

S. Sandwich Is.

60°

PACIFIC-ANTARCTIC RIDGE

S. Shetland Is.

WEDDELL ABYSSAL PLAIN

9

Antarctic Pen.

AMUNDSEN ABYSSAL PLAIN

C. Norvegia

WEDDELL SEA

ROSS SEA

Vinson Massif
5.140 m

80°

10

World - Physical

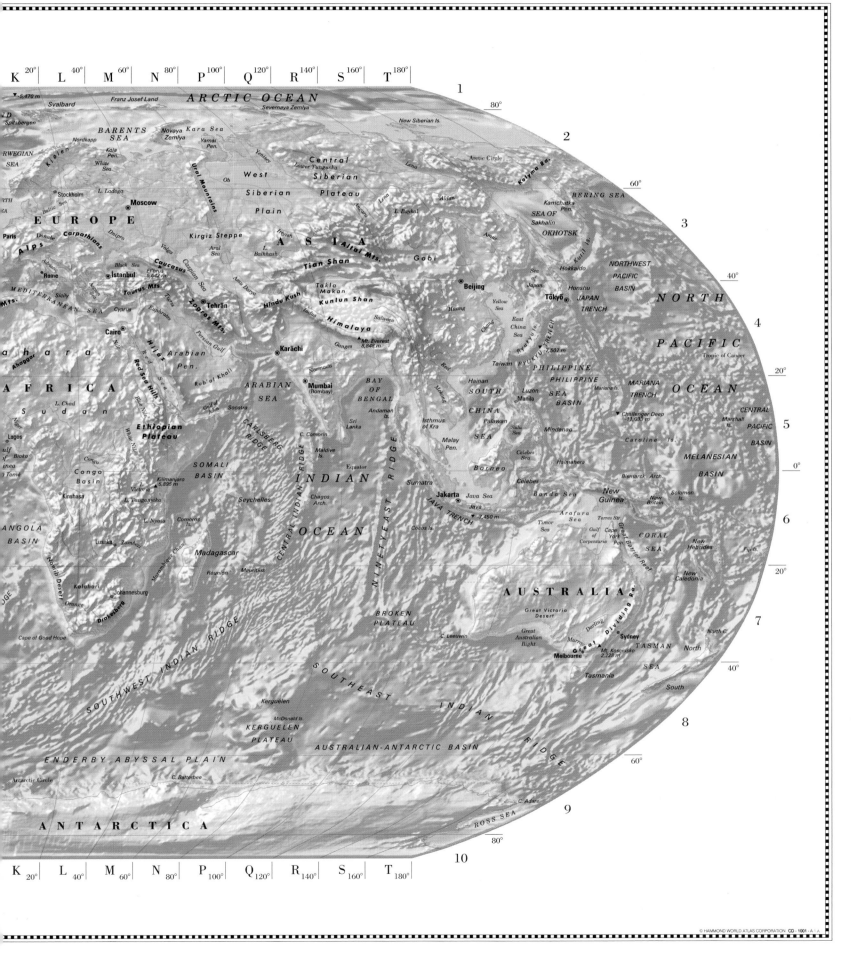

POPULATION OF CITIES AND TOWNS

- ◉ OVER 5,000,000
- ● 2,000,000 - 4,999,999
- ⊙ 500,000 - 1,999,999
- ○ UNDER 500,000

SCALE 1:81,700,000   ROBINSON PROJECTION STANDARD PARALLELS 38°N AND 38°S

MILES   0   1000   2000   3000   4000

KILOMETERS 0   1000   2000   3000   4000

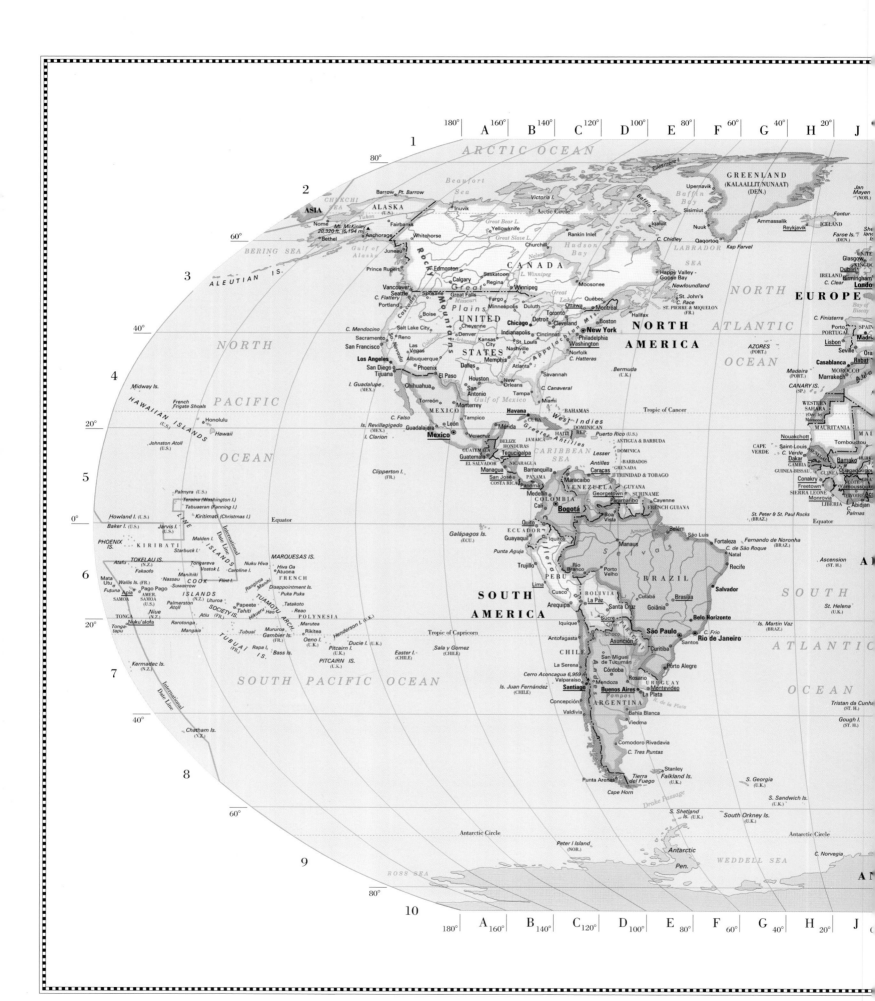

World - Political

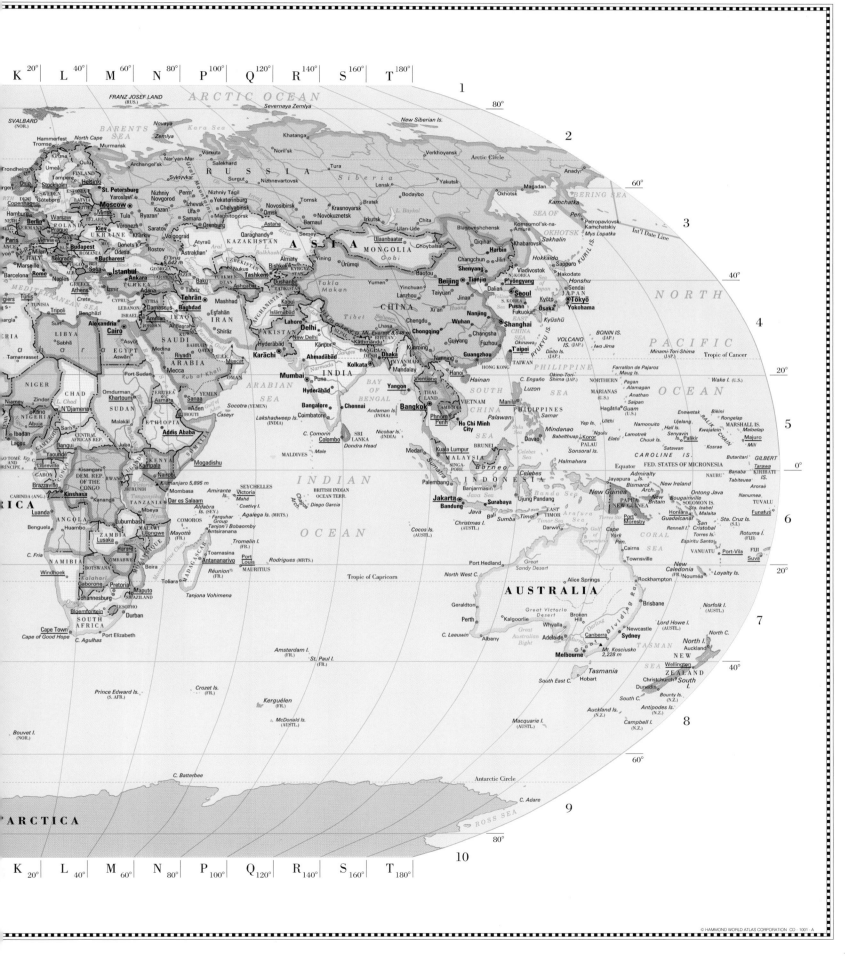

1

FRANZ JOSÉF LAND (RUS.)

ARCTIC OCEAN

Severnaya Zemlya

80°

SVALBARD (NOR.)

BARENTS SEA

Novaya Zemlya

Kara Sea

New Siberian Is.

2

Hammerfest   North Cape   Novaya   Khatanga
Tromsø   Zemlya
Murmansk

Kiruna   Nar'yan-Mar   Vorkuta   Noril'sk   Verkhoyansk   Arctic Circle

Umeå   Salekhard   Anadyr'

Trondheim   Oulu   Archangel'sk   Syktyvkar   Surgut   R U S S I A   S i b e r i a   Tura   Yakutsk   60°   3

FINLAND   Nizhnevartovsk   Lensk   Magadan   BERING SEA

Oslo   Tampere   Helsinki   St. Petersburg   Perm'   Yekaterinburg   Tomsk   Krasnoyarsk   Bratsk   L. Baykal   Chita   SEA OF   Kamchatka   Petropavlovsk-Kamchatskiy   Mys Lopatka

SWEDEN   Göteborg   Yaroslavl'   Nizhniy Novgorod   Izhevsk   Omsk   Novosibirsk   Irkutsk   Ulan-Ude   Blagoveshchensk   OKHOTSK   Komsomol'sk-na-Amure   Int'l Date Line

Copenhagen   ESTONIA   Moscow   Kazan   Ufa   Chelyabinsk   Novokuznetsk   Astana   Semey   Ulaanbaatar   Choybalsan   Qiqihar   Harbin   Khabarovsk   Sakhalin

RTH DENM   LATVIA   Tula   Ryazan'   Samara   Magnitogorsk   Barnaul   MONGOLIA   Gobi   Changchun   Jilin   Vladivostok   Sapporo   40°   4

Hamburg   Warsaw   Minsk   Voronezh   Saratov   Orenburg   Astrakhan'   KAZAKHSTAN   A S I A   Yumen   Baotou   Shenyang   N. KOREA   Hokkaido   Hakodate

NETH.   Berlin   Kiev   Kharkiv   Volgograd   Aral   L.   Almaty   Yining   Ürümqi   Beijing   Tianjin   P'yŏngyang   Honshū   Sendai

GERMANY   POLAND   UKRAINE   Rostov   El'brus 5,642 m   Balkhash   Bishkek   Takla   Yinchuan   Taiyuan   Jinan   Dalian   S. KOREA   Seoul   JAPAN   Tōkyō

Paris   Prague   Vienna   Budapest   Donets'k   Odesa   Astrakhan'   UZBEKISTAN   Tashkent   KYRGYZ   Makan   Lanzhou   Xi'an   Kōbe   Ōsaka   Yokohama

Milan   ROMANIA   Bucharest   Black Sea   GEORGIA   AZER.   Nukus   TURKMEN-   TAJIKISTAN   CHINA   Chengdu   Nanjing   Wuhan   Shanghai   Kyūshū   NORTH

ITALY   Belgrade   Sofia   Istanbul   Ankara   Baku   ISTAN   Ashgabat   Dushanbe   Tibet   Lhasa   Mt. Everest 8,848 m   Chongqing   Changsha   CHINA   Ōita   Fukuoka   20°

Barcelona   Rome   Naples   GREECE   İzmir   TURKEY   Adana   Tehrān   Mashhad   AFGHANISTAN   Kabul   Islāmābād   Salween   Guiyang   Fuzhou   Taipei   VOLCANO   BONIN IS.   Tropic of Cancer

Athens   Crete   CYPRUS   SYRIA   Baghdad   Eşfahān   Kābul   Lahore   NEPAL   Kāthmāndu   Kunming   Guangzhou   Okinawa   IS. (JAP.)   Iwo Jima   Minami-Tori-Shima

MEDITER   LEBANON   Damascus   IRAQ   IRAN   Shīrāz   PAKISTAN   Delhi   BHUTAN   BANGLA-   Nanning   HONG KONG   RYUKYU   Daitō Is.   (JAP.)

TUNISIA   ISRAEL   Amman   Baṣrah   Hyderābād   New Delhi   Kānpur   DESH   Dhaka   MYANMAR   Hanoi   TAIWAN   (JAP.)   Farallon de Pajaros   5

Tripoli   Benghāzī   Alexandria   Cairo   JORDAN   Riyadh   Kuwait   Karāchi   Ahmadābād   Ganges   Kolkata   Mandalay   Hainan   PHILIPPINE   C. Engaño   Maug Is.

Sabhā   LIBYA   EGYPT   Aswān   Medina   SAUDI   BAHRAIN   QATAR   U.A.E.   Muscat   India   Narmada   INDIA   Yangon   THAI-   SOUTH   Alamagan   Anathan

Tamanrasset   NIGER   Port Sudan   Mecca   ARABIA   Rub' al Khali   OMAN   Mumbai   Pune   BAY   LAND   Bangkok   CHINA   Luzon   NORTHERN   Saipan

CHAD   L. Chad   Omdurman   Khartoum   ERITREA   Asmara   YEMEN   ARABIAN   Hyderābād   OF   VIETNAM   Manila   MARIANAS   Guam

NIGERIA   Zinder   N'Djamena   Sarh   Malakāl   Sanaa   Aden   Gulf of Aden   SEA   Bangalore   Chennai   BENGAL   CAMBODIA   Phnom   PHILIPPINES   (U.S.)   Hagåtña   (U.S.)

Niamey   KANO   SUDAN   ETHIOPIA   Socotra (YEMEN)   Lakshadweep Is.   Coimbatore   Andaman Is.   Penh   Ho Chi Minh   Samar   Yap Is.

Abuja   CENTRAL   Juba   DJIBOUTI   Caseyr   (INDIA)   (INDIA)   Palawan   City   Davao   Ulithi   Namonuito   Ujelang

Lagos   AFRICAN REP.   Bangui   SOMALIA   C. Comorin   SRI   Nicobar Is.   BRUNEI   Mindanao   Ngulu   Chuuk Is.   Lamotrek

CAMEROON   Yaoundé   Bangui   UGANDA   KENYA   Mogadishu   Colombo   LANKA   (INDIA)   Kuala Lumpur   MALAYSIA   Koror   Babelthuap   PALAU   Satawan   Sonsorol Is.

SÃO TOMÉ   Libreville   Kisangani   Nairobi   MALDIVES   Male   Dondra Head   SINGA-   Borneo   Celebes   Halmahera   Equator   FED. STATES OF MICRONESIA   0°

AND PRINCIPE   GABON   Kampala   Kilimanjaro 5,895 m   Medan   Sumatra   PORE   INDONESIA   Celebes   Jayapura   Admiralty   New Ireland   NAURU

RICA   Brazzaville   DEM. REP. OF THE CONGO   RWANDA   Mombasa   INDIAN   Palembang   Jakarta   Ujung Pandang   Banda Sea   New Guinea   Is.   Bismarck   Bougainville   Ontong Java

CABINDA (ANG.)   Kinshasa   BURUNDI   Dar es Salaam   SEYCHELLES   Amirante   Victoria   OCEAN   Jakarta   Java   Surabaya   Banjarmasin   Java Sea   PAPUA   New   Arch.   Guadalcanal   Nanumea   TUVALU

Luanda   Kananga   TANZANIA   Mbeya   Is.   Coetivy I.   Mahé   Agalega Is. (MRTS.)   Bandung   Bali   EAST   Torres Str.   NEW GUINEA   Britain   Honiara   Sta. Isabel   6

Benguela   ANGOLA   Huambo   Lubumbashi   MALAWI   COMOROS   Aldabra   Agalega   BRITISH INDIAN   Christmas I.   Sumba   TIMOR   Timor Sea   Port   Moresby   SOLOMON IS.   Rennell I.   Sta. Cruz Is.   Rotuma I.

ZAMBIA   Lilongwe   Mayotte   Is. (SEY.)   Farquhar   Diego Garcia   OCEAN TERR.   (AUSTL.)   Timor   Darwin   Gulf of   Cape   CORAL   San   (S.I.)   (FIJI)

Lusaka   Harare   ZIMBABWE   Beira   MADAGASCAR   Group   Tanjon'i Bobaomby   Chagos   Antananarivo   Cocos Is.   Great   Carpentaria   York   SEA   Cristobal   VANUATU   Port-Vila   FIJI   Suva

NAMIBIA   BOTSWANA   Tromelin I.   (FR.)   Antsiranana   Arch.   (AUSTL.)   Sandy Desert   Pen.   Cairns   Espiritu Santo   Townsville   New

Windhoek   Kalahari   Toamasina   Réunion   Port   Rodrigues (MRTS.)   MAURITIUS   Tropic of Capricorn   Alice Springs   Caledonia   Noumea   Loyalty Is.   20°   7

Gaborone   Pretoria   Maputo   Louis   North West C.   Rockhampton   (FR.)

SOUTH   Johannesburg   SWAZILAND   Antananarivo   Tanjona Vohimena   AUSTRALIA   Norfolk I.   (AUSTL.)

Bloemfontein   LESOTHO   Durban   Geraldton   Great Victoria   Broken   Brisbane   Lord Howe I.   (AUSTL.)

Cape Town   Cape of Good Hope   C. Agulhas   Port Elizabeth   Perth   Desert   Hill   Newcastle   North I.   North C.

SOUTH AFRICA   Amsterdam I.   (FR.)   C. Leeuwin   Kalgoorlie   Whyalla   Canberra   Sydney   Auckland   40°

St. Paul I.   (FR.)   Albany   Great   Adelaide   Mt. Kosciusko   TASMAN   NEW

Australian   Melbourne   2,228 m   ZEALAND   Wellington   South I.

Crozet Is.   (FR.)   Bight   South East C.   Hobart   Christchurch

Prince Edward Is.   (S. AFR.)   Kerguélen   (FR.)   Tasmania   Dunedin   Bounty Is.   (N.Z.)

Bouvet I.   (NOR.)   McDonald Is.   (AUSTL.)   South C.   Antipodes Is.   (N.Z.)

Macquarie I.   (AUSTL.)   Campbell I.   (N.Z.)   8

C. Batterbee   60°

Antarctic Circle   9

ANTARCTICA   ROSS SEA   C. Adare   80°

10

POPULATION OF CITIES AND TOWNS

◉ OVER 5,000,000   ⊙ 500,000 - 1,999,999
● 2,000,000 - 4,999,999   ○ UNDER 500,000

SCALE 1:81,700,000   ROBINSON PROJECTION   STANDARD PARALLELS 38°N AND 38°S

MILES   0   1000   2000   3000   4000

KILOMETERS   0   1000   2000   3000   4000

Europe - Physical

AREA OF OPTIMIZATION
The red band which surrounds these physical and political maps defines the "Area of Optimization." Within this bounding curve is the most accurate conformal map that can be made of the region. Outside the optimized area, distortion increases rapidly, and tears or other irregularities in the grid may occur. (See page 3 for additional information.)

SCALE 1:21,000,000   OPTIMAL CONFORMAL PROJECTION

MILES

KILOMETERS

0   300   600   900

POPULATION OF CITIES AND TOWNS

▣ OVER 3,000,000   ⊛ 500,000 - 999,999   ○ UNDER 100,000
▣ 1,000,000 - 2,999,999   ● 100,000 - 499,999

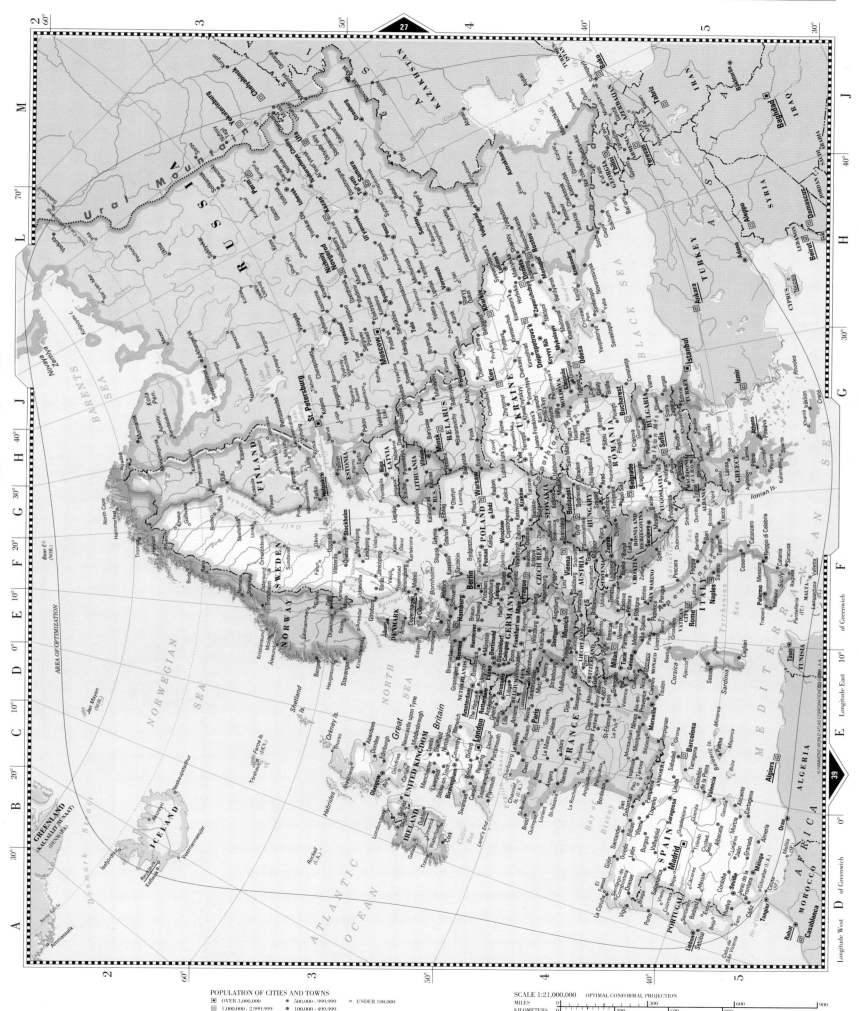

POPULATION OF CITIES AND TOWNS

□ OVER 3,000,000   ● 500,000 - 999,999   ○ UNDER 100,000

▣ 1,000,000 - 2,999,999   ⊙ 100,000 - 499,999

SCALE 1:21,000,000   OPTIMAL CONFORMAL PROJECTION

MILES   0   300   600   900

KILOMETERS   0   300   600   900

Western and Central Europe

POPULATION OF CITIES AND TOWNS

- ■ OVER 2,000,000
- ◉ 500,000 - 999,999
- ● 100,000 - 249,999
- ○ 10,000 - 29,999
- ▣ 1,000,000 - 1,999,999
- ◍ 250,000 - 499,999
- ◔ 30,000 - 99,999
- ○ UNDER 10,000

SCALE 1:7,000,000   LAMBERT CONFORMAL CONIC PROJECTION

MILES 0   100   200   300

KILOMETERS 0   100   200   300

© Hammond World Atlas Corporation   DD-0201-A-A-A

Southern Europe

POPULATION OF CITIES AND TOWNS

- OVER 2,000,000
- 1,000,000 - 1,999,999
- 500,000 - 999,999
- 250,000 - 499,999
- 100,000 - 249,999
- 30,000 - 99,999
- 10,000 - 29,999
- UNDER 10,000

SCALE 1:7,000,000   LAMBERT CONFORMAL CONIC PROJECTION

MILES   0   100   200   300
KILOMETERS   0   100   200   300

© HAMMOND WORLD ATLAS CORPORATION   DD - 0202 - A - A

Scandinavia and Finland, Iceland

Eastern Europe and Turkey

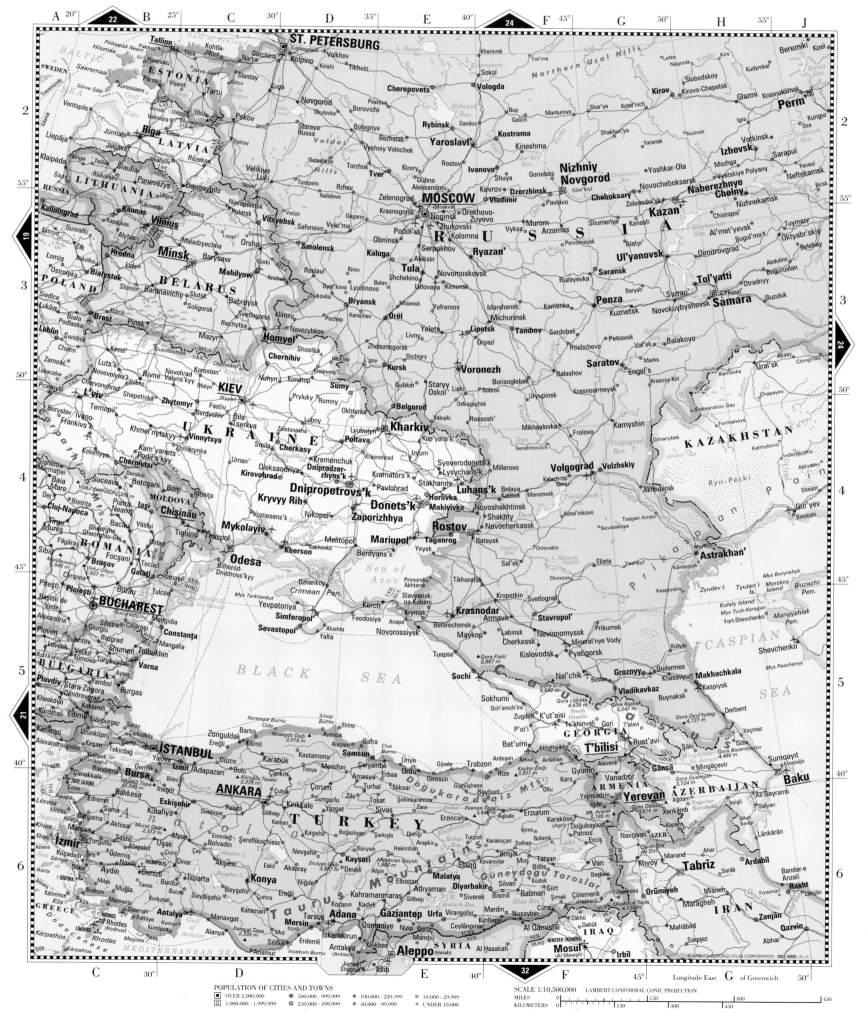

POPULATION OF CITIES AND TOWNS

■	OVER 2,000,000	●	500,000 - 999,999	●	100,000 - 249,999	○	10,000 - 29,999
▣	1,000,000 - 1,999,999	●	250,000 - 499,999	●	30,000 - 99,999	○	UNDER 10,000

SCALE 1:10,500,000   LAMBERT CONFORMAL CONIC PROJECTION

MILES

KILOMETERS

Longitude East of Greenwich

© HAMMOND WORLD ATLAS CORPORATION

Russia and Neighboring Countries

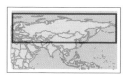

RUSSIA
(Administrative divisions are named only when they differ from their respective capitals.)

1. RESPUBLIKA ADYGEYA
2. RESPUBLIKA KARACHAYEVO-CHERKESIYA
3. RESPUBLIKA KABARDINO-BALKARIYA
4. RESPUBLIKA SEVERNAYA OSETIYA-ALANIYA
5. RESPUBLIKA INGUSHETIYA
6. RESPUBLIKA CHECHNYA
7. RESPUBLIKA DAGESTAN
8. RESPUBLIKA MORDOVIYA
9. RESPUBLIKA CHUVASHIYA
10. RESPUBLIKA MARIY-EL
11. RESPUBLIKA TATARSTAN
12. RESPUBLIKA BASHKORTOSTAN
13. RESPUBLIKA UDMURTIYA
14. KOMI-PERMYATSKIY AVTONOMNYY OKRUG
15. RESPUBLIKA KHAKASIYA
16. UST'-ORDYNSKIY BURYATSKIY AVT. OKRUG
17. AGINSKIY BURYATSKIY AVT. OKRUG

© HAMMOND WORLD ATLAS CORPORATION CD-1029 - A.

POPULATION OF CITIES AND TOWNS
- ■ OVER 2,000,000
- ◉ 500,000 - 999,999
- ○ 50,000 - 99,999
- ▣ 1,000,000 - 1,999,999
- ● 100,000 - 499,999
- ○ UNDER 50,000

SCALE 1:21,000,000   LAMBERT CONFORMAL CONIC PROJECTION

Asia - Physical

AREA OF OPTIMIZATION
The red band which surrounds these physical and political maps defines the "Area of Optimization." Within this bounding curve is the most accurate conformal map that can be made of the region. Outside the optimized area, distortion increases rapidly, and tears or other irregularities in the grid may occur. (See page 3 for additional information.)

SCALE 1:49,000,000   OPTIMAL CONFORMAL PROJECTION

MILES   0   700   1400   2100
KILOMETERS   0   700   1400   2100

POPULATION OF CITIES AND TOWNS
▪ OVER 3,000,000   ● 500,000 - 999,999   ○ UNDER 100,000
▣ 1,000,000 - 2,999,999   ◕ 100,000 - 499,999

Longitude East of Greenwich

© HAMMOND WORLD ATLAS CORPORATION   CD - 1030 - A - A

Asia - Political

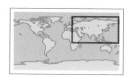

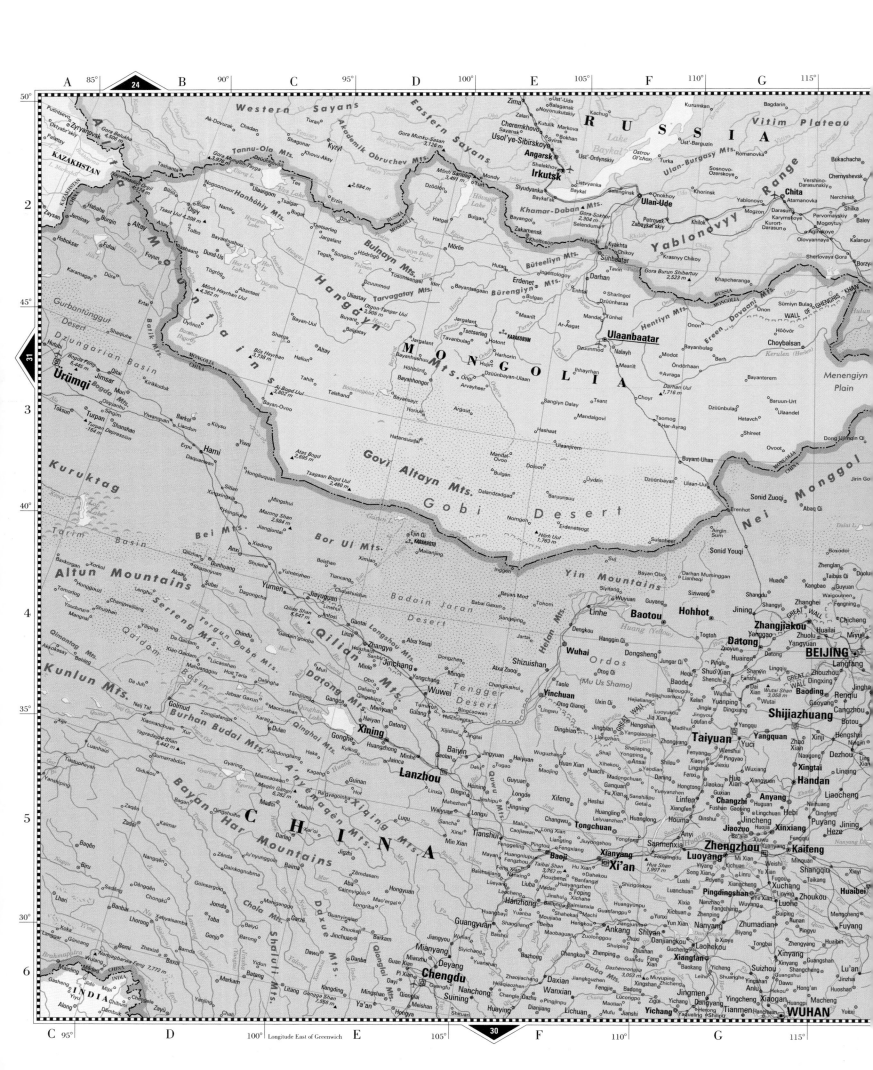

■ OVER 2,000,000   ◉ 500,000 - 999,999   ● 100,000 - 249,999   ○ 10,000 - 29,999
▣ 1,000,000 - 1,999,999   ◉ 250,000 - 499,999   ● 30,000 - 99,999   ○ UNDER 10,000

MILES   150   300   450
KILOMETERS   0   150   300

© HAMMOND WORLD ATLAS CORPORATION CD - 1034 - A/l

Southeastern China, Taiwan, Philippines

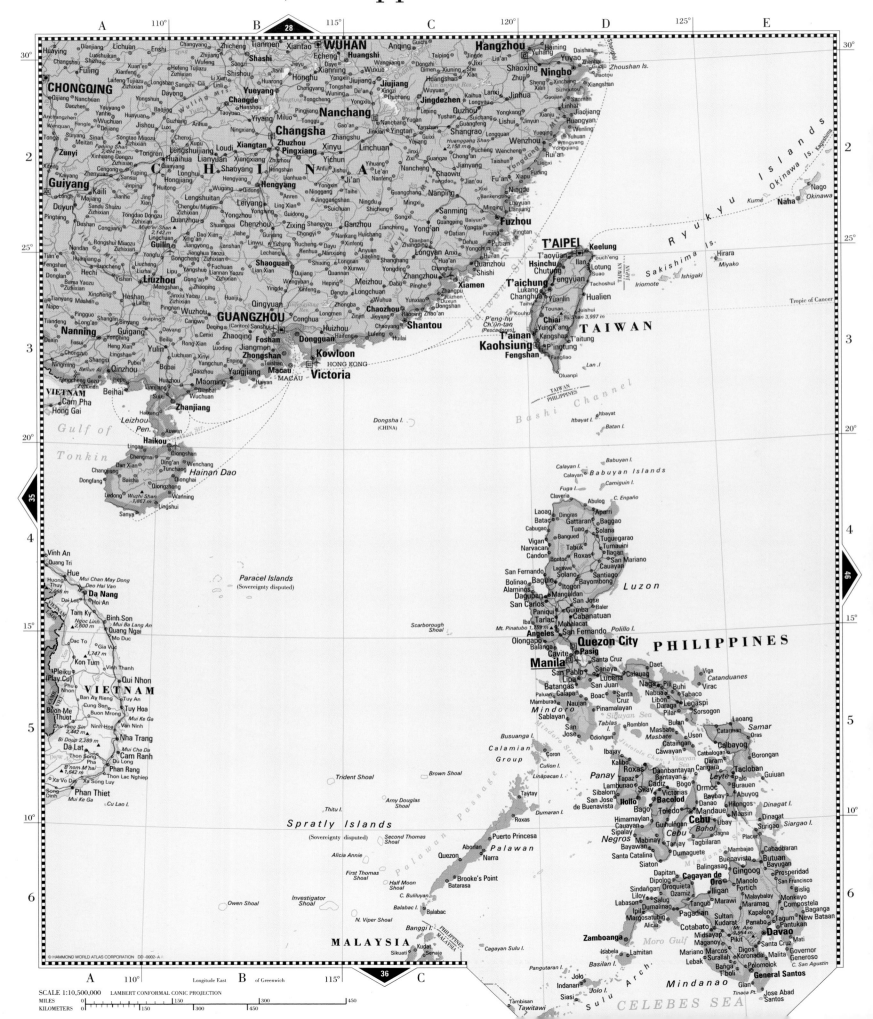

Central Asia

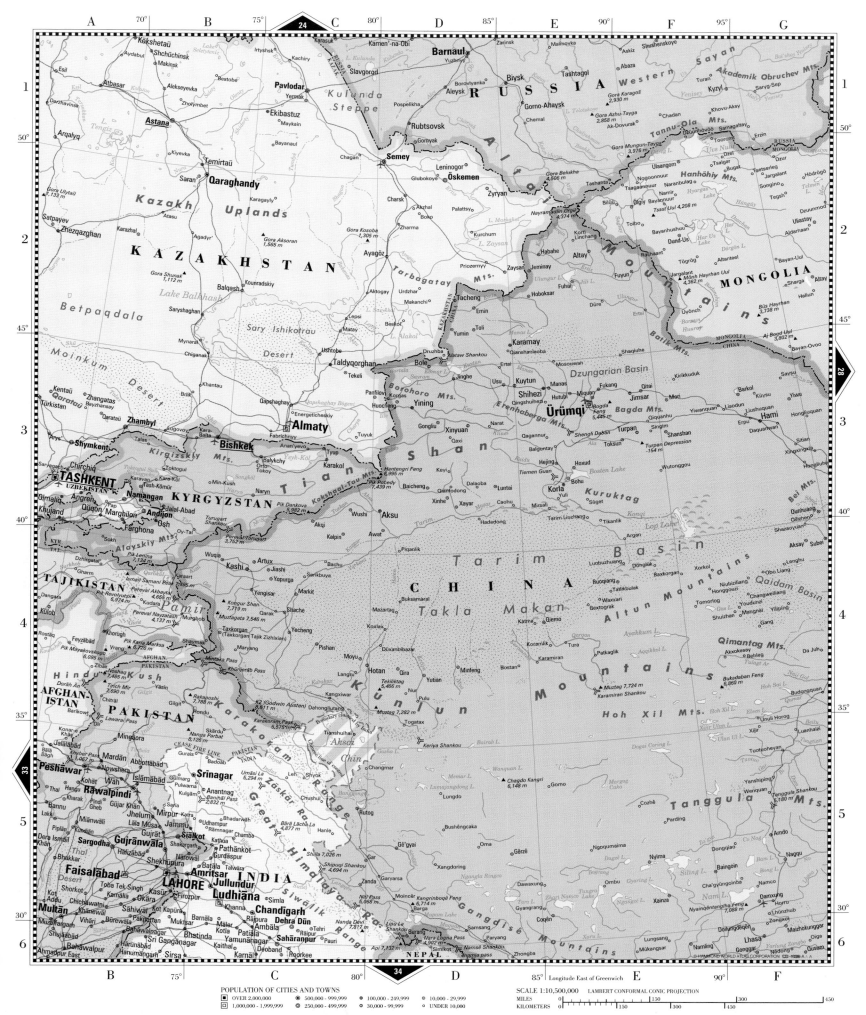

POPULATION OF CITIES AND TOWNS	
■ OVER 2,000,000	● 500,000 - 999,999	● 100,000 - 249,999	○ 10,000 - 29,999
□ 1,000,000 - 1,999,999	● 250,000 - 499,999	● 30,000 - 99,999	○ UNDER 10,000

SCALE 1:10,500,000   LAMBERT CONFORMAL CONIC PROJECTION

MILES 0 ————— 150 ————— 300 ————— 450

KILOMETERS 0 ————— 150 ————— 300 ————— 450

Longitude East of Greenwich

© HAMMOND WORLD ATLAS CORPORATION

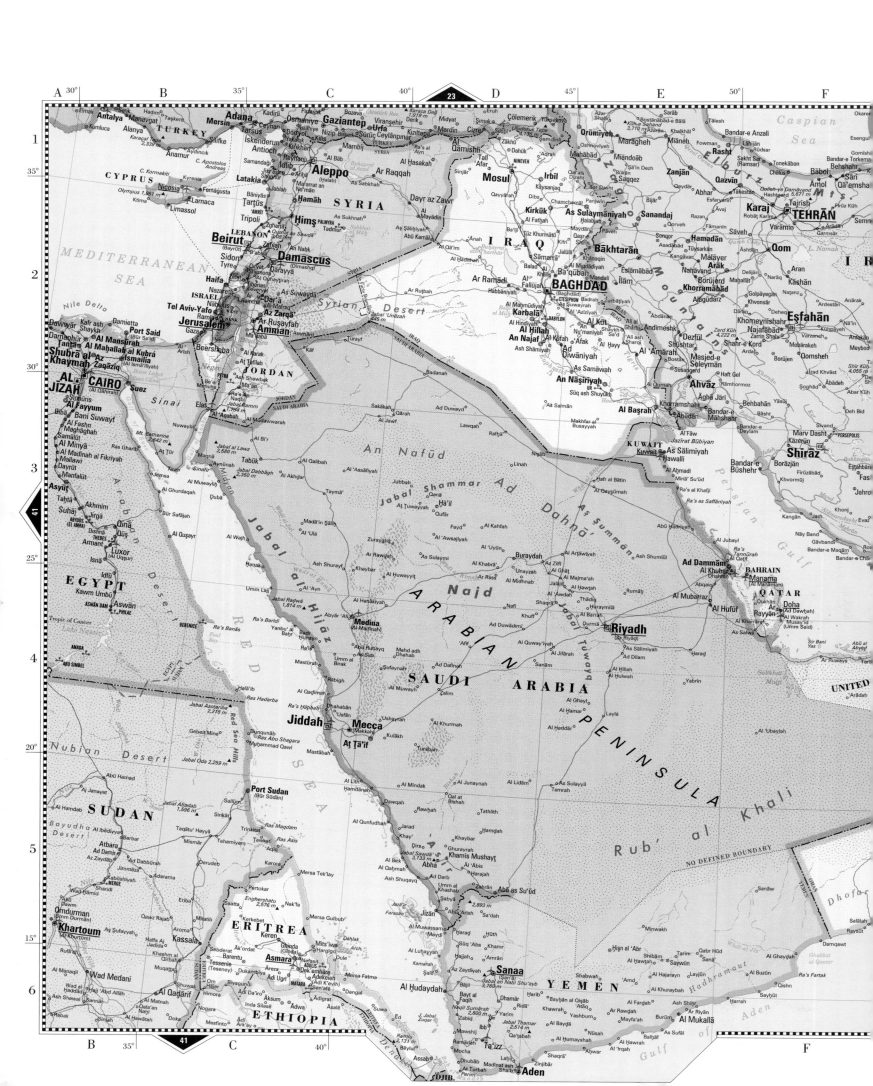

Southwestern Asia

POPULATION OF CITIES AND TOWNS

| ▪ OVER 2,000,000 | ● 500,000 - 999,999 | ● 100,000 - 249,999 | ● 10,000 - 29,999 |
| ▫ 1,000,000 - 1,999,999 | ● 250,000 - 499,999 | ● 30,000 - 99,999 | ○ UNDER 10,000 |

SCALE 1:10,500,000   LAMBERT CONFORMAL CONIC PROJECTION

MILES 0   150   300   450

KILOMETERS 0   150   300   450

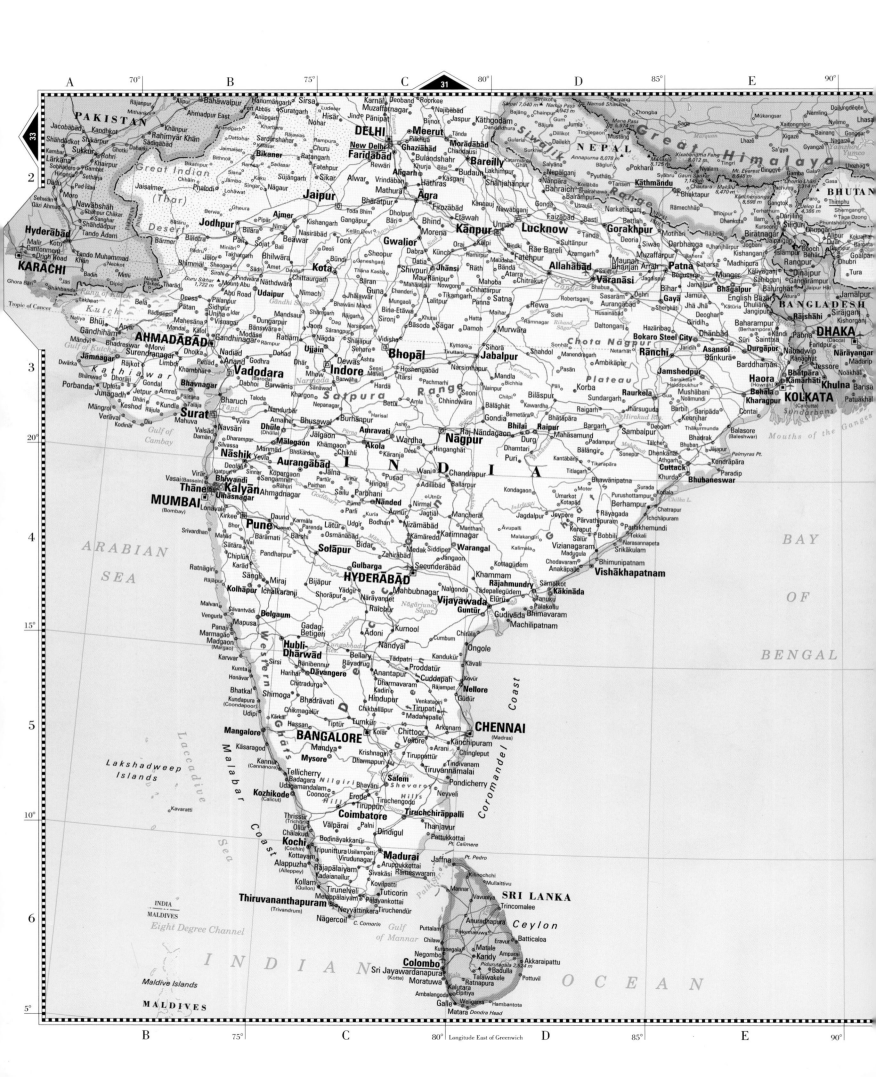

SCALE 1:10,500,000   LAMBERT CONFORMAL CONIC PROJECTION

MILES

KILOMETERS

POPULATION OF CITIES AND TOWNS

■ OVER 2,000,000
▣ 1,000,000 - 1,999,999
◙ 500,000 - 999,999
◉ 250,000 - 499,999
● 100,000 - 249,999
● 30,000 - 99,999
● 10,000 - 29,999
○ UNDER 10,000

Southeastern Asia

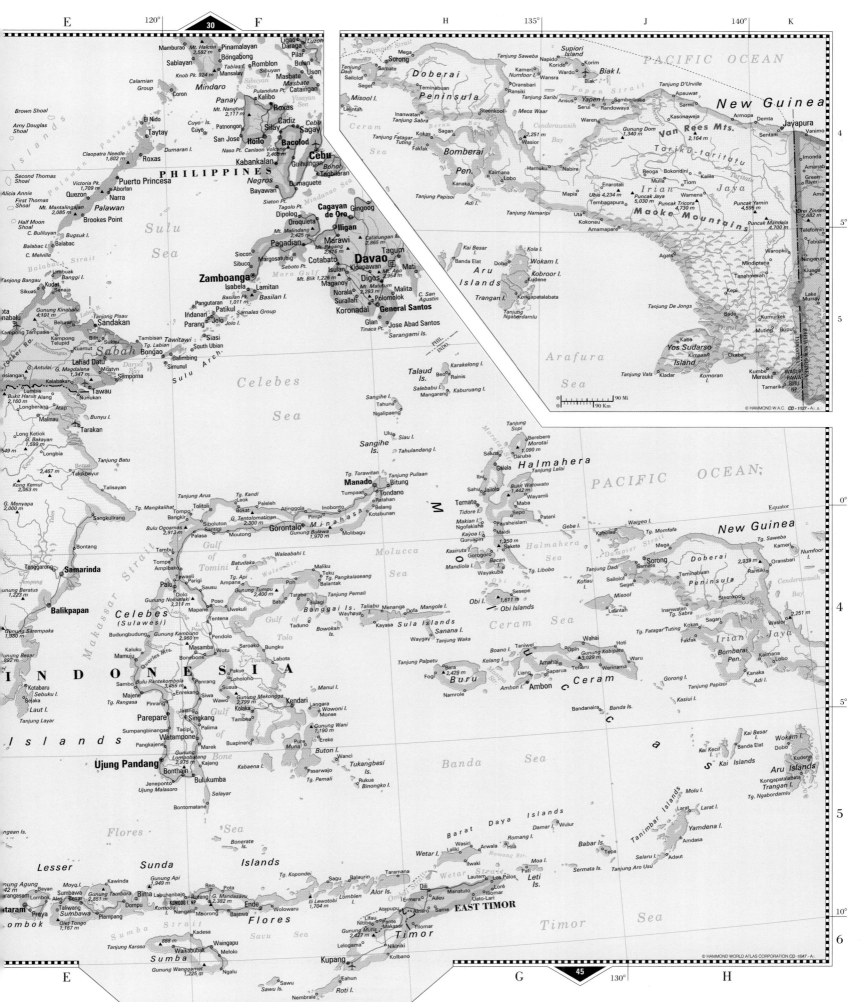

Africa - Physical

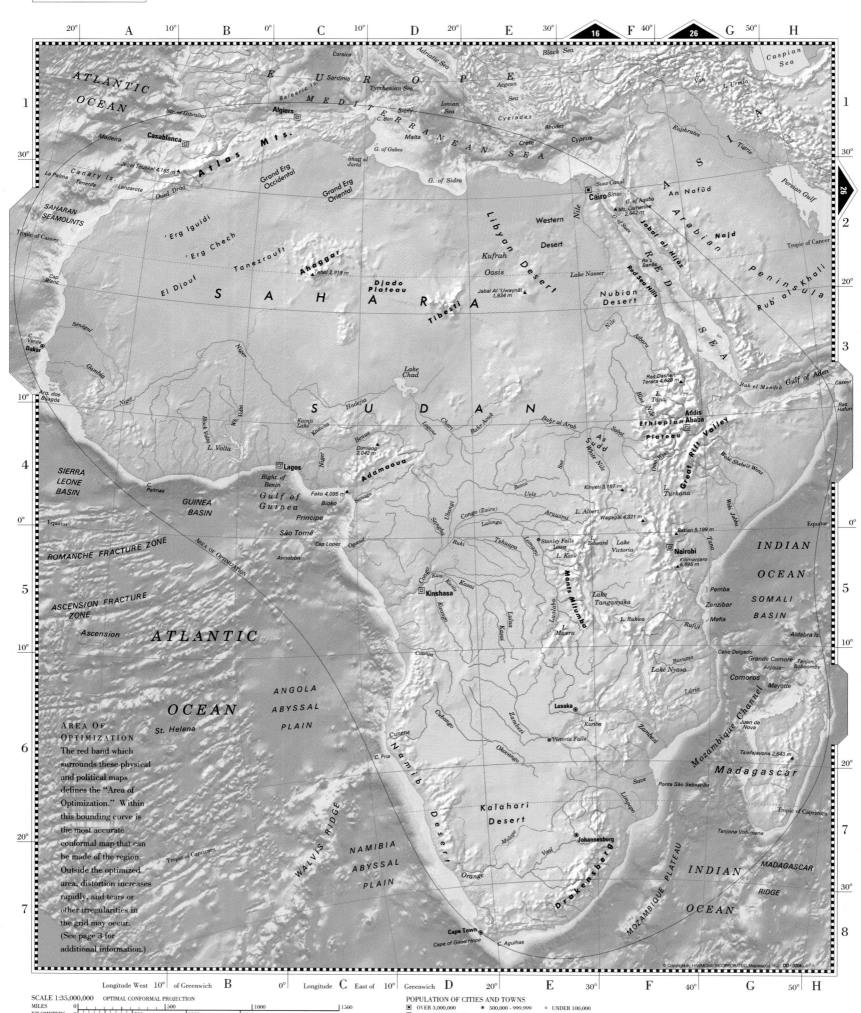

AREA OF OPTIMIZATION
The red band which surrounds these physical and political maps defines the "Area of Optimization." Within this bounding curve is the most accurate conformal map that can be made of the region. Outside the optimized area, distortion increases rapidly, and tears or other irregularities in the grid may occur. (See page 3 for additional information.)

SCALE 1:35,000,000   OPTIMAL CONFORMAL PROJECTION

MILES 0   500   1000   1500
KILOMETERS 0   500   1000   1500

POPULATION OF CITIES AND TOWNS
☐ OVER 3,000,000   ● 500,000 - 999,999   ○ UNDER 100,000
☑ 1,000,000 - 2,999,999   ● 100,000 - 499,999

© Copyright by HAMMOND INCORPORATED, Maplewood, N.J.   DD-0204-AF

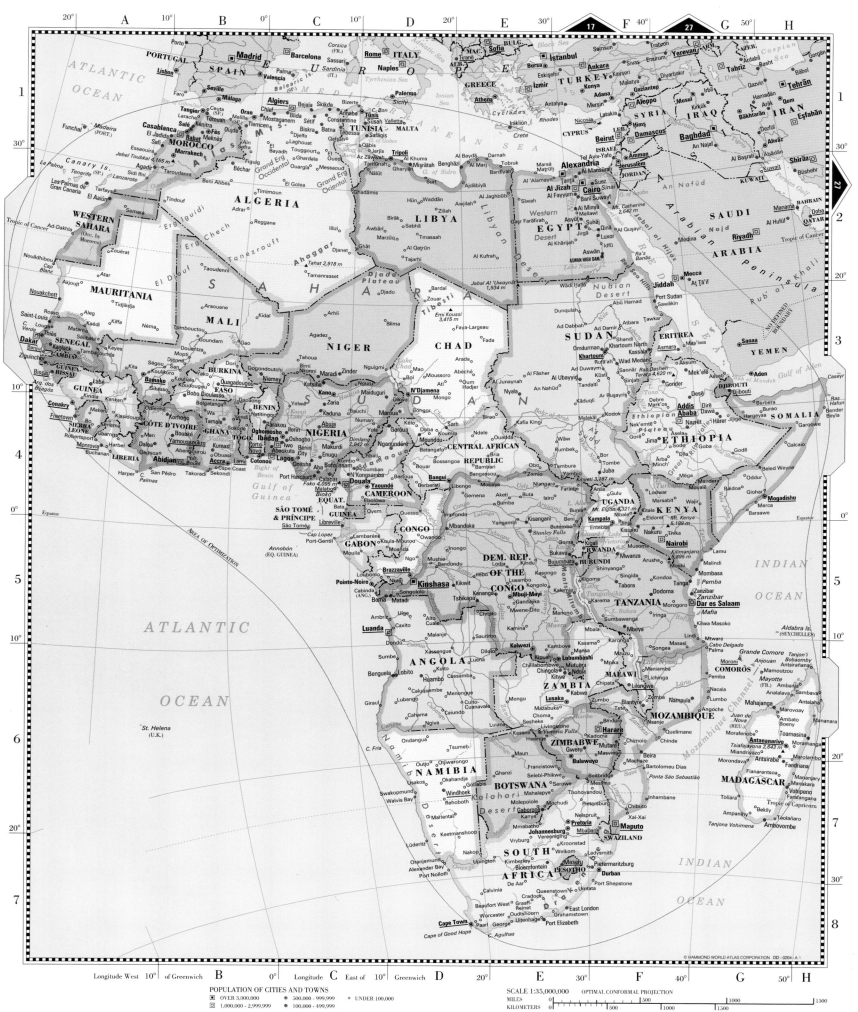

SCALE 1:35,000,000 OPTIMAL CONFORMAL PROJECTION

POPULATION OF CITIES AND TOWNS

| ■ OVER 3,000,000 | ● 500,000 - 999,999 | ○ UNDER 100,000 |
| ▣ 1,000,000 - 2,999,999 | ◉ 100,000 - 499,999 | |

MILES 0   500   1000   1500
KILOMETERS 0 500 1000

© HAMMOND WORLD ATLAS CORPORATION DD - 0204 - A A

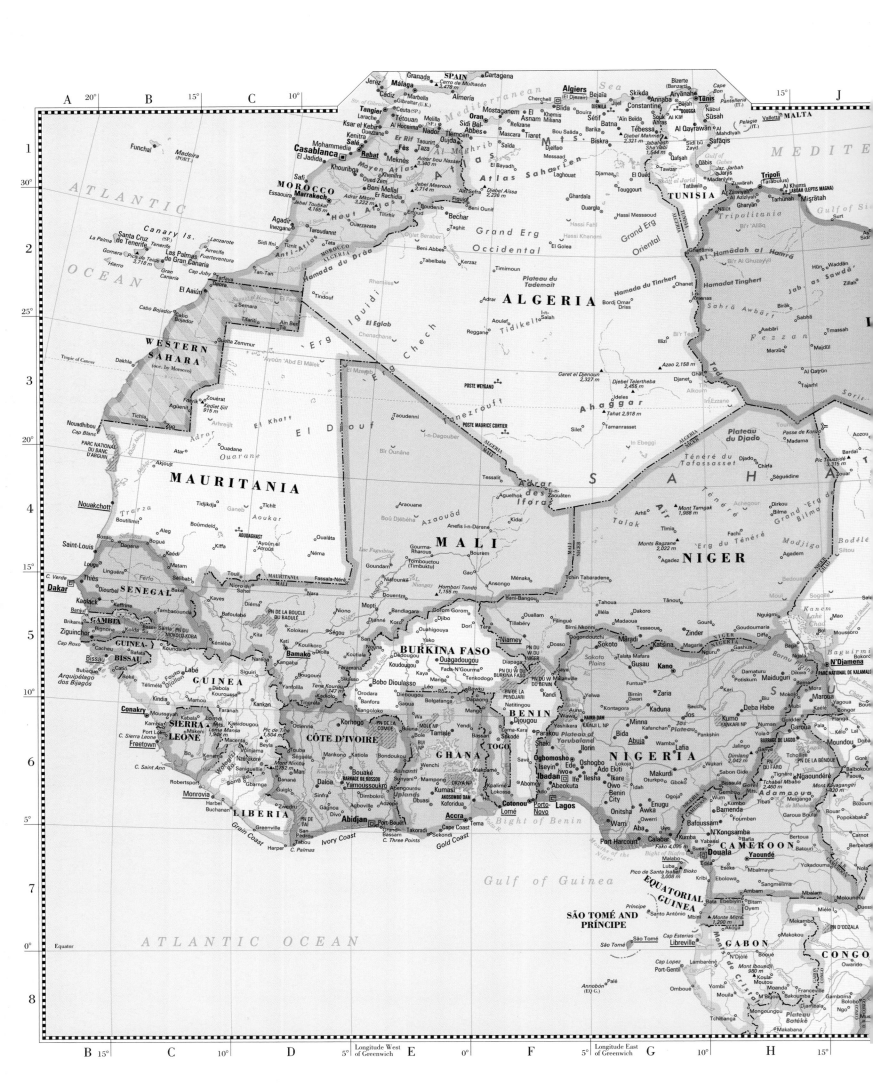

Northern Africa

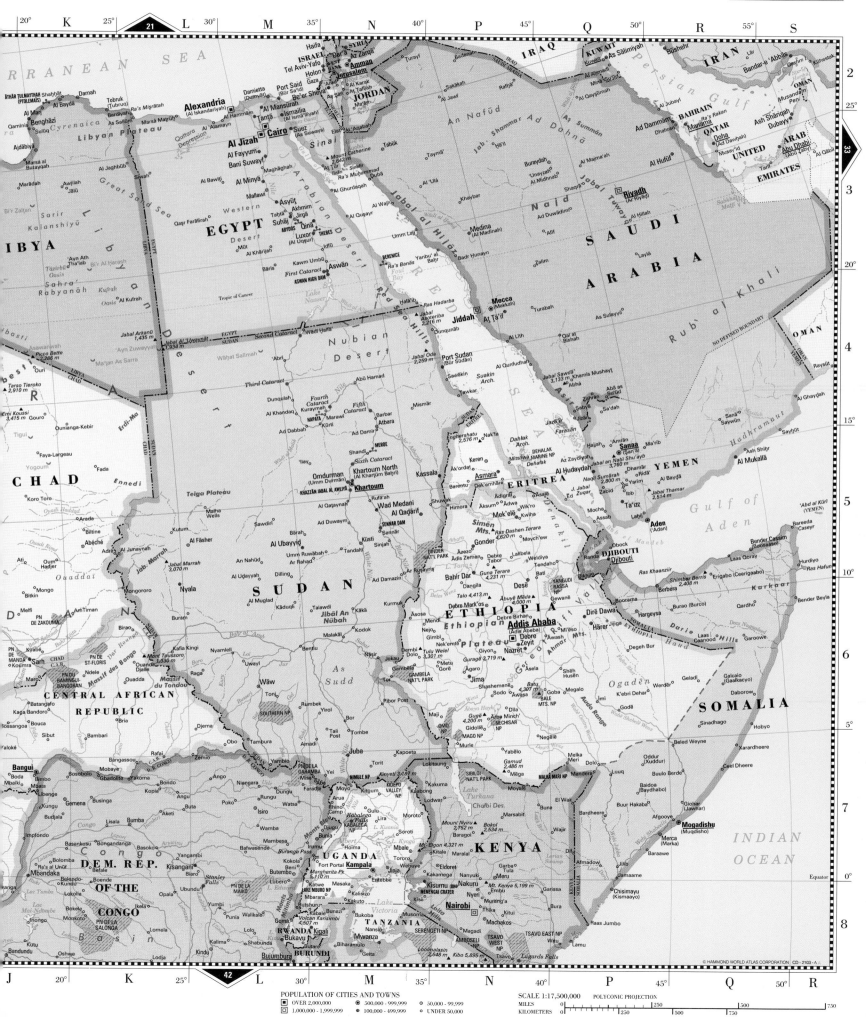

POPULATION OF CITIES AND TOWNS
- ■ OVER 2,000,000
- ▣ 1,000,000 - 1,999,999
- ● 500,000 - 999,999
- ◉ 100,000 - 499,999
- ● 50,000 - 99,999
- ○ UNDER 50,000

SCALE 1:17,500,000   POLYCONIC PROJECTION

MILES   0   250   500   750

KILOMETERS   0   250   500   750

Southern Africa

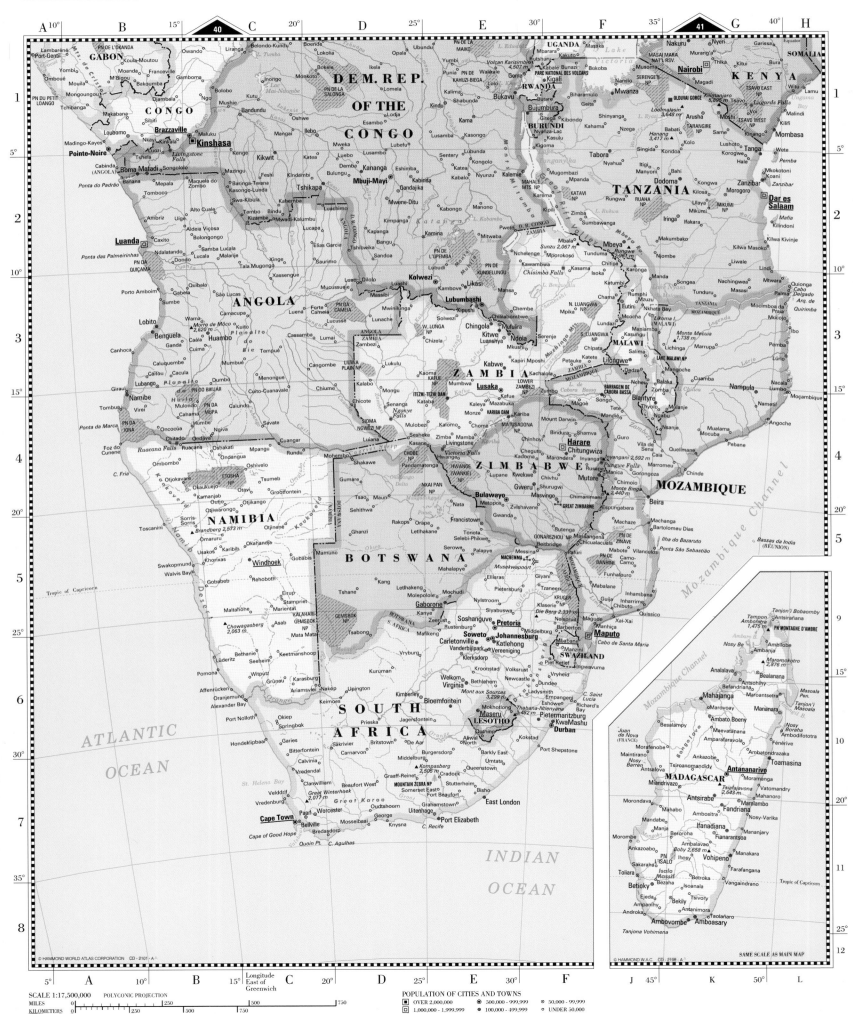

Antarctica

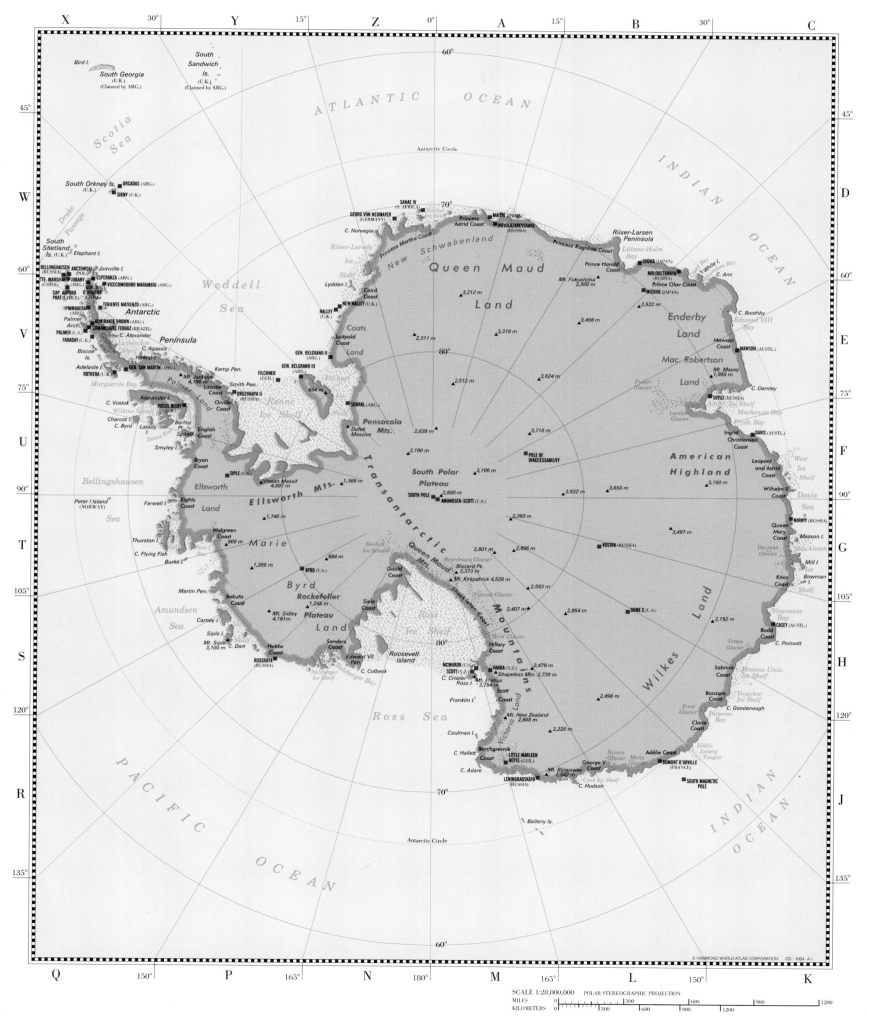

SCALE 1:28,000,000   POLAR STEREOGRAPHIC PROJECTION

MILES 0   300   600   900   1200

KILOMETERS 0   300   600   1200

Australia, New Zealand - Physical

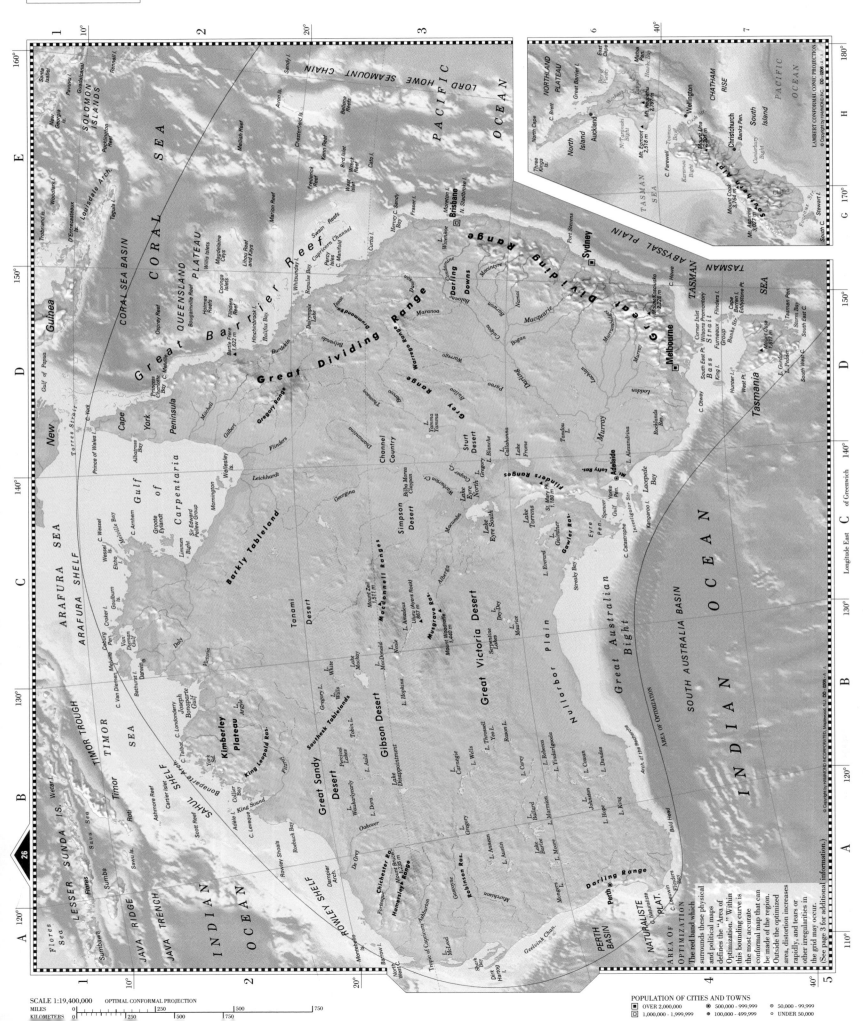

AREA OF OPTIMIZATION
The red band which surrounds these physical and political maps defines the "Area of Optimization." Within this bounding curve is the most accurate conformal map that can be made of the region. Outside the optimized area, distortion increases rapidly, and tears or other irregularities in the grid may occur. (See page 3 for additional information.)

SCALE 1:19,400,000   OPTIMAL CONFORMAL PROJECTION

MILES
0   250   500   750
KILOMETERS
0   250   500   750

LAMBERT CONFORMAL CONIC PROJECTION
© Copyright by HAMMOND INC.   DD-0206-A-1

POPULATION OF CITIES AND TOWNS
□ OVER 2,000,000
▣ 1,000,000 - 1,999,999
◉ 500,000 - 999,999
◉ 100,000 - 499,999
○ 50,000 - 99,999
○ UNDER 50,000

Australia, New Zealand - Political

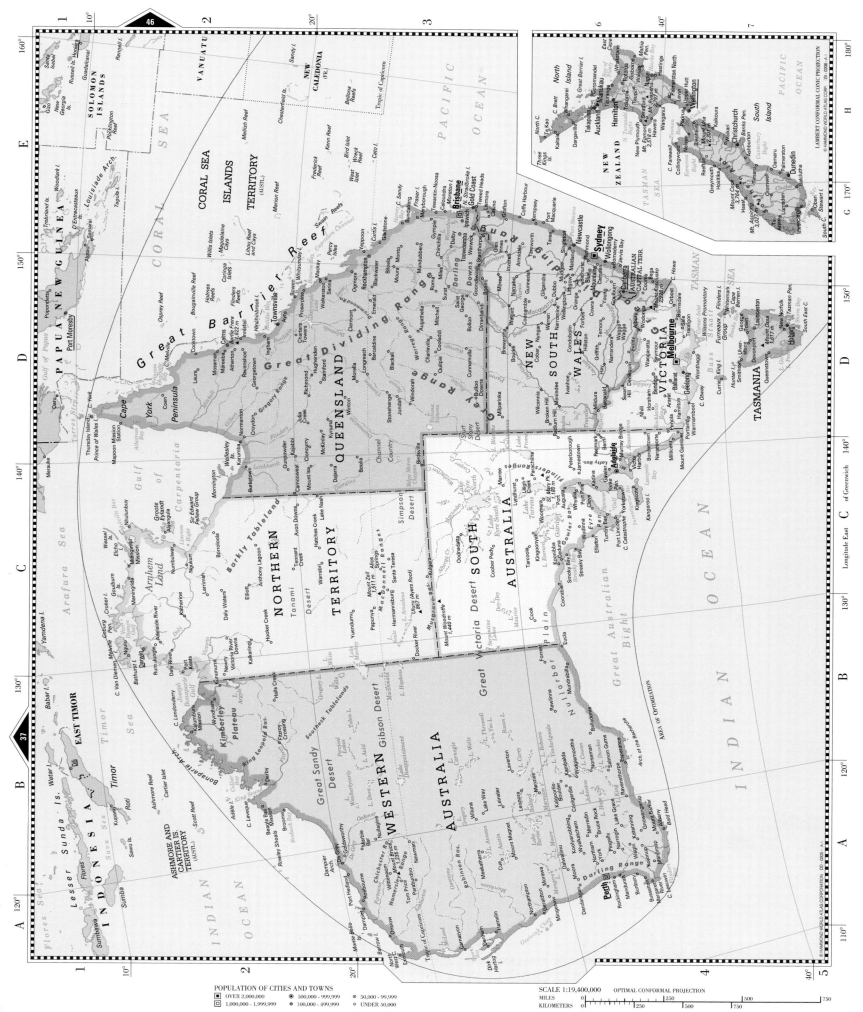

POPULATION OF CITIES AND TOWNS

| ▪ OVER 2,000,000 | ▫ 500,000 - 999,999 | ⊙ 50,000 - 99,999 |
| ◻ 1,000,000 - 1,999,999 | ● 100,000 - 499,999 | ○ UNDER 50,000 |

SCALE 1:19,400,000   OPTIMAL CONFORMAL PROJECTION

MILES 0 · · · 250 · · · 500 · · · 750

KILOMETERS 0 · · · 250 · · · 500 · · · 750

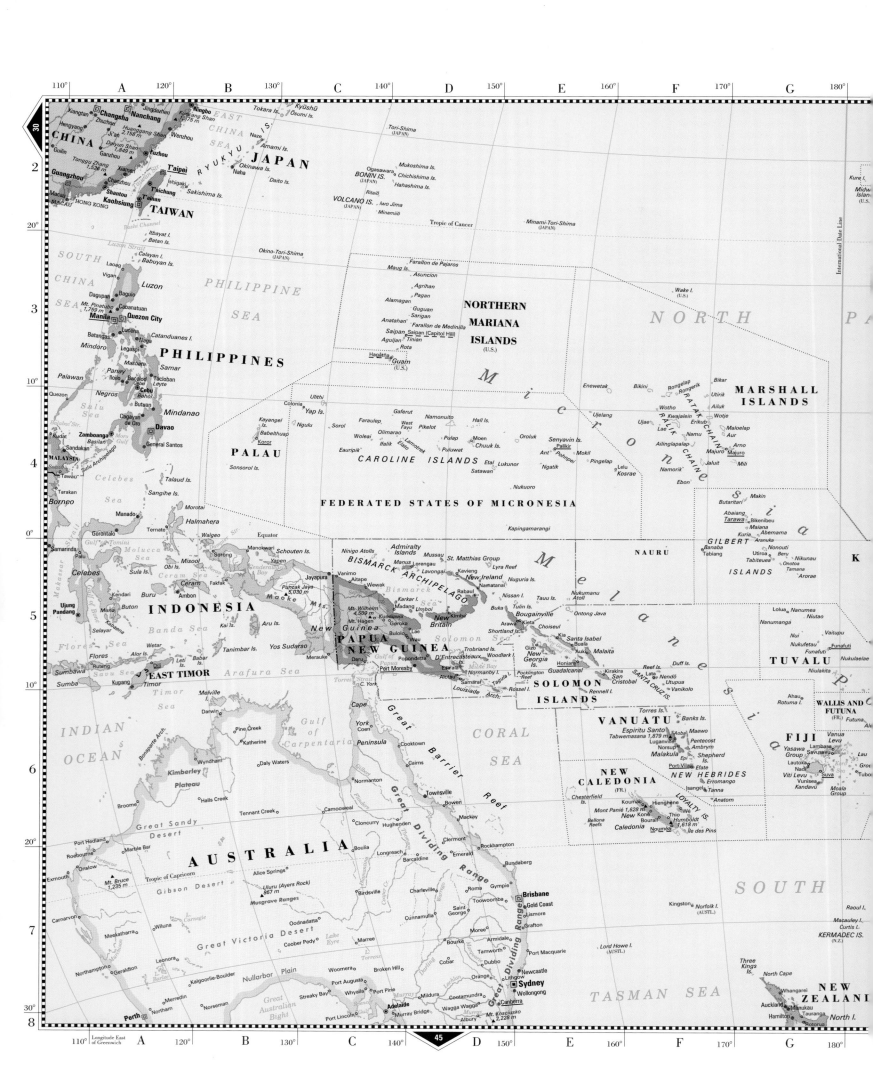

Central Pacific Ocean

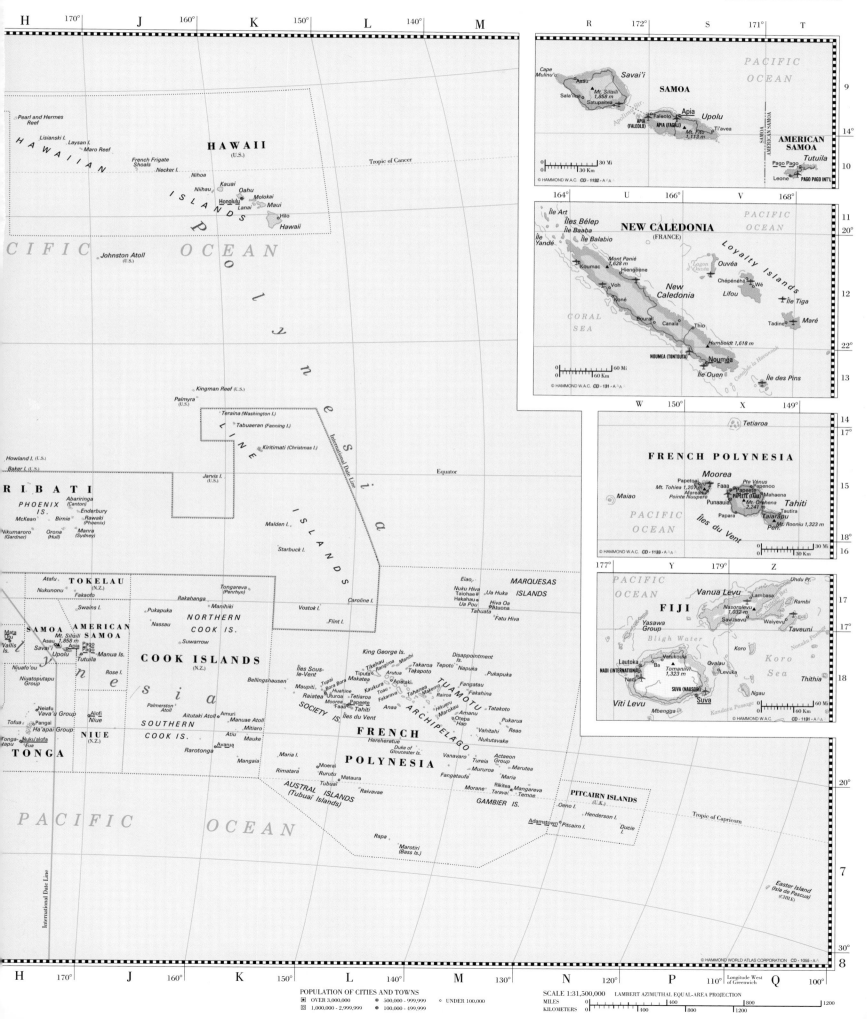

H 170° **J** 160° **K** 150° **L** 140° **M**

R 172° **S** 171° **T**

PACIFIC OCEAN

Cape Mulinu'u
Asau
Sala'ilua
Satupaitea
Savai'i
▲ Mt. Silisili 1,858 m
SAMOA
Faleolo
APIA (FALEOLO)
APIA (FAGALI)
Apia
Upolu
▲ Mt. Fito 1,113 m
Ti'avea

SAMOA / AMERICAN SAMOA

AMERICAN SAMOA
Tutuila
Pago Pago
Leone
PAGO PAGO INT'L

0   30 Mi
0   30 Km
© HAMMOND W.A.C. CD·1132·A/A

9
14°
10

U 166° **V** 168°

Île Art
Îles Bélep
Île Baaba
Île Balabio
PACIFIC OCEAN
NEW CALEDONIA
(FRANCE)
Île Yandé
Koumac
Mont Panié ▲ 1,628 m
Hienghène
Loyalty Islands
Lagon d'Ouvéa
Ouvéa
Chépénéhé
Wé
Voh
Koné
New Caledonia
Lifou
Île Tiga
CORAL SEA
Bourail
Canala
Thio
Tadine
Maré
Humboldt 1,618 m ▲
NOUMEA (TONTOUTA)
Nouméa
Île Ouen
Île des Pins
0   60 Mi
0   60 Km
© HAMMOND W.A.C. CD·131·A·A

11
20°
12
22°
13

W 150° **X** 149°

Tetiaroa
FRENCH POLYNESIA
Papetoai
Moorea
Pte Vénus
Papenoo
Mt. Tohiea 1,207 m ▲
Faaa
PAPEETE (FAA)
Papeete
Afareaitu
Mahaena
Pointe Nuupere
Tahiti
Punaauia
Mt. Orohena ▲ 2,241 m
Tautira
Maiao
Papara
Taiarapu
Pen.
Mt. Rooniu 1,323 m ▲
Îles du Vent
PACIFIC OCEAN
0   30 Mi
© HAMMOND W.A.C. CD·1133·A·A

14
17°
15
18°
16

Y 179° **Z**

PACIFIC OCEAN
Undu Pt.
Vanua Levu
Lambasa
Rambi
Nasorolevu ▲ 1,032 m
FIJI
Yasawa Group
Savusavu
Waiyevu
Taveuni
Bligh Water
Koro
Koro Sea
Lautoka
Vatukoula
Ovalau
Levuka
NADI (INTERNATIONAL)
Ba
Nadi
Tomaniivi ▲ 1,323 m
SUVA (NAUSORI)
Viti Levu
Suva
Ngau
Thithia
Mbengga
Nanuku Passage
Kandavu Passage
0   60 Mi
0   60 Km
© HAMMOND W.A.C. CD·1131·A·A

17
17°
18

Main map

Pearl and Hermes Reef
Lisianski I. Laysan I.
Maro Reef
HAWAIIAN
HAWAII
(U.S.)
French Frigate Shoals
Necker I.
Nihoa
Kauai
Niihau Oahu
Honolulu
Molokai
Lanai Maui
Hilo
Hawaii

Tropic of Cancer

ISLANDS

P O L Y N E S I A

PACIFIC OCEAN

Johnston Atoll *(U.S.)*

L i n e

Kingman Reef (U.S.)
Palmyra (U.S.)
Teraina (Washington I.)
Tabuaeran (Fanning I.)

Howland I. (U.S.)
Baker I. (U.S.)

KIRIBATI
PHOENIX IS.
Abariringa (Canton)
Enderbury
McKean Rawaki (Phoenix)
Nikumaroro (Gardner) Birnie
Orona (Hull) Manra (Sydney)

Kiritimati (Christmas I.)

Jarvis I. (U.S.)

Equator

I s l a n d s

Malden I.

Starbuck I.

Vostok I.
Caroline I.
Flint I.

International Date Line

Atafu **TOKELAU** *(N.Z.)*
Nukunonu
Fakaofo
Swains I.
Pukapuka
Rakahanga
Manihiki
Nassau
Tongareva (Penrhyn)
NORTHERN COOK IS.
Suwarrow

COOK ISLANDS *(N.Z.)*

Eiao
Nuku Hiva Taiohae
Hakahau Ua Huka
Ua Pou Atuona
Hiva Oa
Tahuata Fatu Hiva
MARQUESAS ISLANDS

SAMOA
Mata Utu
Wallis Is.
Asau ▲ Mt. Silisili 1,858 m
Savai'i
Apia Upolu
Pago Pago
AMERICAN SAMOA
Manua Is.
Tutuila
Rose I.

Njuafo'ou
Niuatoputapu Group
Neiafu Vava'u Group
Alofi
Niue
Tofua
Pangai Ha'apai Group
NIUE *(N.Z.)*
Tonga-tapu Nuku'alofa
Eua
TONGA

Palmerston Atoll
Aitutaki Atoll Amuri
Manuae Atoll
Mitiaro
SOUTHERN COOK IS.
Atiu Mauke
Avarua
Rarotonga
Mangaia

King George Is.
Manihi
Tikehau Rangiroa
Tepoto Napuka
Pukapuka
Disappointment Is.
Tiputa
Arutua
Takaroa
Takapoto
Fangatau
Fakahina
Îles Sous-le-Vent
Tupai
Maupiti Bora Bora
Huahine
Kaukura Apataki
Toau
Fakarava
Makatea
Rairoa
Raiatea Uturoa Tetiaroa
Moorea Faaa
Tahanea Makemo
Anaa
Hikueru Takatoto
Marokau
Amanu
Papeete Tahiti
Îles du Vent
Otepa Hao
Karuara
Vahitahi Reao
Nukutavake
FRENCH
Hereheretue
Duke of Gloucester Is.
Vanavaro Tureia
Actaeon Group
Marutea
TUAMOTU ARCHIPELAGO
SOCIETY IS.

POLYNESIA

Maria I.
Moerai
Maria
Rimatara
Rururu Mataura
Tubuai
Fangataufa
Rikitea Mangareva
Morane Temoe
AUSTRAL ISLANDS (Tubuai Islands)
Raivavae Taravai
GAMBIER IS.

PITCAIRN ISLANDS (U.K.)
Oeno I.
Henderson I.
Adamstown Pitcairn I. Ducie I.

Tropic of Capricorn

Rapa
Marotiri (Bass Is.)

PACIFIC OCEAN

International Date Line

Easter Island (Isla de Pascua) (CHILE)

H 170° **J** 160° **K** 150° **L** 140° **M** 130° **N** 120° **P** 110° Longitude West of Greenwich **Q** 100°

POPULATION OF CITIES AND TOWNS

- ■ OVER 3,000,000
- ● 500,000 - 999,999
- ○ UNDER 100,000
- ▣ 1,000,000 - 2,999,999
- ● 100,000 - 499,999

SCALE 1:31,500,000   LAMBERT AZIMUTHAL EQUAL-AREA PROJECTION

MILES   0   400   800   1200
KILOMETERS   0   400   800

North America - Physical

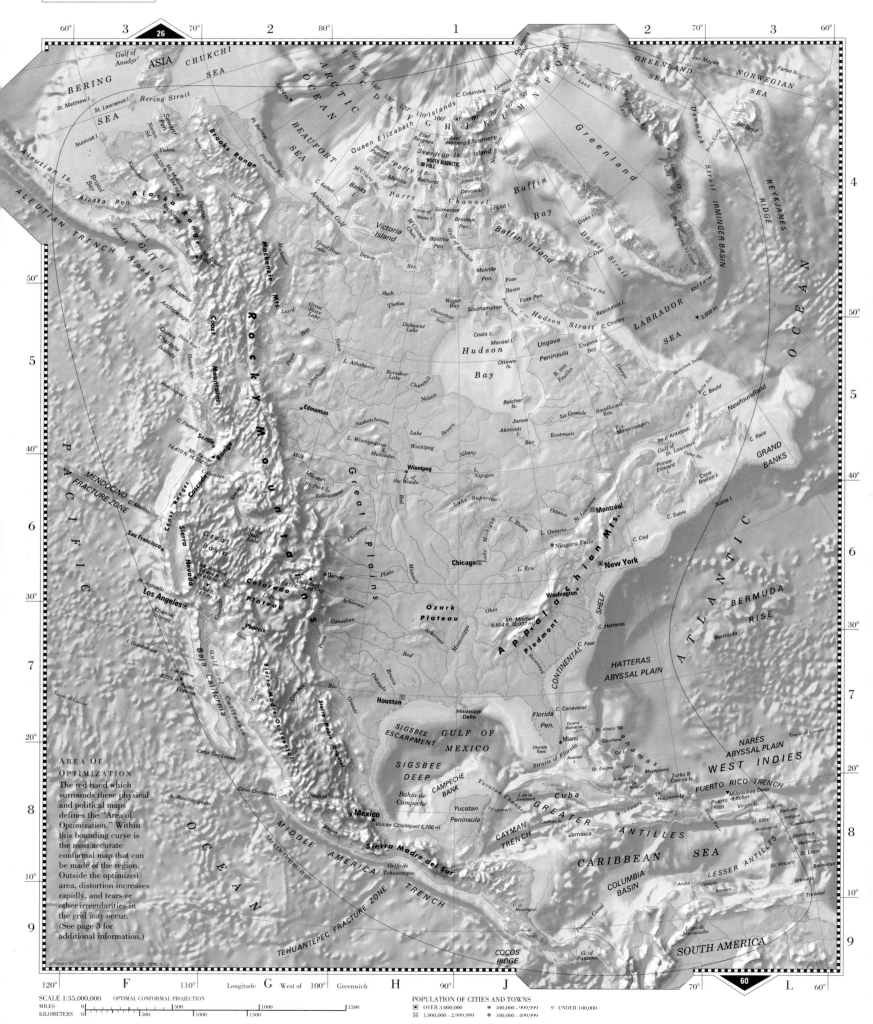

AREA OF OPTIMIZATION

The red band which surrounds these physical and political maps defines the "Area of Optimization." Within this bounding curve is the most accurate conformal map that can be made of the region. Outside the optimized area, distortion increases rapidly, and tears or other irregularities in the grid may occur. (See page 3 for additional information.)

SCALE 1:35,000,000   OPTIMAL CONFORMAL PROJECTION

MILES

KILOMETERS

Longitude   West of   Greenwich

POPULATION OF CITIES AND TOWNS

☐ OVER 3,000,000   ● 500,000 - 999,999   ○ UNDER 100,000
☐ 1,000,000 - 2,999,999   ● 100,000 - 499,999

© HAMMOND WORLD ATLAS CORPORATION CD - 1076 • A • A

North America - Political

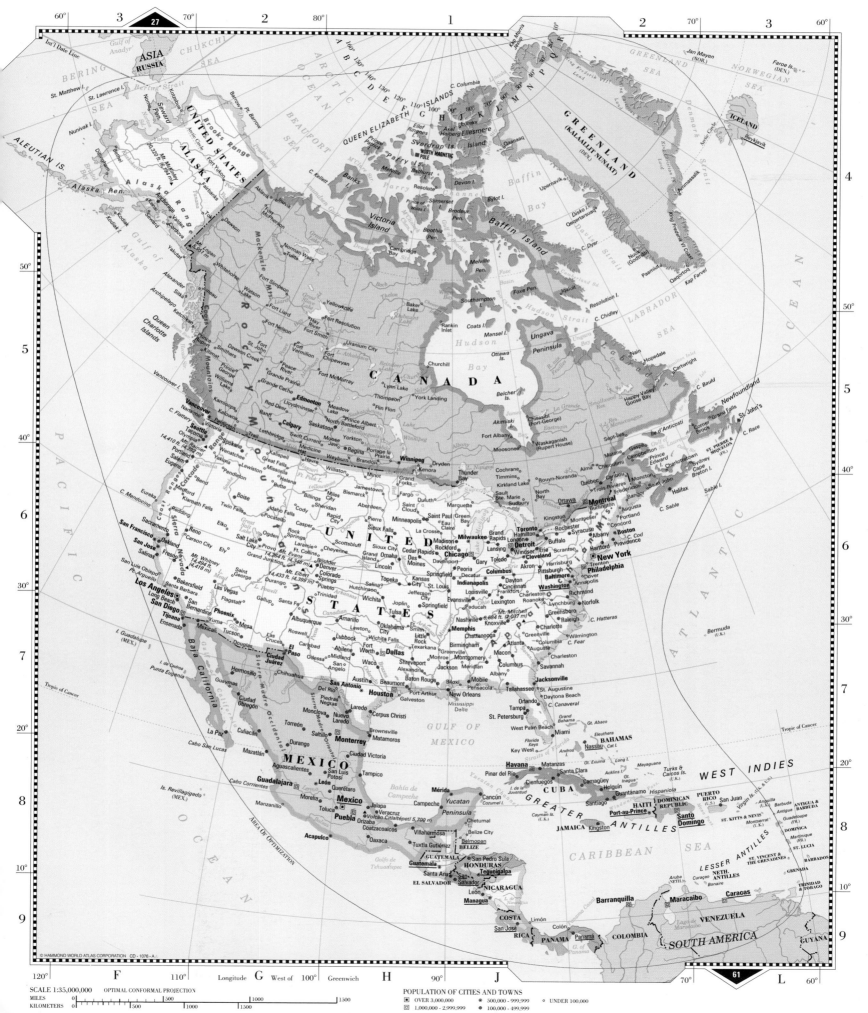

SCALE 1:35,000,000   OPTIMAL CONFORMAL PROJECTION

POPULATION OF CITIES AND TOWNS

Southwestern Canada, Northwestern United States

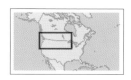

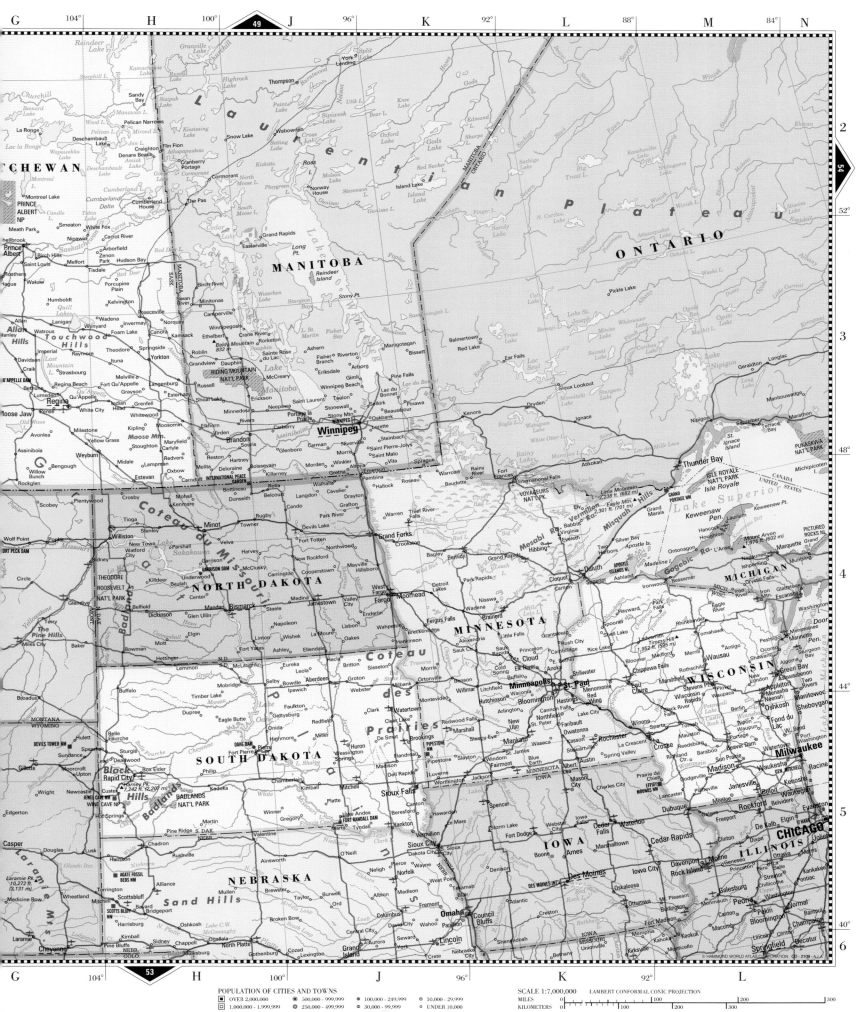

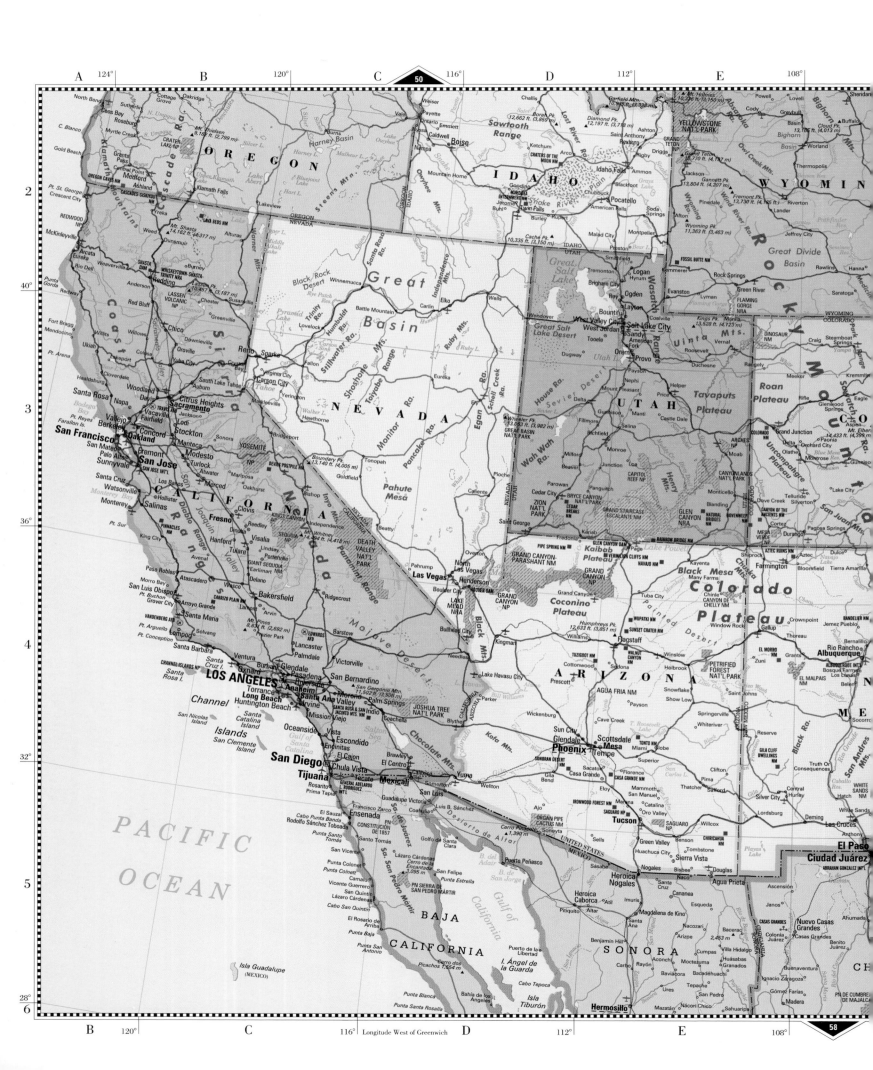

Southwestern United States

POPULATION OF CITIES AND TOWNS

■ OVER 2,000,000	● 500,000 - 999,999	● 100,000 - 249,999	○ 10,000 - 29,999
▣ 1,000,000 - 1,999,999	◉ 250,000 - 499,999	● 30,000 - 99,999	○ UNDER 10,000

SCALE 1:7,000,000   LAMBERT CONFORMAL CONIC PROJECTION

MILES 0   50   100   200   300

KILOMETERS 0   100   200   300

© HAMMOND WORLD ATLAS CORPORATION   CD-2110-A

Southeastern Canada,
Northeastern United States

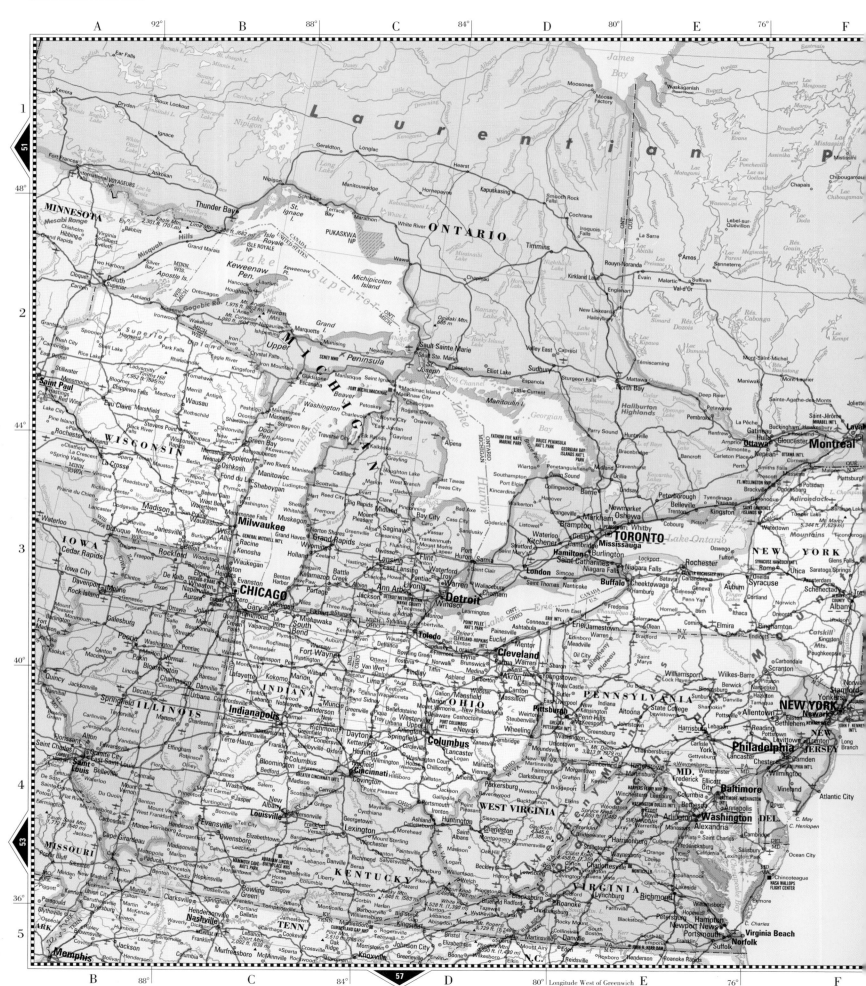

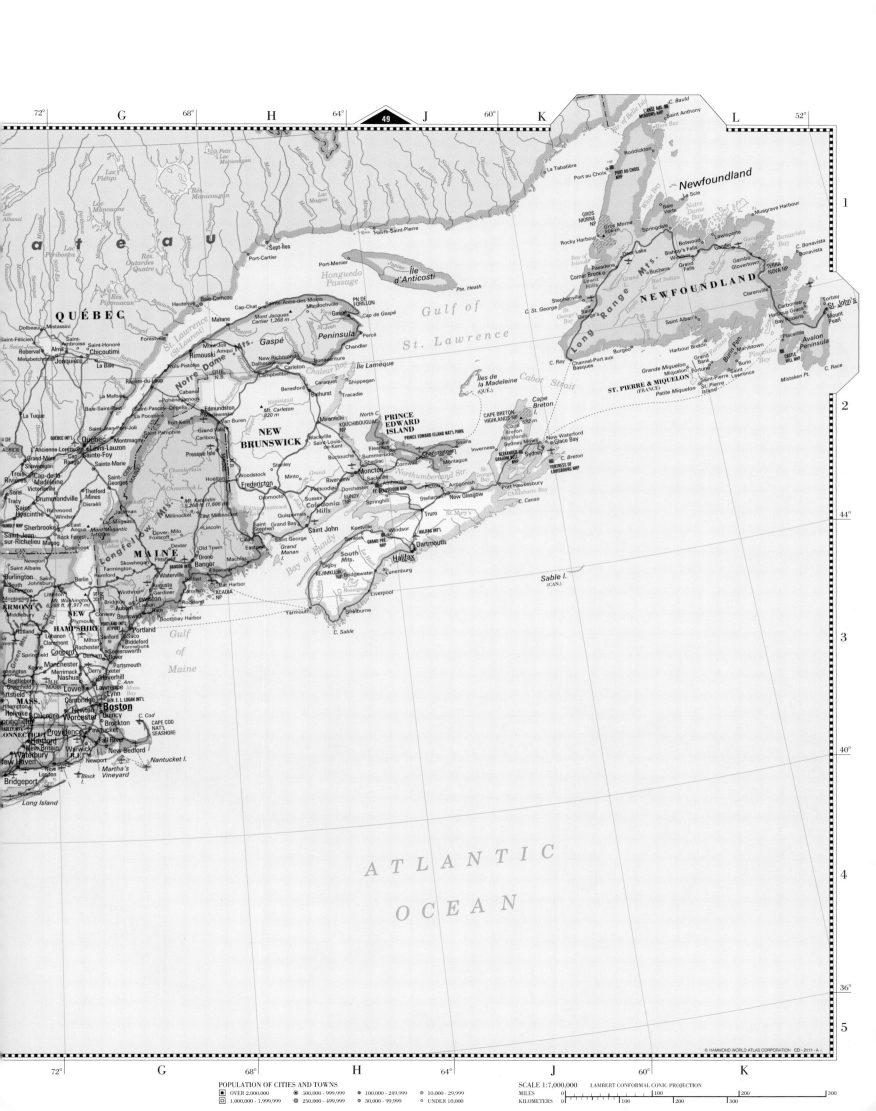

72°   G   68°   H   64°   J   60°   K   L   52°

QUÉBEC

Newfoundland

Plateau

Gulf of
St. Lawrence

NEWFOUNDLAND

Île
d'Anticosti

*Honguedo
Passage*

Gaspé
Peninsula

NEW
BRUNSWICK

PRINCE
EDWARD
ISLAND

Cabot Strait

ST. PIERRE & MIQUELON
(FRANCE)

Avalon
Peninsula

St. John's

NOVA SCOTIA area

Northumberland Str.

Cape
Breton
I.

Charlottetown

Moncton

Fredericton

Saint John

Halifax

Bay of Fundy

MAINE

Gulf
of
Maine

Sable I.
(CAN.)

VERMONT

NEW
HAMPSHIRE

Portland

MASS.

BOSTON

CONNECTICUT

Providence

Cape Cod

Long Island

Nantucket I.

Martha's
Vineyard

Block
I.

A T L A N T I C

O C E A N

72°   G   68°   H   64°   J   60°   K

1

2

44°

3

40°

4

36°

5

© HAMMOND WORLD ATLAS CORPORATION   CD - 2111 - A

POPULATION OF CITIES AND TOWNS

■ OVER 2,000,000   ● 500,000 - 999,999   ● 100,000 - 249,999   ⊙ 10,000 - 29,999
□ 1,000,000 - 1,999,999   ● 250,000 - 499,999   ⊙ 30,000 - 99,999   ○ UNDER 10,000

SCALE 1:7,000,000   LAMBERT CONFORMAL CONIC PROJECTION
MILES   0   100   200   300
KILOMETERS   0   100   200   300

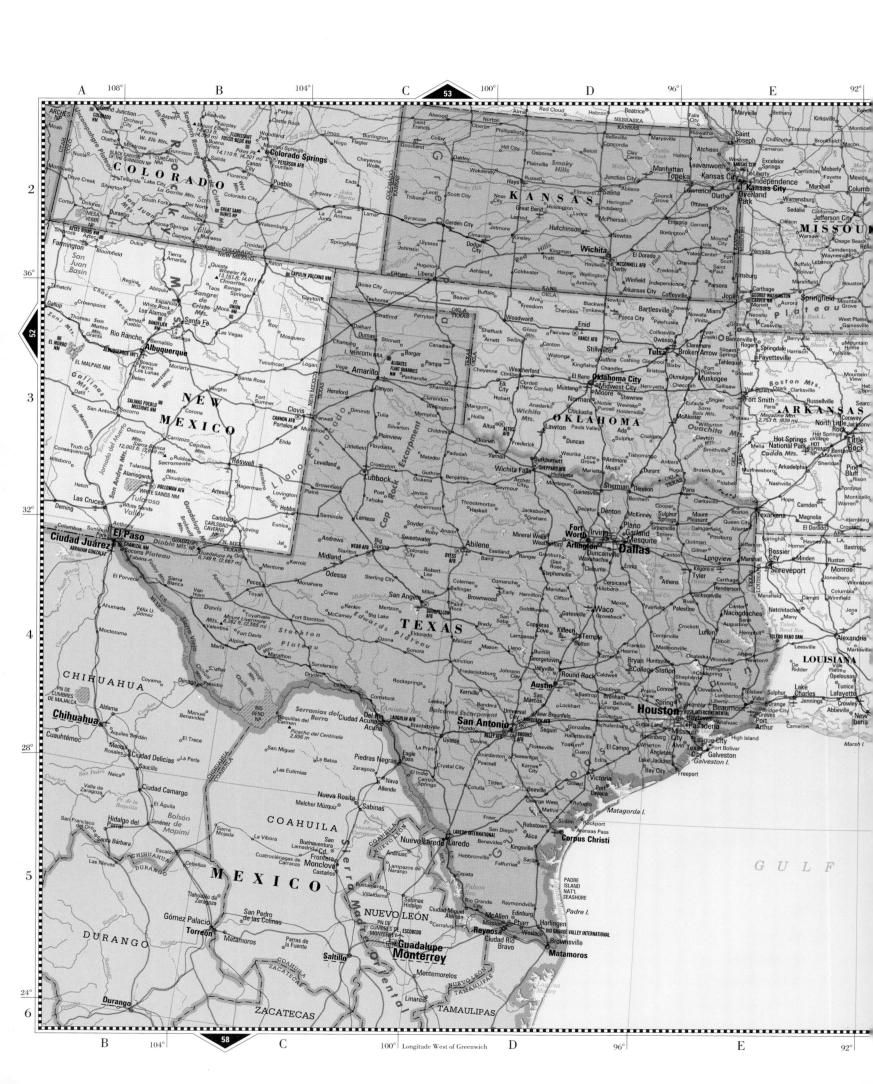

Southeastern United States

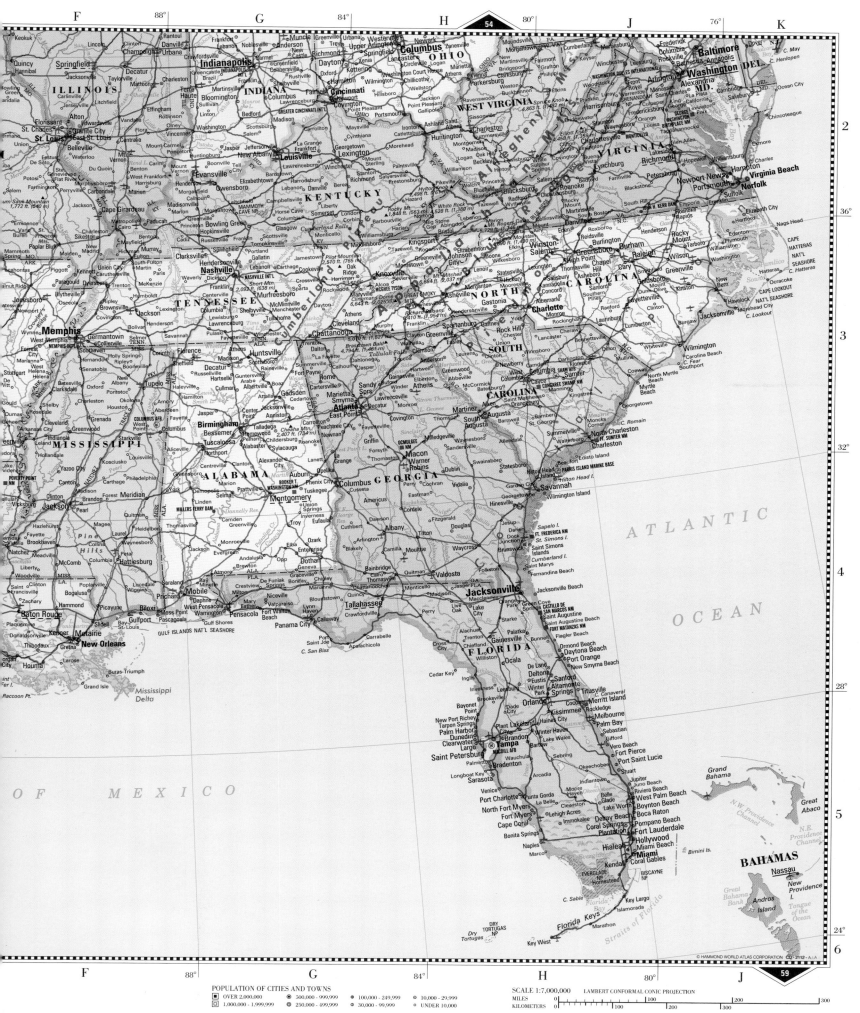

POPULATION OF CITIES AND TOWNS

■ OVER 2,000,000   ◉ 500,000 - 999,999   ● 100,000 - 249,999   ○ 10,000 - 29,999
□ 1,000,000 - 1,999,999   ◐ 250,000 - 499,999   ◔ 30,000 - 99,999   ○ UNDER 10,000

SCALE 1:7,000,000   LAMBERT CONFORMAL CONIC PROJECTION

MILES 0   100   200   300
KILOMETERS 0   100   200   300

Middle America and Caribbean

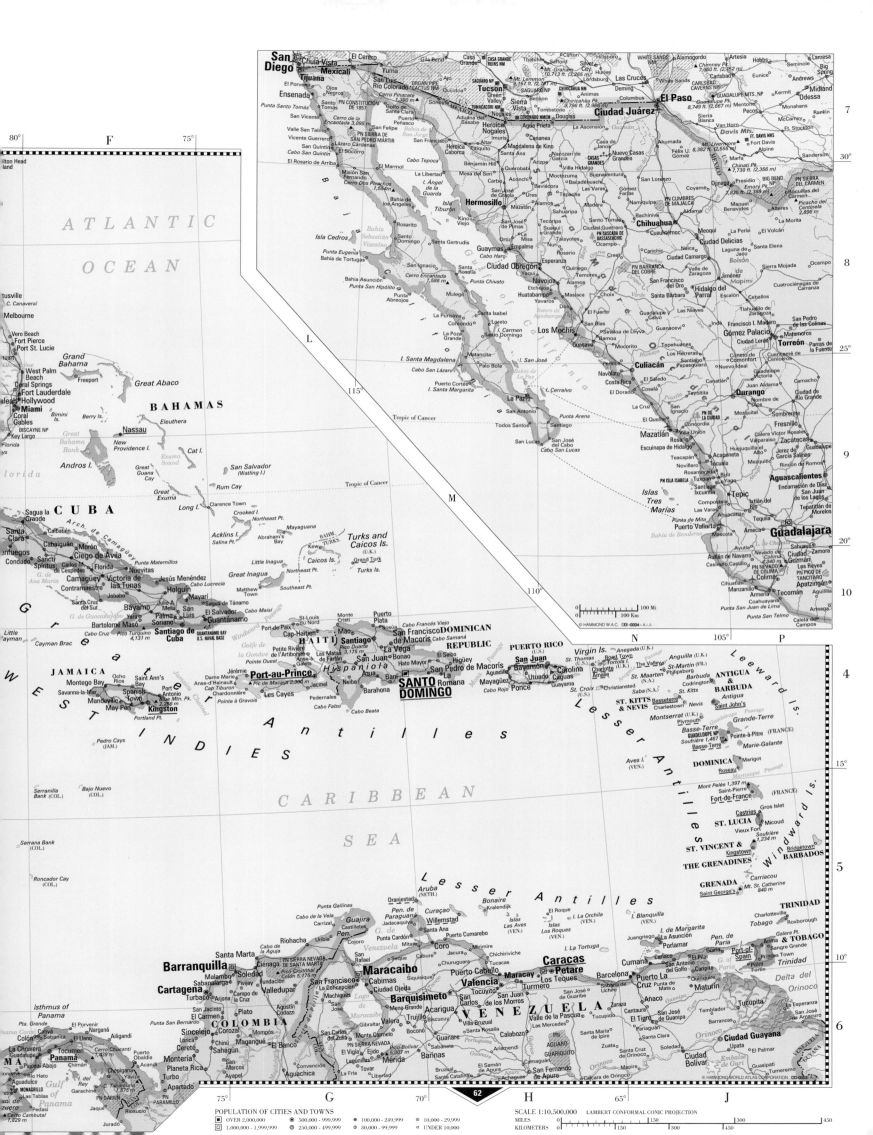

South America - Physical

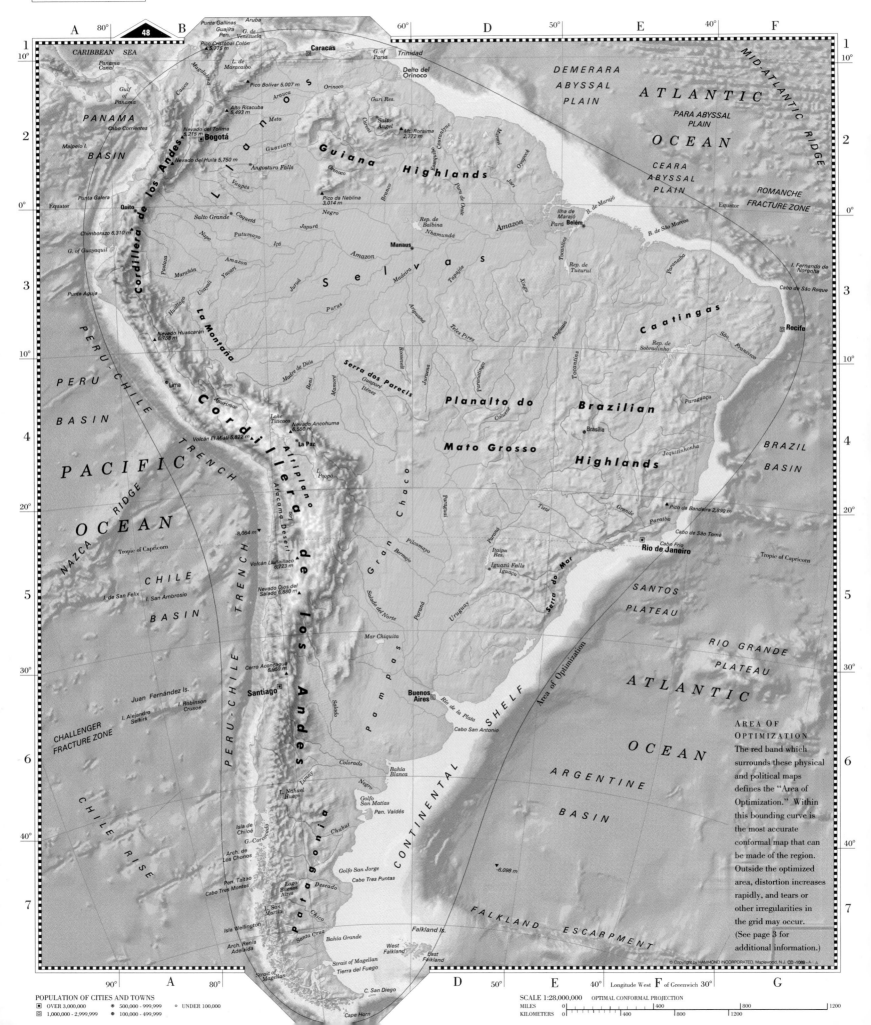

AREA OF OPTIMIZATION

The red band which surrounds these physical and political maps defines the "Area of Optimization." Within this bounding curve is the most accurate conformal map that can be made of the region. Outside the optimized area, distortion increases rapidly, and tears or other irregularities in the grid may occur. (See page 3 for additional information.)

POPULATION OF CITIES AND TOWNS

□ OVER 3,000,000 ● 500,000 - 999,999 ○ UNDER 100,000
■ 1,000,000 - 2,999,999 ● 100,000 - 499,999

SCALE 1:28,000,000 OPTIMAL CONFORMAL PROJECTION

MILES 0   400   800   1200
KILOMETERS 0   400   800   1200

South America - Political

POPULATION OF CITIES AND TOWNS
- ▣ OVER 3,000,000
- ▣ 1,000,000 - 2,999,999
- ● 500,000 - 999,999
- ● 100,000 - 499,999
- ○ UNDER 100,000

SCALE 1:28,000,000   OPTIMAL CONFORMAL PROJECTION

MILES 0   400   800   1200
KILOMETERS 0   400   800   1200

Northern South America

ATLANTIC

OCEAN

St. Peter and
St. Paul Rocks
(BRAZIL)

Equator

Rocas

Fernando de Noronha
(BRAZIL)

New
Amsterdam
Totness
Nieuw-
Nickerie
Paramaribo
Nieuw-
Amsterdam
Albina
Saint-Laurent
du Maroni
Devil's I.
Iles du Salut
Cayenne
Sinnamary
Kourou
Brokopondo
Rémire
Pointe Béhague
SURINAME
Juliana Top
1,230 m
Cottica
FRENCH GUIANA
Régina
Cabo Orange
Wilhelmina Mts.
Saül
Orange
Mts.
Ouaqui
Oiapoque
PN DO
CABO ORANGE
Calçoene
Alalapadu
Tumuc-Humac Mts.
Amapá
Ilha de Maracá
Cabo do Norte

Serra
Tumucumaque
I. Janaucu
I. Caviana
Cabo do Norte
Macapá
I. Mexiana
Mazagão
I. Queimada
Ilha Grande
de Gurupá
Ilha de
Marajó
Soure
Vigia
Salinópolis
Salinópolis
Bragança
Ilhas de São João

Oriximiná
Óbidos
Alenquer
Almeirim
Breves
Portel
Castanhal
Capanema
Cururupu
Parintins
Monte
Alegre
Cametá
Igarapé-Miri
Mocajuba
São Luís
Santarém
Altamira
Paragominas
Pinheiro
Viana
Rosário
Camocim
Juruti
PN DA AMAZÔNIA
(TAPAJÓS)
Tucuruí
Penalva
Santa Inês
Pindaré-Mirim
Santa Luzia
Coroatá
Codó
Caxias
Parnaíba
Granja
Itapipoca
Sobral
Caucaia
Fortaleza
Cascavel
Itaituba
Represa de
Tucuruí
Bacabal
Pedreiras
União
Campo Maior
Piripiri
Tianguá
Ipu
Baturité
Marabá
Barra do
Corda
Presidente
Dutra
Timon
Teresina
Altos
Crateús
Quixeramobim
Boa
Viagem
Mombaça
Canindé
Araxati
Aracati
Mossoró
Ceará-Mirim
Natal
Ipatinga
Itupiranga
Araguatins
Imperatriz
Grajaú
Colinas
Água
Branca
Tauá
Acopiara
Morada
Nova
Açu
Macaíba
Parnamirim
Araguaína
Tocantinópolis
Regeneração
Floriano
Oeiras
Picos
Icó
Cedro
Sousa
Caicó
Currais
Novos
Nova Cruz
Gradaús
Conceição do
Araguaia
Guaraí
Balsas
Represa de Boa
Esperança
Araripina
Várzea Alegre
Crato
Salgueiro
Pombal
Guarabira
Campina
Grande
Timbaúba
João Pessoa
Bayeux
Serra da
Seringa
Miracema
do Tocantins
Juazeiro
do Norte
Serra Talhada
Arcoverde
Vitória de
Santo Antão
Santa
Rita
Recife
Olinda
Paraíso do
Tocantins
Porto Nacional
Ouricuri
Floresta
Belo Jardim
Caruaru
Jaboatão
PN DO
ARAGUAIA
Santa Teresinha
Petrolina
Juazeiro
PN DA SERRA
DA CAPIVARA
Remanso
Sa. Dois Irmãos
Garanhuns
União dos
Palmares
Palmares
Sinop
Barreiras
Corrente
Xique-Xique
Irecê
PN DE PAULO AFONSO
Paulo Afonso
Palmeira dos
Índios
Rio Largo
Maceió
Alta Floresta
PARQUE
NACIONAL
DO XINGU
Ibotirama
Morro do
Chapéu
Senhor do
Bonfim
Campo
Formoso
Ribeira do
Pombal
Cícero
Dantas
Itabaiana
Arapiraca
Penedo
Barra
Jacobina
Tobias
Barreto
Lagarto
Aracaju
Nortelândia
Diamantino
Arenápolis
angaçu da Serra
Barra do
Bugres
Nova Xavantina
Santana
Bom Jesus
da Lapa
Santa
Maria
Riacho de
Santana
Jaguaquara
Serrinha
Esplanada
Alagoinhas
Feira de Santana
Itaberaba
Candeias
Camaçari
Salvador
Cuiabá
Poxoréo
Barra do
Garças
Araguaiana
Goiás
PN DA CHAPADA
DOS VEADEIROS
Uruaçu
Formosa
Januária
Cruz das
Almas
Nazaré
Valença
I. de Tinharé
Pocone
Rondonópolis
Alto Garças
Guiratinga
Iporá
Inhumas
Trindade
Anápolis
Cristalina
Unaí
Montes
Claros
Salinas
Pedra Azul
Guanambi
Caculé
Carinhanha
Espinosa
Monte Azul
Ipiaú
Ubatã
Jequié
Vitória da
Conquista
Itapetinga
Ibicaraí
Itabuna
Ilhéus
Rio Verde de
Mato Grosso
Coxim
PN DAS EMAS
Mineiros
Jataí
Santa Helena
de Goiás
Rio
Verde
Itumbiara
Morrinhos
João Pinheiro
Corinto
Diamantina
Otoni
Teófilo
Otoni
Nanuque
Ponta da Baleia
Pantanal
Alto Araguaia
PN CHAPADA
DIAMANTINA
Barbacena
Paracatu
Ipameri
Catalão
Araguari
Patrocínio
Araxá
Patos de
Minas
Curvelo
Pico do Itambé
2,033 m
Pirapora
Bocaiúva
Itamaraju
PN DE MONTE
PASCOAL
Canavieiras
PN PANTANAL
MATOGROSSENSE
Uberlândia
Ituiutaba
Monte
Carmelo
Abaeté
Sete
Lagoas
Ipatinga
Baixo
Guandu
Governador
Valadares
São Gabriel da Palha
Nova Venécia
São Mateus
Aquidauana
Anastácio
Uberaba
Frutal
Lagoa
da Prata
Contagem
Itabira
Timóteo
Caratinga
Colatina
Aracruz
Campo Grande
Três Lagoas
São José do
Rio Preto
Barretos
Bebedouro
Franca
Formiga
Piumhí
Lafaiete
Ponte
Nova
Manhuaçu
Viçosa
Muriaé
Itapemirim
Vitória
Vila Velha
Argolas
Guarapari
Pico da Bandeira
2,890 m
Bela
Vista
Andradina
Presidente
Epitácio
Nova
Andradina
Dracena
Penápolis
Birigui
Catanduva
Araraquara
Ribeirão
Preto
Poços de
Caldas
Lavras
Varginha
Alfenas
São João
del Rei
Cachoeiro de Itapemirim
Dourados
Presidente
Prudente
Presidente
Venceslau
Tupã
Lins
São Carlos
Mogi-
Guaçu
Pouso
Alegre
Três
Corações
Ubá
Além Paraíba
Itaperuna
Cabo de São Tomé
Pedro Juan
Caballero
Marília
Assis
Bauru
Jaú
Rio Claro
Limeira
Americana
Jundiaí
Barra Mansa
Volta
Redonda
Juiz de
Fora
Nova Friburgo
Campos
Amambaí
Navirai
Paranavaí
Ourinhos
Piracicaba
Campinas
Sorocaba
São José dos Campos
Petrópolis
**Nova
Iguaçu**
Niterói
Rio de Janeiro
Concepção
Maringá
Londrina
Osasco
Santo André
São Paulo
Santos

Ilha da Trindade
(BRAZIL)
Ilhas Martin Vaz
(BRAZIL)

ATLANTIC

OCEAN

Tropic of Capricorn

Z I L

Planalto
do
Mato Grosso

Serra do Cachimbo
Sa. dos Apiacás
Serra Formosa

Planalto
Central

Planalto
Central

Sa. do Espinhaço
Sa. da Mantiqueira

Serra dos Carajás
Serra do Estrondo
Sa. dos Xavantes
Sa. do Roncador

Serra das Alpercatas
Caatingas
Serra do Uruçuí
Planalto da Borborema
Chapada Diamantina

© Hammond World Atlas Corporation/CD - 2107 - A

POPULATION OF CITIES AND TOWNS

■ OVER 2,000,000	● 500,000 - 999,999	○ 50,000 - 99,999
▣ 1,000,000 - 1,999,999	● 100,000 - 499,999	○ UNDER 50,000

SCALE 1:15,000,000   LAMBERT CONFORMAL CONIC PROJECTION

MILES 0 .... 200 .... 400 600
KILOMETERS 0 .... 200 .... 400 600

Southern South America

Index of the World

This index is a comprehensive listing of the places and geographic features found in the atlas. Names are arranged in strict alphabetical order, without regard to hyphens or spaces. Every name is followed by the country or area to which it belongs. Except for cities, towns, countries and cultural areas, all entries include a reference to feature type, such as province, river, island, peak, and so on. The page number and alpha-numeric code appear in blue to the left of each listing. The page number directs you to the largest scale map on which the name can be found. The code refers to the grid squares formed by the horizontal and vertical lines of latitude and longitude on each map. Following the letters from left to right and the numbers from top to bottom helps you to locate quickly the square containing the place or feature. Inset maps have their own alpha-numeric codes. Names that are accompanied by a point symbol are indexed to the symbol's location on the map. Other names are indexed to the initial letter of the name. When a map name contains a subordinate or alternate name, both names are listed in the index. To conserve space and provide room for more entries, many abbreviations are used in this index. The primary abbreviations are listed below.

Index Abbreviations

A
Ab,Can — Alberta
Abor. — Aboriginal
Acad. — Academy
ACT — Australian Capital Territory
A.F.B. — Air Force Base
Afld. — Airfield
Afg. — Afghanistan
Afr. — Africa
Ak,US — Alaska
Al,US — Alabama
Alb. — Albania
Alg. — Algeria
Amm. Dep. — Ammunition Depot
And. — Andorra
Ang. — Angola
Angu. — Anguilla
Ant. — Antarctica
Anti. — Antigua and Barbuda
Ar,US — Arkansas
Arch. — Archipelago
Arg. — Argentina
Arm. — Armenia
Arpt. — Airport
Aru. — Aruba
ASam. — American Samoa
Ash. — Ashmore and Cartier Islands
Aus. — Austria
Austl. — Australia
Aut. — Autonomous
Az,US — Arizona
Azer. — Azerbaijan
Azor. — Azores

B
Bahm. — Bahamas, The
Bahr. — Bahrain
Bang. — Bangladesh
Bar. — Barbados
BC,Can — British Columbia
Bela. — Belarus
Belg. — Belgium
Belz. — Belize
Ben. — Benin
Berm. — Bermuda
Bfld. — Battlefield
Bhu. — Bhutan
Bol. — Bolivia
Bor. — Borough
Bosn. — Bosnia and Herzegovina
Bots. — Botswana
Braz. — Brazil
Brln. — British Indian Ocean Territory
Bru. — Brunei
Bul. — Bulgaria
Burk. — Burkina Faso
Buru. — Burundi
BVI — British Virgin Islands

C
Ca,US — California
CAfr. — Central African Republic
Camb. — Cambodia
Camr. — Cameroon
Can. — Canada
Can. — Canal

Canl. — Canary Islands
Cap. — Capital
Cap. Dist. — Capital District
Cap. Terr. — Capital Territory
Cay. — Cayman Islands
C.d'Iv. — Côte d'Ivoire
C.G. — Coast Guard
Chan. — Channel
Chl. — Channel Islands
Co. — County
Co,US — Colorado
Col. — Colombia
Com. — Comoros
Cont. — Continent
CpV. — Cape Verde Islands
CR — Costa Rica
Cr. — Creek
Cro. — Croatia
CSea. — Coral Sea Islands Territory
Ct,US — Connecticut
Ctr. — Center
Ctry. — Country
Cyp. — Cyprus
Czh. — Czech Republic

D
DC,US — District of Columbia
De,US — Delaware
Den. — Denmark
Depr. — Depression
Dept. — Department
Des. — Desert
DF — Distrito Federal
Dist. — District
Djib. — Djibouti
Dom. — Dominica
Dpcy. — Dependency
D.R.Congo — Democratic Republic of the Congo
DRep. — Dominican Republic

E
Ecu. — Ecuador
Emb. — Embankment
Eng. — Engineering
Eng,UK — England
EqG. — Equatorial Guinea
Erit. — Eritrea
ESal. — El Salvador
Est. — Estonia
Eth. — Ethiopia
Eur. — Europe

F
Falk. — Falkland Islands
Far. — Faroe Islands
Fed. Dist. — Federal District
Fin. — Finland
Fl,US — Florida
For. — Forest
Fr. — France
FrAnt. — French Southern and Antarctic Lands
FrG. — French Guiana
FrPol. — French Polynesia
FYROM — Former Yugoslav Rep. of Macedonia

G
Ga,US — Georgia
Galp. — Galapagos Islands

Gam. — Gambia, The
Gaza — Gaza Strip
GBis. — Guinea-Bissau
Geo. — Georgia
Ger. — Germany
Gha. — Ghana
Gib. — Gibraltar
Glac. — Glacier
Gov. — Governorate
Govt. — Government
Gre. — Greece
Grld. — Greenland
Gren. — Grenada
Grsld. — Grassland
Guad. — Guadeloupe
Guat. — Guatemala
Gui. — Guinea
Guy. — Guyana

H
Har. — Harbor
Hi,US — Hawaii
Hist. — Historic(al)
Hon. — Honduras
Hts. — Heights
Hun. — Hungary

I
Ia,US — Iowa
Ice. — Iceland
Id,US — Idaho
Il,US — Illinois
IM — Isle of Man
In,US — Indiana
Ind. Res. — Indian Reservation
Indo. — Indonesia
Int'l — International
Ire. — Ireland
Isl., Isls. — Island, Islands
Isr. — Israel
Isth. — Isthmus
It. — Italy

J
Jam. — Jamaica
Jor. — Jordan

K
Kaz. — Kazakhstan
Kiri. — Kiribati
Ks,US — Kansas
Kuw. — Kuwait
Ky,US — Kentucky
Kyr. — Kyrgyzstan

L
La,US — Louisiana
Lab. — Laboratory
Lag. — Lagoon
Lakesh. — Lakeshore
Lat. — Latvia
Lcht. — Liechtenstein
Ldg. — Landing
Leb. — Lebanon
Les. — Lesotho
Libr. — Liberia
Lith. — Lithuania
Lux. — Luxembourg

M
Ma,US — Massachusetts
Madg. — Madagascar
Madr. — Madeira
Malay. — Malaysia

Mald. — Maldives
Malw. — Malawi
Mart. — Martinique
May. — Mayotte
Mb,Can — Manitoba
Md,US — Maryland
Me,US — Maine
Mem. — Memorial
Mex. — Mexico
Mi,US — Michigan
Micr. — Micronesia, Federated States of
Mil. — Military
Mn,US — Minnesota
Mo,US — Missouri
Mol. — Moldova
Mon. — Monument
Mona. — Monaco
Mong. — Mongolia
Monts. — Montserrat
Mor. — Morocco
Moz. — Mozambique
Mrsh. — Marshall Islands
Mrta. — Mauritania
Mrts. — Mauritius
Ms,US — Mississippi
Mt. — Mount
Mt,US — Montana
Mtn., Mts. — Mountain, Mountains
Mun. Arpt. — Municipal Airport

N
NAm. — North America
Namb. — Namibia
NAnt. — Netherlands Antilles
Nat'l — National
Nav. — Naval
NB,Can — New Brunswick
Nbrhd. — Neighborhood
NC,US — North Carolina
NCal. — New Caledonia
ND,US — North Dakota
Ne,US — Nebraska
Neth. — Netherlands
Nf,Can — Newfoundland
Nga. — Nigeria
NH,US — New Hampshire
NI,UK — Northern Ireland
Nic. — Nicaragua
NJ,US — New Jersey
NKor. — North Korea
NM,US — New Mexico
NMar. — Northern Mariana Isl.
Nor. — Norway
NP — National Park
NS,Can — Nova Scotia
Nv,US — Nevada
NW,Can — Northwest Territories
NWR — National Wildlife Refuge
NY,US — New York
NZ — New Zealand

O
Obl. — Oblast
Oh,US — Ohio
Ok,US — Oklahoma
On,Can — Ontario
Or,US — Oregon

P
Pa,US — Pennsylvania

PacUS — Pacific Islands, U.S.
Pak. — Pakistan
Pan. — Panama
Par. — Paraguay
Par. — Parish
PE,Can — Prince Edward Island
Pen. — Peninsula
Phil. — Philippines
Phys. Reg. — Physical Region
Pitc. — Pitcairn Islands
Plat. — Plateau
PN — National Park
PNG — Papua New Guinea
Pol. — Poland
Port. — Portugal
Poss. — Possession
Pkwy. — Parkway
PR — Puerto Rico
Pref. — Prefecture
Prov. — Province
Prsv. — Preserve
Pt. — Point

Q
Qu,Can — Quebec

R
Rec. — Recreation(al)
Ref. — Refuge
Reg. — Region
Rep. — Republic
Res. — Reservoir, Reservation
Reun. — Réunion
RI,US — Rhode Island
Riv. — River
Rom. — Romania
Rsv. — Reserve
Rus. — Russia
Rvwy. — Riverway
Rwa. — Rwanda

S
SAfr. — South Africa
Sam. — Samoa
SAm. — South America
SaoT. — São Tomé and Príncipe
SAr. — Saudi Arabia
Sc,UK — Scotland
SC,US — South Carolina
SD,US — South Dakota
Seash. — Seashore
Sen. — Senegal
Sey. — Seychelles
SGeo. — South Georgia and Sandwich Islands
Sing. — Singapore
Sk,Can — Saskatchewan
SKor. — South Korea
SLeo. — Sierra Leone
Slov. — Slovenia
Slvk. — Slovakia
SMar. — San Marino
Sol. — Solomon Islands
Som. — Somalia
Sp. — Spain
Spr., Sprs. — Spring, Springs
SrL. — Sri Lanka
Sta. — Station
StH. — Saint Helena
Str. — Strait
StK. — Saint Kitts and Nevis

StL. — Saint Lucia
StP. — Saint Pierre and Miquelon
StV. — Saint Vincent and the Grenadines
Sur. — Suriname
Sval. — Svalbard
Swaz. — Swaziland
Swe. — Sweden
Swi. — Switzerland

T
Tah. — Tahiti
Tai. — Taiwan
Taj. — Tajikistan
Tanz. — Tanzania
Ter. — Terrace
Terr. — Territory
Thai. — Thailand
Tn,US — Tennessee
Tok. — Tokelau
Trg. — Training
Trin. — Trinidad and Tobago
Trkm. — Turkmenistan
Trks. — Turks and Caicos Islands
Tun. — Tunisia
Tun. — Tunnel
Turk. — Turkey
Tuv. — Tuvalu
Twp. — Township
Tx,US — Texas

U
UAE — United Arab Emirates
Ugan. — Uganda
UK — United Kingdom
Ukr. — Ukraine
Uru. — Uruguay
US — United States
USVI — U.S. Virgin Islands
Ut,US — Utah
Uzb. — Uzbekistan

V
Va,US — Virginia
Val. — Valley
Van. — Vanuatu
VatC. — Vatican City
Ven. — Venezuela
Viet. — Vietnam
Vill. — Village
Vol. — Volcano
Vt,US — Vermont

W
Wa,US — Washington
Wal,UK — Wales
Wall. — Wallis and Futuna
WBnk. — West Bank
Wi,US — Wisconsin
Wild. — Wildlife, Wilderness
WSah. — Western Sahara
WV,US — West Virginia
Wy,US — Wyoming

Y
Yem. — Yemen
Yk,Can — Yukon Territory
Yugo. — Yugoslavia

Z
Zam. — Zambia
Zim. — Zimbabwe

A

18/F4 **Aachen,** Ger.
40/G6 **Aba,** Nga.
32/D5 **Abā as Su'ūd,** SAr.
32/E2 **Abadan,** Iran
24/K4 **Abakan,** Rus.
40/F6 **Abeokuta,** Nga.
18/D2 **Aberdeen,** Sc,UK
51/J4 **Aberdeen,** SD,US
50/B4 **Aberdeen,** Wa,US
18/C3 **Aberystwyth,** Wal,UK
32/D5 **Abhā,** SAr.
40/E6 **Abidjan,** C.d'Iv.
53/H3 **Abilene,** Ks,US
53/H4 **Abilene,** Tx,US
54/D1 **Abitibi** (riv.), On,Can
23/F5 **Abkhazia** (reg.), Geo.
33/K2 **Abottābād,** Pak.
33/F4 **Abu Dhabi** (cap.), UAE
40/G6 **Abuja** (cap.), Nga.
62/E5 **Abunã** (Abuná) (riv.), Braz., Bol.
55/G2 **Acadia Nat'l Pk.,** Me,US
58/B4 **Acapulco,** Mex.
62/G3 **Acarai** (mts.), Braz.
40/E6 **Accra** (cap.), Gha.
24/K4 **Achinsk,** Rus.
59/G3 **Acklins** (isl.), Bah.
64/C3 **Aconcagua** (mt.), Arg.
53/H4 **Ada,** Ok,US
40/H6 **Adamaora** (plat.), Camr., Nga.
47/M7 **Adamstown** (cap.), Pitc.
23/E6 **Adana,** Turk.
23/D5 **Adapazarı,** Turk.
32/D3 **Ad Dahnā** (des.), SAr.
32/F3 **Ad Dammān,** SAr.
41/N6 **Addis Ababa** (cap.), Eth.
45/C4 **Adelaide,** Austl.
41/Q5 **Aden** (gulf), Afr., Asia
32/D6 **Aden,** Yem.
21/F2 **Adige** (riv.), It.
54/F2 **Adirondack** (mts.), NY,US
23/E6 **Adıyahman,** Turk.
46/D5 **Admiralty** (isls.), PNG
54/C3 **Adrian,** Mi,US
21/G2 **Adriatic** (sea), Eur.
21/K4 **Aegean** (sea)
33/H2 **Afghanistan**
39/* **Africa**
40/D1 **Agadir,** Mor.
35/F3 **Agartala,** India
21/J1 **Aggteleki Nat'l Park,** Hun.
34/C2 **Agra,** India
21/G4 **Agrigento,** It.
21/J4 **Agrínion,** Gre.
62/E2 **Aguaro-Guariquito Nat'l Park,** Ven.
58/A3 **Aguascalientes,** Mex.
42/D7 **Agulhas** (cape), SAfr.
40/F3 **Ahaggar** (mts.), Alg.
36/B3 **Ahmadabad,** India
41/P6 **Ahmar** (mts.), Eth.
32/E2 **Ahvaz,** Iran
57/H3 **Aiken,** SC,US
40/G4 **Aïr** (plat.), Niger
20/E3 **Aix-en-Provence,** Fr.
21/F3 **Ajaccio,** Fr.
34/B2 **Ajmer,** India
29/M4 **Akita,** Japan
34/C3 **Akola,** India
54/D3 **Akron,** Oh,US
23/D6 **Akşehir,** Turk.
35/F3 **Akyab,** Myanmar
57/G3 **Alabama** (state), US
57/G4 **Alabama** (riv.), Al,US
63/L6 **Alagoinhas,** Braz.
53/F4 **Alamogordo,** NM,US
53/F3 **Alamosa,** Co,US
22/G3 **Aland** (isls.), Fin.
49/B3 **Alaska** (state), US
49/C4 **Alaska** (gulf), Ak,US
49/B4 **Alaska** (pen.), Ak,US
49/B3 **Alaska** (range), Ak,US
20/C4 **Albacete,** Sp.
21/H3 **Albania**
49/J4 **Albany** (riv.), On,Can
57/G4 **Albany,** Ga,US
54/F3 **Albany** (cap.), NY,US
50/C4 **Albany,** Or,US
32/E2 **Al Başrah,** Iraq
41/M7 **Albert** (lake), Afr.
50/E2 **Alberta** (prov.), Can.
51/K5 **Albert Lea,** Mn,US
64/B7 **Alberto de Agostini Nat'l Park,** Chile
20/C5 **Alborán** (isl.), Sp.
18/G2 **Alborg,** Den.
52/F4 **Albuquerque,** NM,US
20/C3 **Alcalá de Henares,** Sp.
20/B4 **Alcántara** (res.), Sp.
25/N4 **Aldan** (plat.), Rus.
25/P3 **Aldan** (riv.), Rus.
18/D4 **Alderney** (isl.), Chl.
32/C1 **Aleppo,** Syria
64/B5 **Alerces Nat'l Park,** Arg.
49/A4 **Aleutian** (isls.), Ak,US
49/D4 **Alexander** (arch.), Ak,US
41/L1 **Alexandria,** Egypt
56/E4 **Alexandria,** La,US
54/E4 **Alexandria,** Va,US
M2/41 **Al Fayyum,** Egypt
21/H2 **Alfold, Great** (plain), Hun.
33/G3 **Al Fujayrah,** UAE
40/F2 **Algeria**
40/F1 **Algiers** (cap.), Alg.
32/D6 **Al Ḩudaydah,** Yem.
32/E3 **Al Hufūf,** SAr.
20/C4 **Alicante,** Sp.
45/C3 **Alice Springs,** Austl.
36/C2 **Aligarh,** India
41/M2 **Al Jīzah,** Egypt
33/G4 **Al Khābūrah,** Oman
32/F3 **Al Khobar,** SAr.
40/H1 **Al Khums,** Libya
32/E2 **Al Kūt,** Iraq
36/D2 **Allahabad,** India
54/D4 **Allegheny** (mts.), US
54/F3 **Allentown,** Pa,US
34/C6 **Allepey,** India
54/D3 **Alliance,** Oh,US
40/E1 **Al Maghrib** (reg.), Alg., Mor.
32/B2 **Al Mahallah al Kubrá,** Egypt
41/M1 **Al Manşūra,** Egypt
63/J6 **Almas** (riv.), Braz.
24/H5 **Almaty** (cap.), Kaz.
18/F3 **Almelo,** Neth.
20/C4 **Almeria,** Sp.
41/M2 **Al Minyā,** Egypt
32/E3 **Al Mubarraz,** SAr.
32/E6 **Al Mukallā,** Yem.
63/J5 **Alpercatas** (mts.), Braz.
20/E2 **Alps** (mts.), Eur.
20/E2 **Alsace** (reg.), Fr.
28/B2 **Altai** (mts.), Asia
62/E7 **Altiplano** (plat.), Bol., Peru
54/B4 **Alton,** Il,US
54/E3 **Altoona,** Pa,US
28/C4 **Altun** (mts.), China
53/H4 **Altus,** Ok,US
41/L5 **Al Ubayyiḑ,** Sudan
62/D4 **Amacayacú,** Col.
20/A4 **Amadora,** Port.
29/M5 **Amagasaki,** Japan
29/K5 **Amakusa** (sea), Japan
62/F4 **Amaña** (lake), Braz.
53/G4 **Amarillo,** Tx,US
63/H4 **Amazon** (riv.), SAm.
63/G4 **Amazônia Nat'l Park,** Braz.
33/L2 **Ambāla,** India
62/C4 **Ambato,** Ecu.
37/G4 **Ambon,** Indo.
63/J8 **Americana,** Braz.
52/E2 **American Fork,** Ut,US
47/J6 **American Samoa**
57/G3 **Americus,** Ga,US
53/J2 **Ames,** Ia,US
55/H2 **Amherst,** NS,Can
20/D1 **Amiens,** Fr.
32/C2 **Amman** (cap.), Jor.
32/F1 **Āmol,** Iran
34/C3 **Amravati,** India
33/K2 **Amritsar,** India
18/F3 **Amsterdam** (cap.), Neth.
54/F3 **Amsterdam,** NY,US
24/G6 **Amudar'ya** (riv.), Asia
43/S **Amundsen** (sea), Ant.
49/E2 **Amundsen** (gulf), Can.
29/M1 **Amur** (riv.), Asia
50/E4 **Anaconda,** Mt,US
25/T3 **Anadyr',** Rus.
25/R3 **Anadyr** (gulf), Rus.
25/T3 **Anadyr'** (range), Rus.
52/C4 **Anaheim,** Ca,US
63/J7 **Anápolis,** Braz.
23/C6 **Anatolia** (reg.), Turk.
49/C3 **Anchorage,** Ak,US
21/G3 **Ancona,** It.
64/B5 **Ancud** (gulf), Chile
20/B4 **Andalusia** (reg.), Sp.
35/F5 **Andaman** (sea), Asia
35/F5 **Andaman** (isls.), India
54/C3 **Anderson,** In,US
57/H3 **Anderson,** SC,US
61/B3 **Andes** (mts.), SAm.
24/H5 **Andijon,** Uzb.
20/D3 **Andorra**
20/D3 **Andorra la Vella** (cap.), And.
59/F3 **Andros** (isl.), Bahm.
21/K4 **Andros** (isl.), Gre.
59/J4 **Anegada Passage** (chan.), West Indies
20/D3 **Aneto** (peak), Sp.
64/B1 **Angamos** (pt.), Chile
25/L4 **Angara** (riv.), Rus.
28/E1 **Angarsk,** Rus.
62/F2 **Angel** (falls), Ven.
20/C2 **Angers,** Fr.
18/C3 **Anglesea** (isl.), Wal,UK
42/C3 **Angola**
59/J4 **Anguilla** (isl.), UK
23/D6 **Ankara** (cap.), Turk.
55/G3 **Ann** (cape), Ma,US
40/G1 **Annaba,** Alg.
32/D3 **An Nafūd** (des.), SAr.
32/D2 **An Najaf,** Iraq
35/J4 **Annamitique** (mts.), Laos, Viet.
54/E4 **Annapolis** (cap.), Md,US
34/D2 **Annapurna** (mtn.), Nepal
54/D3 **Ann Arbor,** Mi,US
57/G3 **Anniston,** Al,US
30/C1 **Anqing,** China
29/J3 **Anshan,** China
23/E6 **Antakya** (Antioch), Turk.
23/D6 **Antalya,** Turk.
42/K10 **Antananarivo** (cap.), Madg.
43/V **Antarctic** (pen.), Ant.
43/* **Antarctica**
20/E3 **Antibes,** Fr.
55/J1 **Anticosti** (isl.), Qu,Can
59/J4 **Antigua and Barbuda**
23/E6 **Antioch** (Antayka), Turk.
64/B1 **Antofagasta,** Chile
42/K9 **Antsiranana,** Madg.
64/B4 **Antuco** (vol.), Chile
18/F4 **Antwerp,** Belg.
28/G4 **Anyang,** China
24/J4 **Anzhero-Sudzhensk,** Rus.
29/N3 **Aomori,** Japan
20/E2 **Aosta,** It.
18/F3 **Apeldoorn,** Neth.
21/G3 **Apennines** (mts.), It.
47/S9 **Apia** (cap.), Sam.
63/G6 **Apiacás** (mts.), Braz.
49/J6 **Appalachian** (mts.), US
54/B2 **Appleton,** Wi,US
62/E2 **Apure** (riv.), Ven.
32/B3 **Aqaba** (gulf), Asia
24/F5 **Aqtaū,** Kaz.
24/F4 **Aqtöbe,** Kaz.
32/D4 **Arabian** (pen.), Asia
33/H5 **Arabian** (sea), Asia
32/B3 **Arabian** (des.), Egypt
63/L6 **Aracaju,** Braz.
63/H8 **Araçatuba,** Braz.
21/J2 **Arad,** Rom.
46/C5 **Arafura** (sea)
20/C3 **Aragón** (reg.), Sp.
63/J5 **Araguaia** (riv.), Braz.
63/H6 **Araguaia Nat'l Park,** Braz.
32/E3 **Arāk,** Iran
35/F3 **Arakan** (mts.), Myanmar
24/G5 **Aral** (sea), Asia
18/B3 **Aran** (isls.), Ire.
23/F6 **Ararat** (mt.), Turk.
23/G6 **Aras** (riv.), Asia
24/E3 **Archangel'sk,** Rus.
52/E3 **Arches Nat'l Pk.,** Ut,US
14/A1 **Arctic** (ocean)
29/K2 **Arda,** China
23/G6 **Ardabil,** Iran
18/F4 **Ardennes** (for.), Belg.
53/H4 **Ardmore,** Ok,US
62/D7 **Arequipa,** Peru
64/C4 **Argentina**
21/K2 **Arges** (riv.), Rom.
21/J4 **Argos,** Gre.
18/G2 **Arhus,** Den.
62/D7 **Arica,** Chile
62/F5 **Aripuanã** (riv.), Braz.
52/D4 **Arizona** (state), US
53/J4 **Arkadelphia,** Ar,US
53/K4 **Arkansas** (riv.), US
53/J4 **Arkansas** (state), US
24/H2 **Arkticheskiy Institut** (isls.), Rus.
20/E3 **Arles,** Fr.
56/D3 **Arlington,** Tx,US
54/E4 **Arlington,** Va,US
18/C3 **Armagh,** NI,UK
23/F5 **Armavir,** Rus.
23/F5 **Armenia**
62/C3 **Armenia,** Col.
F4/18 **Arnhem,** Neth.
45/C2 **Arnhem Land** (reg.), Austl.
21/F3 **Arno** (riv.), It.
18/C3 **Arran** (isl.), Sc,UK
21/J4 **Arta** (gulf), Gre.
20/D1 **Artois** (reg.), Fr.
37/H5 **Aru** (isls.), Indo.
59/H5 **Aruba** (isl.), Neth.
41/K7 **Aruwimi** (riv.), D.R. Congo
23/F2 **Arzamas,** Rus.
29/N3 **Asahikawa,** Japan
34/E3 **Asansol,** India
14/J6 **Ascension** (isl.), StH.
40/E6 **Ashanti** (reg.), Gha.
57/H3 **Asheville,** NC,US
33/G1 **Ashgabat** (cap.), Trkm.
57/H2 **Ashland,** Ky,US
50/C5 **Ashland,** Or,US
45/B2 **Ashmore and Cartier Is.** (terr.), Austl.
33/G3 **Ash Shāriqah,** UAE
54/D3 **Ashtabula,** Oh,US
27/* **Asia**
32/D5 **'Asīr,** (mts.), SAr., Yem.
32/C5 **Asmara** (cap.), Erit.
52/F3 **Aspen,** Co,US
45/G7 **Aspiring** (mtn.), NZ
32/E3 **As Sālimīyah,** Kuw.
35/F2 **Assam** (state), India
18/F3 **Assen,** Neth.
41/M6 **As Sudd** (reg.), Sudan
31/B1 **Astana** (cap.), Kaz.
50/C4 **Astoria,** Or,US
23/G4 **Astrakhan',** Rus.
64/E2 **Asunción** (cap.), Par.
32/B4 **Aswân,** Egypt
32/B3 **Asyût,** Egypt
64/C1 **Atacama** (des.), Arg.
62/E7 **Atacama** (des.), Chile
23/E6 **Ataturk** (res.), Turk.
41/M4 **'Atbarah, Nahr** (riv.), Sudan
53/J3 **Atchison,** Ks,US
49/F4 **Athabasca** (lake), Can.
21/J4 **Athens** (cap.), Gre.
57/H3 **Athens,** Ga,US
54/D4 **Athens,** Oh,US
21/K3 **Athos** (mt.), Gre.
25/U4 **Atka** (isl.), Ak,US
57/G3 **Atlanta** (cap.), Ga,US
14/G3 **Atlantic** (ocean)
54/F4 **Atlantic City,** NJ,US
40/E1 **Atlas** (mts.), Afr.
40/F1 **Atlas Saharien** (mts.), Alg., Mor.
32/D4 **Aṭ Ṭā'if,** SAr.
25/T5 **Attu** (isl.), Ak,US
64/C4 **Atuel** (riv.), Arg.
57/G3 **Auburn,** Al,US
55/G2 **Auburn,** Me,US
54/E3 **Auburn,** NY,US
45/H6 **Auckland,** NZ
41/P6 **Audo** (range), Eth.
18/G4 **Augsburg,** Ger.
57/H3 **Augusta,** Ga,US
55/G2 **Augusta** (cap.), Me,US
34/C4 **Aurangabad,** India
53/F3 **Aurora,** Co,US
56/D4 **Austin** (cap.), Tx,US
45/* **Australia**
45/D4 **Australian Cap. Terr.,** Austl.
21/G2 **Austria**
62/D6 **Auzangate** (mtn.), Peru
55/L2 **Avalon** (pen.), Nf,Can
20/E3 **Avignon,** Fr.
21/J3 **Axios** (riv.), Gre.
23/C6 **Aydın,** Turk.
45/C3 **Ayers Rock** (mt.), Austl.
35/F4 **Ayeyarwaddy** (riv.), Myanmar
25/S3 **Ayon** (isl.), Rus.
18/C3 **Ayr,** Sc,UK
40/E4 **Azaouâd** (reg.), Mali
23/G5 **Azerbaijan**
14/H4 **Azores** (isls.), Port.
23/E4 **Azov** (sea), Eur.
59/E6 **Azuero** (pen.), Pan.
32/B2 **Az Zagāziq,** Egypt
32/C2 **Az Zarqā',** Jor.

B

41/P5 **Bab el Mandeb** (str.)
32/F1 **Bābol,** Iran
19/M3 **Babruysk,** Bela.
32/D2 **Babylon** (ruins), Iraq
21/K2 **Bacău,** Rom.
30/D5 **Bacolod,** Phil.
20/D3 **Badalona,** Sp.
20/F1 **Baden-Baden,** Ger.
51/H5 **Badlands Nat'l Pk.,** SD,US
49/K2 **Baffin** (isl.), NW,Can
49/L2 **Baffin** (bay), NAm.
32/D2 **Baghdad** (cap.), Iraq
33/J1 **Baghlān,** Afg.
40/J5 **Baguirmi** (reg.), Chad
59/F2 **Bahamas**
33/K3 **Bahawalpur,** Pak.
58/D4 **Bahia** (isls.), Hon.
64/D4 **Bahia Blanca,** Arg.
64/C7 **Bahia Grande** (bay), Arg.
33/G4 **Bahlah,** Oman
32/F3 **Bahrain**
41/L6 **Bahr al 'Arab** (riv.), Sudan
21/J2 **Baia Mare,** Rom.
29/J2 **Baicheng,** China
28/E4 **Baiyin,** China
21/H2 **Baja,** Hun.
59/L8 **Baja California** (pen.), Mex.
47/H4 **Baker** (isl.), PacUS
52/C4 **Bakersfield,** Ca,US
32/E2 **Bakhtarān,** Iran
23/G5 **Baku** (cap.), Azer.
62/E6 **Bala** (mts.), Bol.
23/G3 **Balakovo,** Rus.
21/H2 **Balaton** (lake), Hun.
62/F4 **Balbina** (riv.), Braz.
20/D4 **Balearic** (isls.), Sp.
63/L7 **Baleia** (pt.), Braz.
36/D5 **Bali** (isl.), Indo.
36/D5 **Bali** (sea), Indo.
23/C6 **Balıkesir,** Turk.
37/E4 **Balikpapan,** Indo.
21/J3 **Balkan** (mts.), Bulg.
31/B2 **Balkhash** (lake), Kaz.
19/L5 **Bălţi,** Mol.
19/J2 **Baltic** (sea), Eur.
54/E4 **Baltimore,** Md,US
40/D5 **Bamako** (cap.), Mali
18/G4 **Bamberg,** Ger.
41/J6 **Bamingui-Bangoran Nat'l Park,** CAfr.
46/F5 **Banaba** (isl.), Kiri.
63/H6 **Bananal** (isl.), Braz.
37/G5 **Banda** (sea), Indo.
36/A2 **Banda Aceh,** Indo.
33/G3 **Bandar-e 'Abbās,** Iran
32/F3 **Bandar-e Būshehr,** Iran
36/D3 **Bandar Seri Begawan** (cap.), Bru.
63/K8 **Bandeira** (peak), Braz.
36/C5 **Bandung,** Indo.
50/E2 **Banff Nat'l Pk.,** Ab,Can
34/C5 **Bangalore,** India
37/F4 **Banggai** (isls.), Indo.
36/C4 **Bangka** (isl.), Indo.
35/H5 **Bangkok** (cap.), Thai.
34/E3 **Bangladesh**
18/C3 **Bangor,** NI,UK
55/G2 **Bangor,** Me,US
41/J7 **Bangui** (cap.), CAfr.
41/L2 **Banī Suwayf,** Egypt
21/H2 **Banja Luka,** Bosn.
36/D4 **Banjarmasin,** Indo.
41/B5 **Banjul** (cap.), Gam.
49/E2 **Banks** (isl.), Can.
19/J4 **Banská Bystrica,** Slvk.
36/A3 **Banyak** (isls.), Indo.
28/H4 **Baoding,** China
28/F5 **Baoji,** China
28/G3 **Baotou,** China
36/E4 **Barabai,** Indo.
20/C3 **Baracaldo,** Sp.
19/L3 **Baranavichy,** Bela.
59/K5 **Barbados**
54/D3 **Barberton,** Oh,US
20/D3 **Barcelona,** Sp.
62/F1 **Barcelona,** Ven.
34/C2 **Bareilly,** India
17/H1 **Barents** (sea), Eur.
55/G2 **Bar Harbor,** Me,US
21/H3 **Bari,** It.
62/D2 **Barinas,** Ven.
34/F3 **Barisāl,** Bang.
36/B4 **Barisan** (mts.), Indo.
36/D4 **Barito** (riv.), Indo.
57/G2 **Barkley** (lake), Ky,Tn,US
45/C2 **Barkly Tableland** (plat.), Austl.
24/J4 **Barnaul,** Rus.
34/B3 **Baroda,** India
62/E1 **Barquisimeto,** Ven.
62/D2 **Barrancabermeja,** Col.
62/D1 **Barranquilla,** Col.
54/E2 **Barrie,** On,Can
49/B2 **Barrow** (pt.), Ak,US
18/D3 **Barrow-in-Furness,** Eng,UK
52/C4 **Barstow,** Ca,US
53/H3 **Bartlesville,** Ok,US
19/M3 **Barysaw,** Bela.
20/E2 **Basel,** Swi.
30/D3 **Bashi** (chan.), Phil., Tai.
18/D4 **Basingstoke,** Eng,UK
45/D4 **Bass** (str.), Austl.
35/F4 **Bassein,** Myanmar
59/J4 **Basse-Terre** (cap.), Guad.
59/J4 **Basse-Terre** (isl.), Guad.
59/J4 **Basseterre** (cap.), StK.
21/F3 **Bastia,** Fr.
56/F3 **Bastrop,** La,US
58/E3 **Batabanó** (gulf), Cuba
33/L2 **Batāla,** India
40/H8 **Batéké** (plat.), Congo
18/D4 **Bath,** Eng,UK
49/G2 **Bathurst** (isl.), Can.
55/H2 **Bathurst,** NB,Can
23/F6 **Batman,** Turk.
40/G1 **Batna,** Alg.
57/F4 **Baton Rouge** (cap.), La,US
54/C3 **Battle Creek,** Mi,US
36/B3 **Batu** (bay), Malay.
23/F5 **Batumi,** Geo.
63/J8 **Baurú,** Braz.
59/F3 **Bayamo,** Cuba
59/H4 **Bayamón,** PR
28/D5 **Bayan Har** (mts.), China
54/D3 **Bay City,** Mi,US
24/G3 **Baydaratskaya** (bay), Rus.
28/F1 **Baykal** (lake), Rus.
25/L4 **Baykal** (mts.), Rus.
24/G5 **Baykonyr,** Kaz.
20/C2 **Bayonne,** Fr.
18/G4 **Bayreuth,** Ger.
56/E4 **Baytown,** Tx,US
23/G5 **Bazardyuzyu, Gora** (mt.), Azer.
52/E2 **Bear** (lake), US
50/F3 **Bearpaw** (mts.), Mt,US
53/H2 **Beatrice,** Ne,US
49/C2 **Beaufort** (sea), NAm.
57/H3 **Beaufort,** SC,US
56/E4 **Beaumont,** Tx,US
40/E1 **Bechar,** Alg.
54/D4 **Beckley,** WV,US
18/D3 **Bedford,** Eng,UK
32/B2 **Beersheba,** Isr.
25/M2 **Begichev** (isl.), Rus.
63/H3 **Béhague** (pt.), FrG.
35/J3 **Beihai,** China
28/H4 **Beijing** (Peking) (cap.), China
29/J3 **Beipiao,** China
32/C2 **Beirut** (cap.), Leb.
40/G1 **Bejaïa,** Alg.
36/C5 **Bekasi,** Indo.
19/L3 **Belarus**
63/J4 **Belém,** Braz.
18/C3 **Belfast** (cap.), NI,UK
55/G2 **Belfast,** Me,US
34/B4 **Belgaum,** India
18/E4 **Belgium**
23/E3 **Belgorod,** Rus.
21/J2 **Belgrade** (cap.), Yugo.
36/C4 **Belitung** (isl.), Indo.
58/D4 **Belize**
58/D4 **Belize City,** Belz.
25/P2 **Bel'kovskiy** (isl.), Rus.
34/C4 **Bellary,** India
54/E2 **Belleville,** On,Can
54/B4 **Belleville,** Il,US
50/C3 **Bellingham,** Wa,US
43/U **Bellingshausen** (sea), Ant.
62/C2 **Bello,** Col.
58/D4 **Belmopan** (cap.), Belz.
63/K7 **Belo Horizonte,** Braz.
54/B3 **Beloit,** Wi,US
24/J5 **Belovo,** Rus.
23/E1 **Beloye** (lake), Rus.
24/G2 **Belyy** (isl.), Rus.
51/K4 **Bemidji,** Mn,US
34/D2 **Benares** (Varanasi), India
50/C4 **Bend,** Or,US
34/E4 **Bengal** (bay), Asia
29/H5 **Bengbu,** China
41/K1 **Benghazi,** Libya
42/B3 **Benguela,** Ang.
62/E6 **Beni** (riv.), Bol.
40/F5 **Benin**
40/F6 **Benin** (bight), Afr.
40/G6 **Benin City,** Nga.
18/C2 **Ben Nevis** (mt.), Sc,UK
55/F3 **Bennington,** Vt,US
53/J4 **Benton,** Ar,US
54/C3 **Benton Harbor,** Mi,US
40/G6 **Benue** (riv.), Nga.
29/J3 **Benxi,** China
29/L5 **Beppu,** Japan
21/J3 **Berat,** Alb.
37/H4 **Berau** (bay), Indo.
19/H5 **Berchtesgaden Nat'l Park,** Ger.
54/C4 **Berea,** Ky,US
19/M3 **Berezina** (riv.), Bela.
23/J2 **Berezniki,** Rus.
21/F2 **Bergamo,** It.
22/C3 **Bergen,** Nor.
34/D4 **Berhampur,** India
25/T4 **Bering** (sea)
25/V3 **Bering** (str.)
25/S4 **Bering** (isl.), Rus.
52/B3 **Berkeley,** Ca,US
19/H3 **Berlin** (cap.), Ger.
55/G2 **Berlin,** NH,US
64/D2 **Bermejo** (riv.), Arg.
49/L6 **Bermuda** (isl.), UK
20/E2 **Bern** (cap.), Swi.
64/B6 **Bernardo O'Higgins Nat'l Park,** Chile
20/E2 **Besançon,** Fr.
57/G3 **Bessemer,** Al,US
54/F3 **Bethlehem,** Pa,US
23/D6 **Beyşehir,** Turk.
34/E2 **Bhagalpur,** India
34/E2 **Bhaktapur,** Nepal
33/L2 **Bhatinda,** India
34/E3 **Bhātpāra,** India
34/B3 **Bhavnagar,** India
34/D3 **Bhilai,** India
34/C3 **Bhopal,** India
34/E3 **Bhubaneswar,** India
34/E2 **Bhutan**
40/G7 **Biafra** (bight), Afr.
37/J4 **Biak** (isl.), Indo.
19/K3 **Bialystok,** Pol.
55/G3 **Biddeford,** Me,US
42/C3 **Bie** (plat.), Ang.
18/G3 **Bielefeld,** Ger.
19/J4 **Bielsko-Biala,** Pol.
35/J5 **Bien Hoa,** Viet.
56/C4 **Big Bend Nat'l Pk.,** Tx,US
50/G4 **Bighorn** (riv.), US
50/F4 **Bighorn** (mts.), Wy,US
56/C3 **Big Spring,** Tx,US
40/B5 **Bijagós** (arch.), GBis.
34/B2 **Bikaner,** India
46/F3 **Bikini** (atoll), Mrsh.
42/C4 **Bikuar Nat'l Park,** Ang.
34/D3 **Bilāspur,** India
23/D4 **Bila Tserkva,** Ukr.
35/G5 **Bilaukraung** (range), Myanmar, Thai.
20/C4 **Bilbao,** Sp.
50/F4 **Billings,** Mt,US
57/F4 **Biloxi,** Ms,US
59/F2 **Biminis** (isls.), Bahm.
54/F3 **Binghamton,** NY,US
64/B4 **Bio-Bio** (riv.), Chile
18/D3 **Birmingham,** Eng,UK
57/G3 **Birmingham,** Al,US
52/E5 **Bisbee,** Az,US
20/B2 **Biscay** (bay), Eur.
57/H5 **Biscayne Nat'l Pk.,** Fl,US
31/B3 **Bishkek** (cap.), Kyr.
42/E7 **Bisho,** SAfr.
40/F1 **Biskra,** Alg.
46/D5 **Bismarck** (arch.), PNG
51/H4 **Bismarck** (cap.), ND,US
40/B5 **Bissau** (cap.), GBis.
21/J3 **Bitola,** FYROM
50/E4 **Bitterroot** (range), US
37/G3 **Bitung,** Indo.
24/J4 **Biysk,** Rus.
40/G1 **Bizerte,** Tun.
23/D5 **Black** (sea)
18/G5 **Black** (for.), Ger.
50/E5 **Blackfoot,** Id,US
51/H5 **Black Hills** (mts.), US
18/D3 **Blackpool,** Eng,UK
57/H2 **Blacksburg,** Va,US
40/E5 **Black Volta** (riv.), Afr.
21/F2 **Blagoevgrad,** Bulg.
29/K1 **Blagoveshchensk,** Rus.
20/E2 **Blanc** (mt.), Eur.
62/C5 **Blanca** (mts.), Peru
62/B4 **Blanco** (cape), Ecu.
42/G4 **Blantyre,** Malw.
41/L7 **Bleu** (mts.), D.R. Congo
40/F1 **Blida,** Alg.
55/G3 **Block** (isl.), RI,US
42/E6 **Bloemfontein,** SAfr.
54/B3 **Bloomington,** Il,US
54/C4 **Bloomington,** In,US
51/K4 **Bloomington,** Mn,US
50/D4 **Blue** (mts.), Or,US
57/H2 **Bluefield,** WV,US
41/M5 **Blue Nile** (riv.), Afr.
57/H2 **Blue Ridge** (mts.), US
64/G2 **Blumenau,** Braz.
53/K4 **Blytheville,** Ar,US
63/J5 **Boa Esperança** (res.), Braz.
40/E5 **Bobo-Dioulasso,** Burk.
57/H5 **Boca Raton,** Fl,US
22/E2 **Bodø,** Nor.
57/F4 **Bogalusa,** La,US
28/B3 **Bogda Feng** (mtn.), Mong.
36/C5 **Bogor,** Indo.
62/D3 **Bogotá** (cap.), Col.
29/H4 **Bo Hai** (gulf), China
19/H4 **Bohemia** (reg.), Czh.
50/D5 **Boise** (cap.), Id,US
62/D2 **Bolivar** (mt.), Ven.
62/D2 **Bolívar** (peak), Ven.
62/F7 **Bolivia**
21/F2 **Bologna,** It.
25/L2 **Bol'shevik** (isl.), Rus.
25/Q2 **Bol'shoy Lyakhovskiy** (isl.), Rus.
21/F2 **Bolzano,** It.
34/B4 **Bombay** (Mumbai), India
37/H4 **Bomberai** (pen.), Indo.
63/K5 **Bom Jesus do Gurgueia** (mts.), Braz.
40/H1 **Bon** (cape), Tun.
59/H5 **Bonaire** (isl.), NAnt.
45/B2 **Bonaparte** (arch.), Austl.
37/F5 **Bone** (gulf), Indo.
42/K10 **Bongolava** (uplands), Madg.
41/K6 **Bongos, Massif des** (plat.), CAfr.
21/F3 **Bonifacio** (str.), Eur.
46/D2 **Bonin** (isls.), Japan
18/F4 **Bonn,** Ger.
50/C4 **Bonneville** (dam), US
37/E5 **Bonthain,** Indo.
53/J2 **Boone,** Ia,US
47/K6 **Bora Bora** (isl.), FrPol.
50/E4 **Borah** (peak), Id,US
63/L5 **Borborema** (plat.), Braz.
20/C2 **Bordeaux,** Fr.
56/C3 **Borger,** Tx,US
37/E3 **Borneo** (isl.), Asia
22/E5 **Bornholm** (isl.), Den.
40/H5 **Bornu** (plains), Nga.
32/E2 **Borūjerd,** Iran
21/H3 **Bosnia and Herzegovina**
23/C5 **Bosporus** (str.), Turk.
56/E3 **Bossier City,** La,US
55/G3 **Boston** (cap.), Ma,US
22/F3 **Bothnia** (gulf), Eur.
21/K2 **Botoşani,** Rom.
28/H4 **Botou,** China
42/D5 **Botswana**
40/E6 **Bouaké,** C.d'Iv.
40/E5 **Boucle du Baoulé Nat'l Park,** Mali
46/E5 **Bougainville** (isl.), PNG
53/F2 **Boulder,** Co,US
52/D4 **Boulder City,** Nv,US
20/D1 **Boulogne-sur-Mer,** Fr.
52/E2 **Bountiful,** Ut,US
20/D2 **Bourges,** Fr.
18/D4 **Bournemouth,** Eng,UK
15/K8 **Bouvet** (isl.), Nor.
57/G2 **Bowling Green,** Ky,US
54/D3 **Bowling Green,** Oh,US
57/H5 **Boynton Beach,** Fl,US
50/F4 **Bozeman,** Mt,US
21/H3 **Brač** (isl.), Cro.
57/H5 **Bradenton,** Fl,US
18/D3 **Bradford,** Eng,UK
20/A3 **Braga,** Port.
35/F2 **Brahmaputra** (riv.), Asia
21/K2 **Brăila,** Rom.
62/F4 **Branco** (riv.), Braz.
54/D3 **Brantford,** On,Can
63/J7 **Brasília** (cap.), Braz.
63/J7 **Brasília Nat'l Park,** Braz.
21/K2 **Braşov,** Rom.
19/J4 **Bratislava** (cap.), Slvk.
25/L4 **Bratsk,** Rus.
55/F3 **Brattleboro,** Vt,US
18/G3 **Braunschweig,** Ger.
62/F7 **Bravo** (mtn.), Bol.
61/D3 **Brazil**
56/D4 **Brazos** (riv.), Tx,US
42/C1 **Brazzaville** (cap.), Congo
18/D4 **Brecon Beacons Nat'l Park,** Wal,UK
18/F4 **Breda,** Neth.
18/G3 **Bremen,** Ger.
18/G3 **Bremerhaven,** Ger.
50/C4 **Bremerton,** Wa,US
21/F2 **Brescia,** It.
19/K3 **Brest,** Bela.
20/B1 **Brest,** Fr.
55/F3 **Bridgeport,** Ct,US
59/K5 **Bridgetown** (cap.), Bar.
52/D2 **Brigham City,** Ut,US
18/D4 **Brighton,** Eng,UK
21/H3 **Brindisi,** It.
45/E3 **Brisbane,** Austl.
18/C4 **Bristol** (chan.), UK
18/D4 **Bristol,** Eng,UK
49/A4 **Bristol** (bay), Ak,US
57/H2 **Bristol,** Tn,US
57/H2 **Bristol,** Va,US
50/C3 **British Columbia** (prov.), Can.
27/G10 **British Indian Ocean Terr.,** UK
20/C2 **Brittany** (reg.), Fr.
19/J4 **Brno,** Czh.
55/G3 **Brockton,** Ma,US
53/J3 **Broken Arrow,** Ok,US
45/D4 **Broken Hill,** Austl.
51/J4 **Brookings,** SD,US
49/B3 **Brooks** (range), Ak,US
56/D5 **Brownsville,** Tx,US
56/D4 **Brownwood,** Tx,US
18/E4 **Brugge,** Belg.
36/D2 **Brunei**
64/B7 **Brunswick** (pen.), Chile
57/H4 **Brunswick,** Ga,US
55/G3 **Brunswick,** Me,US
18/F4 **Brussels** (cap.), Belg.
56/D4 **Bryan,** Tx,US
23/D3 **Bryansk,** Rus.
52/D3 **Bryce Canyon Nat'l Pk.,** Ut,US
62/D2 **Bucaramanga,** Col.
21/K2 **Bucharest** (cap.), Rom.
21/H2 **Budapest** (cap.), Hun.
62/C3 **Buenaventura,** Col.
64/E3 **Buenos Aires** (cap.), Arg.
64/B6 **Buenos Aires** (lake), Arg., Chile
54/E3 **Buffalo,** NY,US
19/K3 **Bug** (riv.), Eur.
42/E1 **Bujumbura** (cap.), Buru.
42/E1 **Bukavu,** D.R. Congo
24/G6 **Bukhoro,** Uzb.
21/J2 **Bükki Nat'l Park,** Hun.
42/E5 **Bulawayo,** Zim.
21/K3 **Bulgaria**
28/D2 **Bulnayn** (mts.), Mong.
37/F5 **Bulukumba,** Indo.
32/D3 **Buraydah,** SAr.
52/C4 **Burbank,** Ca,US
34/E3 **Burdwan,** India
K3/21 **Burgas,** Bulg.
20/C3 **Burgos,** Sp.
20/E2 **Burgundy** (reg.), Fr.
40/E5 **Burkina Faso**
54/E3 **Burlington,** On,Can
53/K2 **Burlington,** Ia,US
57/J2 **Burlington,** NC,US
55/F2 **Burlington,** Vt,US
23/C5 **Bursa,** Turk.
37/G4 **Buru** (isl.), Indo.
42/E1 **Burundi**
54/E3 **Butler,** Pa,US
30/E6 **Butuan,** Phil.
37/F5 **Butung** (isl.), Indo.
21/K2 **Buzău,** Rom.
19/J3 **Bydgoszcz,** Pol.
24/K2 **Byrranga** (mts.), Rus.
19/J3 **Bytom,** Pol.

C

63/K5 **Caatingas** (reg.), Braz.
62/D1 **Cabimas,** Ven.
42/B2 **Cabinda,** Ang.
64/C7 **Cabo de Hornos Nat'l Park,** Chile
54/E2 **Cabonga** (res.), Qu,Can
63/H3 **Cabo Orange Nat'l Park,** Braz.
42/F4 **Cabora Bassa** (lake), Moz.
55/J2 **Cabot** (str.), Can.
21/J3 **Čačak,** Yugo.
63/G5 **Cachimbo** (mts.), Braz.
20/B4 **Cádiz,** Sp.
20/B4 **Cádiz** (gulf), Sp.
20/C1 **Caen,** Fr.
30/D6 **Cagayan de Oro,** Phil.
21/F4 **Cagliari,** It.
59/H4 **Caguas,** PR
63/H7 **Caiapó** (mts.), Braz.
59/G3 **Caicos** (isls.), Trks.
45/D2 **Cairns,** Austl.
32/B3 **Cairo** (cap.), Egypt
54/B4 **Cairo,** Il,US
40/G7 **Calabar,** Nga.
21/H4 **Calabria** (reg.), It.
20/D1 **Calais,** Fr.
55/H2 **Calais,** Me,US
64/C2 **Calalaste** (mts.), Arg.
34/E3 **Calcutta** (Kolkata), India
50/D5 **Caldwell,** Id,US
50/E3 **Calgary,** Ab,Can
62/C3 **Cali,** Col.
34/C5 **Calicut** (Kozhikode), India
59/M8 **California** (gulf), Mex.
52/B3 **California** (state), US
62/C6 **Callao,** Peru
59/F3 **Camagüey,** Cuba
59/F3 **Camagüey** (arch.), Cuba
34/B3 **Cambay** (gulf), India
35/H5 **Cambodia**
18/D3 **Cambrian** (mts.), Wal,UK
18/E3 **Cambridge,** Eng,UK
55/G3 **Cambridge,** Ma,US
54/E4 **Cambridge,** Md,US
53/J4 **Camden,** Ar,US
55/F4 **Camden,** NJ,US
57/H3 **Camden,** SC,US
42/D3 **Cameia Nat'l Park,** Ang.
40/H7 **Cameroon**
64/B4 **Campanario** (mtn.), Arg.
58/C4 **Campeche,** Mex.
58/C4 **Campeche** (bay), Mex.
63/L5 **Campina Grande,** Braz.
64/G1 **Campinas,** Braz.
63/H8 **Campo Grande,** Braz.
63/K8 **Campos,** Braz.
35/J5 **Cam Ranh,** Viet.
49/G4 **Canada**
53/G3 **Canadian** (riv.), US
62/F2 **Canaima Nat'l Park,** Ven.
40/B2 **Canary** (isls.), Sp.
45/D4 **Canberra** (cap.), Austl.
58/D3 **Cancún,** Mex.
64/C2 **Candado** (mtn.), Arg.
28/H4 **Cangzhou,** China
20/E3 **Cannes,** Fr.
64/F2 **Canoas,** Braz.
20/B3 **Cantabrica, Cordillera** (range), Sp.
45/H7 **Canterbury** (bight), NZ
18/E4 **Canterbury,** Eng,UK
35/J6 **Can Tho,** Viet.
47/H5 **Canton** (isl.), Kiri.
54/D3 **Canton,** Oh,US

67

Canto – Fürth

30/B3 **Canton** (Guangzhou), China
52/E3 **Canyonlands Nat'l Pk.,** Ut,US
55/J2 **Cape Breton** (isl.), NS,Can
57/H5 **Cape Coral,** Fl,US
57/F2 **Cape Girardeau,** Mo,US
42/C7 **Cape Town** (cap.), SAfr.
14/H5 **Cape Verde**
45/D2 **Cape York** (pen.), Austl.
59/G4 **Cap-Haïtien,** Haiti
63/J4 **Capim** (riv.), Braz.
52/E3 **Capitol Reef Nat'l Pk.,** Ut,US
63/H8 **Capivara** (res.), Braz.
42/D4 **Caprivi Strip** (reg.), Namb.
62/D4 **Caquetá** (riv.), Col.
62/E1 **Caracas** (cap.), Ven.
63/H5 **Carajás** (mts.), Braz.
54/B4 **Carbondale,** Il,US
20/D3 **Carcassonne,** Fr.
18/D4 **Cardiff** (cap.), Wal,UK
18/C3 **Cardigan** (bay), Wal,UK
59/G4 **Caribbean** (sea)
50/C2 **Cariboo** (mts.), BC,Can
55/G2 **Caribou,** Me,US
18/D3 **Carlisle,** Eng,UK
54/E3 **Carlisle,** Pa,US
18/C3 **Carlow,** Ire.
53/F4 **Carlsbad,** NM,US
53/F4 **Carlsbad Caverns Nat'l Pk.,** NM,US
59/H4 **Carolina,** PR
46/D4 **Caroline** (isls.), Micr.
19/J4 **Carpathians** (mts.), Eur.
45/C2 **Carpentaria** (gulf), Austl.
21/F2 **Carrara,** It.
52/C3 **Carson** (sink), Nv,US
52/C3 **Carson City** (cap.), Nv,US
62/C1 **Cartagena,** Col.
20/C4 **Cartagena,** Sp.
58/E6 **Cartago,** CR
40/D1 **Casablanca,** Mor.
52/E4 **Casa Grande,** Az,US
50/C5 **Cascade** (range), US
64/F1 **Cascavel,** Braz.
50/G5 **Casper,** Wy,US
24/F6 **Caspian** (sea)
20/D3 **Castellón de la Plana,** Sp.
59/J5 **Castries** (cap.), StL.
20/D3 **Catalonia** (reg.), Sp.
21/G4 **Catania,** It.
21/H4 **Catanzaro,** It.
32/B3 **Catherine** (mt.), Egypt
55/F3 **Catskill** (mts.), NY,US
23/F5 **Caucasus** (mts.), Eur.
63/J3 **Caviana** (isl.), Braz.
34/D2 **Cawnpore** (Kanpur), India
63/K4 **Caxias,** Braz.
64/F2 **Caxias do Sul,** Braz.
62/C3 **Cayambe** (mtn.), Ecu.
63/H3 **Cayenne** (cap.), FrG.
58/E4 **Cayman Islands,** UK
30/D5 **Cebu,** Phil.
52/D3 **Cedar City,** Ut,US
53/J2 **Cedar Falls,** Ia,US
53/K2 **Cedar Rapids,** Ia,US
59/L8 **Cedros** (isl.), Mex.
37/F3 **Celebes** (sea), Asia
37/E4 **Celebes** (isl.), Indo.
18/C4 **Celtic** (sea), Eur.
37/H4 **Cenderawasih** (bay), Indo.
41/J6 **Central African Republic**
62/C5 **Central, Cordillera** (mts.), SAm.
54/B4 **Centralia,** Il,US
50/C4 **Centralia,** Wa,US
33/H3 **Central Makrān** (mts.), Pak.
63/J7 **Central, Planalto** (plat.), Braz.
25/L2 **Central Siberian** (plat.), Rus.
37/G4 **Ceram** (isl.), Indo.
37/G4 **Ceram** (sea), Indo.
64/C4 **Cerro Colorados** (res.), Arg.
19/H4 **České Budějovice,** Czh.
20/B5 **Ceuta,** Sp.
34/D6 **Ceylon** (isl.)
64/D1 **Chaco Austral** (reg.), Arg.
62/G8 **Chaco Boreal** (reg.), Par.
64/D1 **Chaco Central** (reg.), Arg.
64/D2 **Chaco, Gran** (reg.), SAm.
64/E2 **Chaco Nat'l Park,** Arg.
41/J4 **Chad**
40/H5 **Chad** (lake), Afr.
27/G10 **Chagos** (arch.), BrIn.
54/E4 **Chambersburg,** Pa,US
42/F3 **Chambeshi** (riv.), Zam.
20/E1 **Champagne** (reg.), Fr.
54/B3 **Champaign,** Il,US
54/F2 **Champlain** (lake), NAm.
62/C5 **Chan Chan** (ruins), Peru
33/L2 **Chandigarh,** India
34/C3 **Chandrapur,** India
29/K3 **Changchun,** China
30/D3 **Changhua,** Tai.
27/L6 **Chang Jiang** (Yangtze) (riv.), China
35/K2 **Changsha,** China
28/G4 **Changzhi,** China
29/H5 **Changzhou,** China
64/C1 **Chañi** (mtn.), Arg.
52/C4 **Channel** (isls.), Ca,US
45/D3 **Channel Country** (reg.), Austl.
18/D4 **Channel Islands,** UK
63/K6 **Chapada Diamantina Nat'l Park,** Braz.
63/J6 **Chapada dos Veadeiros Nat'l Park,** Braz.
57/J3 **Chapel Hill,** NC,US
40/J5 **Chari** (riv.), Afr.
18/F4 **Charleroi,** Belg.
57/J3 **Charleston,** SC,US
54/D4 **Charleston** (cap.), WV,US
57/H3 **Charlotte,** NC,US
59/J4 **Charlotte Amalie** (cap.), USVI
57/J2 **Charlottesville,** Va,US
55/J2 **Charlottetown** (cap.), PE,Can
20/D1 **Chartres,** Fr.
55/H2 **Chatham,** NB,Can
57/G4 **Chattahoochee** (riv.), US
57/G4 **Chattahoochee,** Fl,US
57/G3 **Chattanooga,** Tn,US
25/T3 **Chaunskaya** (bay), Rus.
23/D2 **Cheboksary,** Rus.
54/C2 **Cheboygan,** Mi,US
40/E2 **Chech, Erg** (des.), Alg.
54/E3 **Cheektowaga,** NY,US
50/C4 **Chehalis,** Wa,US
29/K5 **Cheju,** SKor.
29/K5 **Cheju** (isl.), SKor.
29/K5 **Cheju** (str.), SKor.
50/C4 **Chelan** (lake), Wa,US
18/D4 **Cheltenham,** Eng,UK
24/G4 **Chelyabinsk,** Rus.
25/L2 **Chelyuskina** (cape), Rus.
34/D5 **Chennai** (Madras), India
19/H4 **Chemnitz,** Ger.
29/H6 **Chengde,** China
28/E5 **Chengdu** (Chengtu), China
20/C1 **Cherbourg,** Fr.
23/E2 **Cherepovets,** Rus.
23/D4 **Cherkasy,** Ukr.
23/F5 **Cherkessk,** Rus.
23/D3 **Chernihiv,** Ukr.
23/C4 **Chernivtsi,** Ukr.
23/D4 **Cherry Hill,** NJ,US
25/Q3 **Cherskiy** (range), Rus.
54/E4 **Chesapeake** (bay), US
18/D3 **Chester,** Eng,UK
58/D4 **Chetumal,** Mex.
53/F2 **Cheyenne** (riv.), US
53/F2 **Cheyenne** (cap.), Wy,US
35/G4 **Chiang Mai,** Thai.
30/D3 **Chiayi,** Tai.
29/N4 **Chiba,** Japan
54/C3 **Chicago,** Il,US
58/D3 **Chichén-Itzá** (ruins), Mex.
45/A3 **Chichester** (range), Austl.
53/H4 **Chickasha,** Ok,US
62/C5 **Chiclayo,** Peru
64/C5 **Chico** (riv.), Arg.
52/B3 **Chico,** Ca,US
54/F3 **Chicopee,** Ma,US
55/G1 **Chicoutimi,** Qu,Can
29/H3 **Chifeng,** China
63/K7 **Chifre** (mts.), Braz.
59/N8 **Chihuahua,** Mex.
61/B6 **Chile**
64/B4 **Chillán,** Chile
54/D4 **Chillicothe,** Oh,US
64/A5 **Chiloé** (isl.), Chile
62/C4 **Chimborazo** (mt.), Ecu.
62/C5 **Chimbote,** Peru
27/J6 **China, People's Rep. of**
30/D3 **China, Rep. of** (Taiwan)
33/K2 **Chiniot,** Pak.
24/G5 **Chirchiq,** Uzb.
58/E6 **Chiriquí** (gulf), Pan.
19/M5 **Chişinău** (cap.), Mold.
28/G1 **Chita,** Rus.
35/F3 **Chittagong,** Bang.
42/D4 **Chobe Nat'l Park,** Bots.
35/H5 **Chon Buri,** Thai.
29/K3 **Chŏngjin,** NKor.
29/K4 **Chŏngju,** SKor.
30/A2 **Chongqing** (Chungking), China
29/K4 **Chŏnju,** SKor.
64/A6 **Chonos** (arch.), Arg.
33/M3 **Chota Nagur** (plat.), India
28/G2 **Choybalsan,** Mong.
45/H7 **Christchurch,** NZ
27/K11 **Christmas** (isl.), Austl.
64/C5 **Chubut** (riv.), Arg.
25/U3 **Chukchi** (pen.), Rus.
25/U3 **Chukchi** (sea), Rus.
52/C4 **Chula Vista,** Ca,US
24/J4 **Chulym** (riv.), Rus.
29/K4 **Ch'unch'ŏn,** SKor.
49/H4 **Churchill,** Can.
49/H4 **Churchill** (riv.), Can.
36/C5 **Ciamis,** Indo.
36/C5 **Cianjur,** Indo.
59/E3 **Cienfuegos,** Cuba
36/C5 **Cilacap,** Indo.
53/G3 **Cimarron** (riv.), US
54/C4 **Cincinnati,** Oh,US
21/F3 **Cinto** (mt.), Fr.
36/C5 **Cirebon,** Indo.
58/B4 **Citlaltépetl** (mt.), Mex.
62/F2 **Ciudad Bolívar,** Ven.
62/F2 **Ciudad Guayana,** Ven.
59/N7 **Ciudad Juárez,** Mex.
58/B3 **Ciudad Madero,** Mex.
59/N8 **Ciudad Obregón,** Mex.
20/B4 **Ciudad Real,** Sp.
58/B3 **Ciudad Victoria,** Mex.
55/F3 **Claremont,** NH,US
53/J3 **Claremore,** Ok,US
54/D4 **Clarksburg,** WV,US
57/F3 **Clarksdale,** Ms,US
57/G2 **Clarksville,** Tn,US
18/B4 **Clear** (cape), Ire.
57/H5 **Clearwater,** Fl,US
50/D4 **Clearwater** (mts.), Id,US
20/D2 **Clermont-Ferrand,** Fr.
55/D3 **Cleveland,** Oh,US
57/G3 **Cleveland,** Tn,US
53/K2 **Clinton,** Ia,US
14/D5 **Clipperton** (isl.), Fr.
52/C3 **Clovis,** Ca,US
53/G4 **Clovis,** NM,US
21/J2 **Cluj-Napoca,** Rom.
18/C3 **Clyde, Firth of** (inlet), Sc,UK
50/A2 **Coast** (mts.), Can.
49/E5 **Coast** (ranges), US
57/H4 **Coastal** (plain), US
62/E7 **Cochabamba,** Bol.
34/C6 **Cochin,** India
58/E5 **Coco** (riv.), Hon., Nic.
27/J11 **Cocos** (isls.), Austl.
55/G3 **Cod** (cape), Ma,US
50/F4 **Cody,** Wy,US
50/D4 **Coeur d'Alene,** Id,US
53/J3 **Coffeyville,** Ks,US
34/C5 **Coimbatore,** India
21/A3 **Coimbra,** Port.
62/E2 **Cojedes** (riv.), Ven.
59/P10 **Colima,** Mex.
56/D4 **College Station,** Tx,US
20/E1 **Colmar,** Fr.
18/F4 **Cologne** (Köln), Ger.
62/C3 **Colombia**
34/C6 **Colombo** (cap.), SrL.
59/F6 **Colón,** Pan.
64/D4 **Colorado** (riv.), Arg.
52/E3 **Colorado** (plat.), US
52/D4 **Colorado** (riv.), US
52/F3 **Colorado** (state), US
56/D4 **Colorado** (riv.), Tx,US
53/F3 **Colorado Springs,** Co,US
50/C2 **Columbia** (mts.), BC,Can
50/C4 **Columbia** (riv.), NAm.
53/J3 **Columbia,** Mo,US
50/D4 **Columbia** (plat.), Or,Wa,US
57/H3 **Columbia** (cap.), SC,US
57/G3 **Columbia,** Tn,US
57/G3 **Columbus,** Ga,US
54/C4 **Columbus,** In,US
57/F3 **Columbus,** Ms,US
54/D4 **Columbus** (cap.), Oh,US
21/F2 **Como** (lake), It.
64/C6 **Comodoro Rivadavia,** Arg.
40/E6 **Comoe Nat'l Park,** C.d'Iv.
34/C6 **Comorin** (cape), India
39/G6 **Comoros**
21/D1 **Compiègne,** Fr.
41/C6 **Conakry** (cap.), Gui.,
62/F7 **Concepción** (lake), Bol.
64/B4 **Concepción,** Chile
52/B3 **Concord,** Ca,US
55/G3 **Concord** (cap.), NH,US
57/H3 **Concord,** NC,US
30/B3 **Conghua,** China
39/E5 **Congo, Dem. Rep. of the**
39/D4 **Congo, Rep. of the**
39/D4 **Congo** (riv.), Afr.
41/K7 **Congo** (basin), D.R. Congo
18/B3 **Connacht** (reg.), Ire.
55/G2 **Connecticut** (riv.), US
55/F3 **Connecticut** (state), US
18/G5 **Constance** (lake), Eur.
21/L2 **Constanta,** Rom.
41/G1 **Constantine,** Alg.
63/K7 **Contagem,** Braz.
50/C2 **Continental** (ranges), Ab,BC,Can
53/J4 **Conway,** Ar,US
45/G7 **Cook** (mt.), NZ
45/H7 **Cook** (str.), NZ
47/J6 **Cook Islands,** NZ
50/B5 **Coos Bay,** Or,US
19/H2 **Copenhagen** (cap.), Den.
46/E6 **Coral** (sea)
57/H5 **Coral Gables,** Fl,US
45/E2 **Coral Sea Is.** (terr.), Austl.
57/H5 **Coral Springs,** Fl,US
62/D3 **Cordillera de los Picachos Nat'l Park,** Col.
64/D3 **Córdoba,** Arg.
64/D3 **Córdoba** (mts.), Arg.
20/B4 **Córdoba,** Sp.
21/H4 **Corfu** (Kérkira), Gre.
21/J4 **Corinth,** Gre.
21/J4 **Corinth** (gulf), Gre.
18/B4 **Cork,** Ire.
55/K1 **Corner Brook,** Nf,Can
54/E3 **Corning,** NY,US
54/F2 **Cornwall,** On,Can
62/E1 **Coro,** Ven.
34/D5 **Coromandel** (coast), India
58/E6 **Coronado** (bay), CR
62/D7 **Coropuna** (mtn.), Peru
56/D5 **Corpus Christi,** Tx,US
64/E2 **Corrientes,** Arg.
21/F3 **Corsica** (isl.), Fr.
56/D3 **Corsicana,** Tx,US
54/E3 **Cortland,** NY,US
23/D5 **Çorum,** Turk.
63/J7 **Corumba** (riv.), Braz.
50/C4 **Corvallis,** Or,US
21/G3 **Cosenza,** It.
54/D3 **Coshocton,** Oh,US
58/E5 **Costa Rica**
40/D6 **Côte d'Ivoire**
20/C1 **Cotentin** (pen.), Fr.
40/F6 **Cotonou,** Benin
19/H4 **Cottbus,** Ger.
53/J2 **Council Bluffs,** Ia,US
18/D3 **Coventry,** Eng,UK
54/C4 **Covington,** Ky,US
58/D3 **Cozumel** (isl.), Mex.
21/J2 **Craiova,** Rom.
50/E3 **Cranbrook,** BC,Can
50/C5 **Crater Lake Nat'l Pk.,** Or,US
54/C3 **Crawfordsville,** In,US
21/G2 **Cres** (isl.), Cro.
21/K5 **Crete** (isl.), Gre.
21/K4 **Crete** (sea), Gre.
23/D4 **Crimea** (pen.), Ukr.
40/H8 **Cristal** (mts.), Gabon
62/D1 **Cristóbal Colón** (peak), Col.
21/G2 **Croatia**
37/E3 **Crocker** (range), Malay.
56/E4 **Crowley,** La,US
42/C2 **Cuango** (riv.), Ang.
42/B2 **Cuanza** (riv.), Ang.
59/F3 **Cuba**
42/C4 **Cubango** (riv.), Ang.
62/D2 **Cucuta,** Col.
62/C4 **Cuenca,** Ecu.
58/B4 **Cuernavaca,** Mex.
63/G7 **Cuiabá,** Braz.
63/H6 **Culene** (riv.), Braz.
45/D3 **Culgoa** (riv.), Austl.
59/N9 **Culiacán,** Mex.
57/G3 **Cullman,** Al,US
62/F1 **Cumaná,** Ven.
57/G3 **Cumberland** (plat.), US
57/G2 **Cumberland** (riv.), US
54/E4 **Cumberland,** Md,US
18/D3 **Cumbrian** (mts.), Eng,UK
59/H5 **Curaçao** (isl.), NAnt.
64/G2 **Curitiba,** Braz.
62/D6 **Cusco,** Peru
34/E3 **Cuttack,** India
21/K4 **Cyclades** (isls.), Gre.
32/B1 **Cyprus**
41/K1 **Cyrenaica** (reg.), Libya
19/H4 **Czech Republic**
19/J4 **Czestochowa,** Pol.

D

21/G3 **D'Abruzzo Nat'l Park,** It.
34/E4 **Dacca** (Dhaka) (cap.), Bang.
18/G4 **Dachau,** Ger.
35/J2 **Dafang,** China
29/J2 **Da Hinggang** (mts.), China
46/C2 **Daito** (isls.), Japan
40/B5 **Dakar** (cap.), Sen.
35/J5 **Da Lat,** Viet.
55/H1 **Dalhousie,** NB,Can
29/J4 **Dalian,** China
56/D3 **Dallas,** Tx,US
21/G2 **Dalmatia** (reg.), Cro.
45/D3 **Dalrymple** (lake), Austl.
57/G3 **Dalton,** Ga,US
34/B3 **Damān,** India
32/B2 **Damanhur,** Egypt
32/C2 **Damascus** (cap.), Syria
32/F1 **Damavand** (mt.), Iran
32/B2 **Damietta,** Egypt
37/H4 **Dampier** (str.), Indo.
41/P5 **Danakil** (reg.), Djib., Eth.
35/E2 **Da Nang,** Viet.
29/J3 **Dandong,** China
21/L2 **Danube** (riv.), Eur.
55/C3 **Danville,** Il,US
54/E4 **Danville,** Va,US
29/K2 **Daqing,** China
34/E2 **Darbhanga,** India
23/C6 **Dardanelles** (str.), Turk.
42/G2 **Dar es Salaam** (cap.), Tanz.
28/F2 **Darhan,** Mong.
41/Q6 **Darie** (hills), Som.
59/F6 **Darien Nat'l Park,** Pan.
34/E2 **Darjiling,** India
45/A4 **Darling** (range), Austl.
45/D4 **Darling** (riv.), Austl.
45/D3 **Darling Downs** (ridge), Austl.
18/D3 **Darlington,** Eng,UK
18/G4 **Darmstadt,** Ger.
18/C4 **Dartmoor Nat'l Park,** Eng,UK
55/J2 **Dartmouth,** NS,Can
45/C2 **Darwin,** Austl.
64/B7 **Darwin** (mts.), Chile
41/N5 **Dashen Terara, Ras** (peak), Eth.
24/F5 **Dashhowuz,** Trkm.
33/F2 **Dasht-e Kavīr** (des.), Iran
33/G2 **Dasht-e Lūt** (des.), Iran
28/G3 **Datong,** China
19/L2 **Daugava** (Western Dvina) (riv.), Lat.
19/L3 **Daugavpils,** Lat.
30/E6 **Davao,** Phil.
53/K2 **Davenport,** Ia,US
58/E6 **David,** Pan.
43/F **Davis** (sea), Ant.
49/M3 **Davis** (str.), NAm.
52/B3 **Davis,** Ca,US
49/D3 **Dawson,** Can.
50/C2 **Dawson Creek,** BC,Can
28/F5 **Daxian,** China
54/C4 **Dayton,** Oh,US
57/H4 **Daytona Beach,** Fl,US
32/C2 **Dead** (sea), Asia
52/C3 **Death Valley Nat'l Mon.,** Ca,Nv,US
21/J2 **Debrecen,** Hun.
57/G3 **Decatur,** Al,US
57/G3 **Decatur,** Ga,US
54/B4 **Decatur,** Il,US
34/C5 **Deccan** (plat.), India
54/C3 **Defiance,** Oh,US
33/L2 **Dehra Dun,** India
54/B3 **De Kalb,** Il,US
57/H4 **De Land,** Fl,US
54/F4 **Delaware** (bay), US
54/F3 **Delaware** (riv.), US
54/F4 **Delaware** (state), US
54/D3 **Delaware,** Oh,US
21/J4 **Delfoi** (ruins), Gre.
64/D5 **Delgada** (pt.), Arg.
34/C2 **Delhi,** India
21/F2 **Dello Stelvio Nat'l Park,** It.
57/H5 **Delray Beach,** Fl,US
56/C4 **Del Rio,** Tx,US
41/P5 **Denakil** (reg.), Erit., Eth.
18/F3 **Den Helder,** Neth.
23/C6 **Denizli,** Turk.
18/G3 **Denmark**
14/A2 **Denmark** (str.)
56/D3 **Denton,** Tx,US
53/F3 **Denver** (cap.), Co,US
33/J3 **Dera Ghāzi Khān,** Pak.
23/G5 **Derbent,** Rus.
18/D3 **Derby,** Eng,UK
18/B3 **Derg, Lough** (lake), Ire.
56/E4 **De Ridder,** La,US
55/G3 **Derry,** NH,US
64/C6 **Deseado** (riv.), Arg.
53/J2 **Des Moines** (cap.), Ia,US
23/D3 **Desna** (riv.), Eur.
64/A7 **Desolación** (isl.), Chile
18/H4 **Dessau,** Ger.
54/D3 **Detroit,** Mi,US
63/H2 **Devil's** (isl.), FrG.
49/J2 **Devon** (isl.), Can.
32/E2 **Dezfūl,** Iran
25/T3 **Dezhnaya** (cape), Rus.
28/H4 **Dezhou,** China
32/E3 **Dhahran,** SAr.
34/E3 **Dhaka** (Dacca) (cap.), Bang.
34/E3 **Dhānbād,** India
32/F5 **Dhofar** (reg.), Oman
34/B3 **Dhulia,** India
63/K6 **Diamantina** (uplands), Braz.
51/H4 **Dickinson,** ND,US
27/G10 **Diego Garcia** (isls.), BrIn.
35/H3 **Dien Bien Phu,** Viet.
20/D1 **Dieppe,** Fr.
37/J5 **Digul** (riv.), Indo.
20/E2 **Dijon,** Fr.
37/G5 **Dili** (cap.), E. Timor
25/P2 **Dimitriya Lapteva** (str.), Rus.
21/H2 **Dinaric Alps** (mts.), Eur.
41/N5 **Dinder Nat'l Park,** Sudan
18/B3 **Dingle** (bay), Ire.
52/E2 **Dinosaur Nat'l Mon.,** Co,Ut,US
41/P6 **Dire Dawa,** Eth.
63/J8 **Divinópolis,** Braz.
62/D5 **Divisor** (mts.), Braz.
54/B3 **Dixon,** Il,US
23/F6 **Diyarbakir,** Turk.
40/H3 **Djado** (plat.), Niger
36/C5 **Djakarta** (Jakarta), Indo.
41/P5 **Djibouti**
41/P5 **Djibouti** (cap.), Djib.
36/D5 **Djokjakarta** (Yogyakarta), Indo.
23/D4 **Dnipro** (riv.), Eur.
23/D4 **Dniprodzerzhyns'k,** Ukr.
23/D4 **Dnipropetrovs'k,** Ukr.
23/C4 **Dnister** (riv.), Eur.
37/H4 **Doberai** (pen.), Indo.
63/K7 **Doce** (riv.), Braz.
21/K4 **Dodecanese** (isls.), Gre.
53/G3 **Dodge City,** Ks,US
23/E5 **Dogukaradeniz** (mts.), Turk.
32/F3 **Doha** (cap.), Qatar
63/K5 **Dois Irmãos** (mts.), Braz.
64/C1 **Domeyko** (mts.), Chile
59/J4 **Dominica**
59/H4 **Dominican Republic**
23/F4 **Don** (riv.), Rus.
34/D6 **Dondra** (head), SrL.
18/B3 **Donegal** (bay), Ire.
23/E4 **Donets** (riv.), Ukr.
23/E4 **Donets'k,** Ukr.
30/B3 **Dongguan,** China
29/H4 **Dongying,** China
21/D2 **Dordogne** (riv.), Fr.
18/F4 **Dortmund,** Ger.
57/G4 **Dothan,** Al,US
40/G7 **Douala,** Camr.
18/C3 **Douglas** (cap.), IM,UK
52/E5 **Douglas,** Az,US
20/B3 **Douro** (riv.), Port.
18/E4 **Dover** (str.), Eur.
18/E4 **Dover,** Eng,UK
54/F4 **Dover** (cap.), De,US
55/G3 **Dover,** NH,US
64/C8 **Drake** (passage)
42/E6 **Drakensburg** (range), SAfr.
21/H2 **Drāva** (riv.), Eur.
19/H4 **Dresden,** Ger.
21/H2 **Drina** (riv.), Bosn.
45/D3 **Drummond** (range), Austl.
33/G3 **Dubayyi** (Dubai), UAE
18/C3 **Dublin** (cap.), Ire.
57/H3 **Dublin,** Ga,US
21/H3 **Dubrovnik,** Cro.
53/K2 **Dubuque,** Ia,US
24/J3 **Dudinka,** Rus.
20/E2 **Dufourspitze** (mt.), Eur.
62/E3 **Duida Marahuaca Nat'l Park,** Ven.
18/F4 **Duisburg,** Ger.
51/L4 **Duluth,** Mn,US
18/D3 **Dumfries,** Sc,UK
53/H4 **Duncan,** Ok,US
18/C3 **Dundalk,** Ire.
18/D2 **Dundee,** Sc,UK
45/H7 **Dunedin,** NZ
57/H4 **Dunedin,** Fl,US
20/D1 **Dunkirk** (Dunkerque), Fr.
59/P9 **Durango,** Mex.
52/F3 **Durango,** Co,US
53/H4 **Durant,** Ok,US
42/F6 **Durban,** SAfr.
34/E3 **Durgapur,** India
18/D3 **Durham,** Eng,UK
57/J3 **Durham,** NC,US
55/G3 **Durham,** NH,US
21/H3 **Durrës,** Alb.
24/G6 **Dushanbe** (cap.), Taj.
18/F4 **Düsseldorf,** Ger.
17/J2 **Dvina, Northern** (Dvina Severnaya) (riv.), Rus.
23/C2 **Dvina, Western** (Dvina Zapadnaya) (riv.), Bela.
23/F2 **Dzerzhinsk,** Rus.
25/P4 **Dzhugdzhur** (range), Rus.

E

56/C4 **Eagle Pass,** Tx,US
27/M6 **East China** (sea), Asia
47/Q7 **Easter** (isl.), Chile
34/C5 **Eastern Ghats** (mts.), India
64/E7 **East Falkland** (isl.), Falk.
18/F3 **East Frisian** (isls.), Ger.
54/C3 **East Lansing,** Mi,US
54/D3 **East Liverpool,** Oh,US
42/E7 **East London,** SAfr.
57/G3 **East Point,** Ga,US
25/S2 **East Siberian** (sea), Rus.
54/B4 **East St. Louis,** Il,US
37/G5 **East Timor**
54/B2 **Eau Claire,** Wi,US
20/D3 **Ebro** (riv.), Sp.
58/B4 **Ecatepec,** Mex.
20/E2 **Ecrins Nat'l Park,** Fr.
62/C4 **Ecuador**
57/J2 **Eden,** NC,US
57/J2 **Edenton,** NC,US
56/D5 **Edinburg,** Tx,US
18/D3 **Edinburgh** (cap.), Sc,UK
23/C5 **Edirne,** Turk.
50/C4 **Edmonds,** Wa,US
50/E2 **Edmonton** (cap.), Ab,Can
55/G2 **Edmundston,** NB,Can
23/C6 **Edremit,** Turk.
56/C4 **Edwards** (plat.), Tx,US
54/B4 **Edwardsville,** Il,US
52/B3 **Eel** (riv.), Ca,US
54/B4 **Effingham,** Il,US
21/G4 **Egadi** (isls.), It.
45/H6 **Egmont** (mt.), NZ
41/L2 **Egypt**
18/F4 **Eifel** (plat.), Ger.
18/F4 **Eindhoven,** Neth.
40/F1 **El Asnam,** Alg.
32/B3 **Elat** (Elath), Isr.
23/E6 **Elazig,** Turk.
21/F3 **Elba** (isl.), It.
18/G3 **Elbe** (riv.), Ger.
52/F3 **Elbert** (mt.), Co,US
19/J3 **Elblag,** Pol.
23/F5 **El'brus** (mt.), Rus.
32/E1 **Elburz** (mts.), Iran
52/C4 **El Cajon,** Ca,US
52/D4 **El Centro,** Ca,US
62/D2 **El Cocuy Nat'l Park,** Col.
40/D3 **El Djouf** (des.), Mrta.
53/J4 **El Dorado,** Ar,US
17/H3 **Elektrostal',** Rus.
59/F2 **Eleuthera** (isl.), Bahm.
54/B3 **Elgin** (mt.), Il,US
41/M7 **Elgon** (mt.), Ugan.
57/J2 **Elizabeth City,** NC,US
54/C3 **Elkhart,** In,US
40/C3 **El Khatt** (escarp.), Mrta.
50/C4 **Ellensburg,** Wa,US
49/J2 **Ellesmere** (isl.), Can.
43/U **Ellsworth Land** (reg.), Ant.
54/E3 **Elmira,** NY,US
62/D7 **El Misti** (vol.), Peru
64/C4 **El Nevado** (mtn.), Arg.
56/A4 **El Paso,** Tx,US
52/H4 **El Reno,** Ok,US
58/D5 **El Salvador**
62/E2 **El Tuparro Nat'l Park,** Col.
62/D2 **El Viejo** (mtn.), Col.
54/D3 **Elyria,** Oh,US
63/H7 **Emas Nat'l Park,** Braz.
18/F3 **Emden,** Ger.
18/F3 **Emmen,** Neth.
53/H3 **Emporia,** Ks,US
18/F3 **Ems** (riv.), Eur.
43/D **Enderby Land** (reg.), Ant.
54/E3 **Endicott,** NY,US
46/F3 **Enewetak** (atoll), Mrsh.
23/G3 **Engel's,** Rus.
18/D3 **England,** UK
18/C4 **English** (chan.), Eur.
53/H3 **Enid,** Ok,US
41/K4 **Ennedi** (plat.), Chad
18/C3 **Enniskillen,** NI,UK
18/F3 **Enschede,** Neth.
59/L7 **Ensenada,** Mex.
41/M8 **Entebbe,** Ugan.
40/G6 **Enugu,** Nga.
32/E1 **Enzeli** (Bandar-e Anzali), Iran
20/E1 **Épinal,** Fr.
40/G7 **Equatorial Guinea**
28/E2 **Erdenet,** Mong.
63/G4 **Erepecu** (lake), Braz.
18/G4 **Erfurt,** Ger.
40/D3 **Erg Chech** (des.), Alg., Mali
40/D2 **Erg Iguidi** (des.), Alg., Mrta.
54/D3 **Erie** (lake), NAm.
54/D3 **Erie,** Pa,US
32/C5 **Eritrea**
18/G4 **Erlangen,** Ger.
34/C5 **Erode,** India
18/B3 **Erris Head** (pt.), Ire.
19/H4 **Erzgebirge** (mts.), Eur.
23/F6 **Erzurum,** Turk.
22/H3 **Esbo** (Espoo), Fin.
54/C2 **Escanaba,** Mi,US
52/C4 **Escondido,** Ca,US
32/F2 **Esfahān,** Iran
23/D6 **Eskişehir,** Turk.
62/C3 **Esmeraldas,** Ecu.
63/K7 **Espinhaço** (mts.), Braz.
46/F6 **Espiritu Santo** (isl.), Van.
22/H3 **Espoo** (Esbo), Fin.
18/F4 **Essen,** Ger.
62/G2 **Essequibo** (riv.), Guy.
64/D7 **Estados** (isl.), Arg.
19/L2 **Estonia**
20/A3 **Estrella** (mts.), Port.
63/J5 **Estrondo** (mts.), Braz.
41/N5 **Ethiopia**
41/N6 **Ethiopian** (plat.), Eth.
21/G4 **Etna** (vol.), It.
42/C4 **Etosha Nat'l Park,** Namb.
21/K4 **Euboea** (Évvoia) (isl.), Gre.
54/D3 **Euclid,** Oh,US
50/C4 **Eugene,** Or,US
56/E4 **Eunice,** La,US
27/D6 **Euphrates** (riv.), Asia
52/A2 **Eureka,** Ca,US
17/* **Europe**
53/F3 **Evans** (mt.), Co,US
54/C3 **Evanston,** Il,US
54/C4 **Evansville,** In,US
34/E2 **Everest** (mt.), Asia
50/C3 **Everett,** Wa,US
57/H5 **Everglades Nat'l Pk.,** Fl,US
20/B4 **Évora,** Port.
21/K4 **Évvoia** (isl.), Gre.
18/D4 **Exeter,** Eng,UK
55/G3 **Exeter,** NH,US
18/D4 **Exmoor Nat'l Park,** Eng,UK
45/C3 **Eyre** (lake), Austl.
45/C4 **Eyre** (pen.), Austl.

F

49/C3 **Fairbanks,** Ak,US
54/C4 **Fairfield,** Oh,US
50/D4 **Fairmont,** WV,US
33/K2 **Faisalabad,** Pak.
56/D5 **Falcon** (res.), NAm.
18/C3 **Falkirk,** Sc,UK
64/D7 **Falkland Islands,** UK
55/G3 **Fall River,** Ma,US
18/C4 **Falmouth,** Eng,UK
32/B1 **Famagusta,** Cyp.
42/K11 **Fandriana,** Madg.
47/K4 **Fanning** (Tabuaeran) (isl.), Kiri.
52/B3 **Farallon** (isls.), Ca,US
31/B3 **Farghona,** Uzb.
51/J4 **Fargo,** ND,US
51/K5 **Faribault,** Mn,US
34/C2 **Farīdābād,** India
52/E3 **Farmington,** NM,US
20/B4 **Faro,** Port.
17/D2 **Faroe** (isls.), Den.
53/J3 **Fayetteville,** Ar,US
57/J3 **Fayetteville,** NC,US
18/G3 **Fehmarn** (isl.), Ger.
29/J3 **Fengcheng,** China
51/K4 **Fergus Falls,** Mn,US
21/F2 **Ferrara,** It.
64/C3 **Fertil** (val.), Arg.
40/E1 **Fès,** Mor.
40/H2 **Fezzan** (reg.), Libya
42/K11 **Fianarantsoa,** Madg.
63/L6 **Fiera de Santana,** Braz.
46/G6 **Fiji**
21/K3 **Filippoi** (ruins), Gre.
54/D3 **Findlay,** Oh,US
20/A3 **Finisterre** (cape), Sp.
22/H2 **Finland**
22/H4 **Finland** (gulf), Eur.
21/F3 **Firenze** (Florence), It.
33/K2 **Firozpur,** India
21/G2 **Fiume** (Rijeka), Cro.
52/E4 **Flagstaff,** Az,US
52/E2 **Flaming Gorge** (res.), US
50/B3 **Flattery** (cape), Wa,US
18/G3 **Flensburg,** Ger.
45/D4 **Flinders** (isl.), Austl.
45/C4 **Flinders** (ranges), Austl.
54/D3 **Flint,** Mi,US
57/G3 **Florence,** Al,US
57/J3 **Florence,** SC,US
21/F3 **Florence** (Firenze), It.
37/F5 **Flores** (isl.), Indo.
37/E5 **Flores** (sea), Indo.
64/G2 **Florianópolis,** Braz.
58/E3 **Florida** (str.), Cuba, Fl,US
57/H4 **Florida** (state), US
57/H5 **Florida** (bay), Fl,US
53/K3 **Florissant,** Mo,US
21/G3 **Foggia,** It.
54/B3 **Fond du Lac,** Wi,US
58/D5 **Fonseca** (gulf), NAm.
20/D1 **Fontainebleau,** Fr.
30/C2 **Foochow** (Fuzhou), China
21/G2 **Forli,** It.
63/G6 **Formosa** (mts.), Braz.
63/L4 **Fortaleza,** Braz.
52/F2 **Ft. Collins,** Co,US
59/J5 **Ft.-de-France** (cap.), Mart.
53/J2 **Ft. Dodge,** Ia,US
18/D2 **Forth** (firth), Sc,UK
18/D2 **Forth, Firth of** (inlet), Sc,UK
57/H5 **Ft. Lauderdale,** Fl,US
50/E3 **Ft. Macleod,** Ab,Can
53/K2 **Ft. Madison,** Ia,US
49/F4 **Ft. McMurray,** Can
57/H5 **Ft. Myers,** Fl,US
50/G4 **Ft. Peck Lake** (res.), Mt,US
57/H5 **Ft. Pierce,** Fl,US
49/F4 **Ft. Smith,** NW,Can
53/J4 **Ft. Smith,** Ar,US
57/G4 **Ft. Walton Beach,** Fl,US
54/C3 **Ft. Wayne,** In,US
18/C2 **Fort William,** Sc,UK
56/D3 **Ft. Worth,** Tx,US
30/B3 **Foshan,** China
54/D3 **Fostoria,** Oh,US
40/C5 **Fouta Djallon** (reg.), Gui.
45/G7 **Foveaux** (str.), NZ
49/J3 **Foxe** (basin), Can
62/E7 **Frailes** (mts.), Bol.
63/J8 **França,** Braz.
20/D2 **France**
51/J5 **Francis Case** (lake), SD,US
42/E5 **Francistown,** Bots.
54/C3 **Frankfort,** In,US
54/C4 **Frankfort** (cap.), Ky,US
18/G4 **Frankfurt am Main,** Ger.
19/H3 **Frankfurt an der Oder,** Ger.
50/D3 **Franklin D. Roosevelt** (lake), Wa,US
24/F2 **Franz Josef Land** (isls.), Rus.
50/C3 **Fraser** (riv.), BC,Can
22/D5 **Fredericia,** Den.
54/E4 **Frederick,** Md,US
54/E4 **Fredericksburg,** Va,US
55/H2 **Fredericton** (cap.), NB,Can
22/D4 **Frederikshavn,** Den.
59/F2 **Freeport,** Bah.
54/B3 **Freeport,** Il,US
40/C6 **Freetown** (cap.), SLeo.
18/F5 **Freiburg,** Ger.
50/B3 **Fremont,** Ca,US
53/H2 **Fremont,** Ne,US
63/H3 **French Guiana**
47/M6 **French Polynesia**
52/C3 **Fresno,** Ca,US
20/E2 **Fribourg,** Swi.
45/D4 **Frome** (lake), Austl.
53/F2 **Front** (range), Co,US
57/J2 **Front Royal,** Va,US
29/M4 **Fukui,** Japan
29/L5 **Fukuoka,** Japan
29/N4 **Fukushima,** Japan
33/J2 **Fūlādī** (mtn.), Afg.
53/K3 **Fulton,** Mo,US
46/G5 **Funafuti** (cap.), Tuv.
40/B1 **Funchal,** Port.
55/H2 **Fundy** (bay), NAm.
55/H2 **Fundy Nat'l Park,** NB,Can
63/J8 **Furnas** (res.), Braz.
45/D4 **Furneaux Group** (isls.), Austl.
18/G4 **Fürth,** Ger.

Fushu – Kikwi

29/J3 Fushun, China
29/J3 Fuxin, China
30/C2 Fuzhou, China

G

40/H7 Gabon
42/E5 Gaborone (cap.), Bots.
57/G3 Gadsden, Al,US
21/G3 Gaeta (gulf), It.
57/H3 Gaffney, SC,US
57/H4 Gainesville, Fl,US
57/H3 Gainesville, Ga,US
45/C4 Gairdner (lake), Austl.
14/E6 Galápagos (isls.), Ecu.
21/K2 Galaţi, Rom.
54/B3 Galesburg, Il,US
57/G2 Gallatin, Tn,US
34/D6 Galle, SrL.
64/B7 Gallegos (riv.), Arg.
62/D1 Gallinas (pt.), Col.
23/C5 Gallipoli, Turk.
52/E4 Gallup, NM,US
52/E4 Galveston, Tx,US
18/B3 Galway, Ire.
41/M6 Gambela Nat'l Park, Eth.
40/B5 Gambia
40/B5 Gambia (riv.), Gam., Sen.
47/M7 Gambier (isls.), FrPol.
23/G5 Gäncä, Azer.
55/L1 Gander, Nf,Can
34/B3 Gandhinagar, India
31/D5 Gangdise (mts.), China
27/H7 Ganges (riv.), Asia
34/E3 Ganges, Mouths of the (delta), Bang., India
34/E2 Gangtok, India
30/C2 Ganzhou, China
20/E2 Gap, Fr.
24/F5 Garabogazköl (gulf), Trkm.
41/L7 Garamba Nat'l Park, D.R. Congo
21/F2 Garda (lake), It.
53/G3 Garden City, Ks,US
52/D3 Garland, Tx,US
21/F2 Garmisch-Partenkirchen, Ger.
20/D2 Garonne (riv.), Fr.
54/C3 Gary, In,US
36/C4 Gaspar (str.), Indo.
55/H1 Gaspé (pen.), Qu,Can
57/H3 Gastonia, NC,US
35/F2 Gauhāti, India
45/C4 Gawler (range), Austl.
34/E3 Gaya, India
32/B2 Gaza, Gaza
32/B2 Gaza Strip
23/E6 Gaziantep, Turk.
19/J3 Gdańsk, Pol.
19/J3 Gdańsk (gulf), Pol.
19/J3 Gdynia, Pol.
45/D4 Geelong, Austl.
35/H3 Gejiu, China
42/D6 Gemsbok Nat'l Park, Bots.
64/B6 General Carrera (lake), Chile
20/E2 Geneva, Swi.
54/E3 Geneva, NY,US
20/E2 Geneva (Léman) (lake), Eur.
21/F2 Genoa (Genova), It.
21/F2 Genova (gulf), It.
58/E4 George Town (cap.), Cay.
62/G2 Georgetown (cap.), Guy.
36/B2 George Town (Pinang), Malay.
23/F5 Georgia
50/C3 Georgia (str.), BC,Can
57/G3 Georgia (state), US
54/D2 Georgian (bay), On,Can
18/H4 Gera, Ger.
63/J6 Geral de Goias (mts.), Braz.
18/G4 Germany
54/E4 Gettysburg, Pa,US
40/E6 Ghana
34/C2 Ghaziābād, India
33/J2 Ghazni, Afg.
18/E4 Ghent, Belg.
20/B5 Gibraltar (str.)
20/B4 Gibraltar, UK
45/B3 Gibson (des.), Austl.
29/M4 Gifu, Japan
20/B3 Gijón, Sp.
52/D4 Gila (riv.), US
46/G5 Gilbert Is. (Kiribati)
50/G4 Gillette, Wy,US
20/D3 Girona (Gerona), Sp.
20/C3 Gironde (riv.), Fr.
25/R3 Gizhiga (bay), Rus.
55/K2 Glace Bay, NS,Can
64/B6 Glaciares Nat'l Park, Arg.
50/D2 Glacier Nat'l Pk., BC,Can
50/E3 Glacier Nat'l Pk., Mt,US
18/C3 Glasgow, Sc,UK
52/D4 Glendale, Az,US
52/C4 Glendale, Ca,US
55/F3 Glens Falls, NY,US
18/D4 Gloucester, Eng,UK
34/B4 Goa (dist.), India
63/J7 Goânia, Braz.
28/E3 Gobi (des.), Asia
34/D4 Godavari (riv.), India
64/C3 Godoy Cruz, Arg.
49/M3 Godthåb (Nuuk) (cap.), Grld.
33/L1 Godwin Austen (K2) (mt.), Asia
63/J7 Goiânia, Braz.
45/E3 Gold Coast, Austl.
40/E7 Gold Coast (reg.), Gha.
53/F3 Golden, Co,US
57/J3 Goldsboro, NC,US
59/G4 Gonâve (gulf), Haiti
41/N5 Gonder, Eth.
42/C7 Good Hope (cape), SAfr.
52/B2 Goose (lake), US
49/L4 Goose Bay-Happy Valley, Nf,Can
34/D2 Gorakhpur, India
33/F2 Gorgān, Iran
23/F2 Gor'kiy (res.), Rus.
23/F2 Gor'kiy (Nizhniy Novgorod), Rus.
37/F3 Gorontalo, Indo.
23/C4 Goryn (riv.), Ukr.
19/H4 Gorzow Wielkopolski, Pol.
21/J3 Gostivar, FYROM
22/D4 Göteborg, Swe.
22/F4 Gotland (isl.), Swe.
18/G4 Göttingen, Ger.
19/L4 Goverla, Gora (mt.), Ukr.
63/K7 Governador Baladares, Braz.
28/D3 Govi Altayn (mts.), Mong.
24/G1 Graham Bell (isl.), Rus.
40/D6 Grain Coast (reg.), Libr.
18/C2 Grampian (mts.), Sc,UK
20/C4 Granada, Sp.
64/C6 Gran Altiplanicie Central (plat.), Arg.
64/C6 Gran Bajo Oriental (val.), Arg.
40/B2 Gran Canaria (isl.), Sp.
64/D2 Gran Chaco (reg.), SAm.
59/F2 Grand Bahama (isl.), Bahm.
52/D3 Grand Canyon Nat'l Pk., Az,US
58/E4 Grand Cayman (isl.), Cay.
62/F7 Grande (riv.), Bol.
63/J7 Grande (riv.), Braz.
63/K6 Grande (riv.), Braz.
50/D2 Grande Prairie, Ab,Can
40/H4 Grand 'Erg de Bilma (des.), Niger
40/E1 Grand Erg Occidental (des.), Alg.
40/G1 Grand Erg Oriental (des.), Alg., Tun.
56/C4 Grande, Rio (riv.), NAm.
59/J4 Grande-Terre (isl.), Guad.
51/J4 Grand Forks, ND,US
53/H2 Grand Island, Ne,US
52/E3 Grand Junction, Co,US
55/H2 Grand Manan (isl.), NB,Can
54/C3 Grand Rapids, Mi,US
50/F5 Grand Teton Nat'l Pk., Wy,US
59/G3 Grand Turk (cap.), Trks.
57/F2 Granite City, Il,US
62/F3 Gran Sabana, La (plain), Ven.
52/F4 Grants, NM,US
50/C5 Grants Pass, Or,US
62/C5 Gran Vilaya (ruins), Peru
20/E3 Grasse, Fr.
21/G2 Graz, Aus.
59/F2 Great Abaco (isl.), Bahm.
45/B4 Great Australian (bight), Austl.
45/D2 Great Barrier (reef), Austl.
50/C2 Great Basin (basin), US
52/D3 Great Basin Nat'l Park, Nv,US
49/E3 Great Bear (lake), Can.
53/H3 Great Bend, Ks,US
18/D2 Great Britain (isl.), UK
45/D4 Great Dividing (range), Austl.
59/F3 Greater Antilles (isls.), NAm.
36/C4 Greater Sunda (isls.), Indo.
59/F3 Great Exuma (isl.), Bahm.
50/F4 Great Falls, Mt,US
59/G3 Great Inagua (isl.), Bahm.
34/B2 Great Indian (Thar) (des.), India
42/D7 Great Karoo (reg.), SAfr.
53/G2 Great Plains (plains), US
42/F2 Great Rift (val.), Afr.
41/N6 Great Rift (val.), Djib., Eth.
52/D2 Great Salt (lake), Ut,US
41/K2 Great Sand Sea (des.), Afr.
45/B2 Great Sandy (des.), Austl.
49/F3 Great Slave (lake), NW,Can
57/H3 Great Smoky Mts. Nat'l Pk., NC,Tn,US
45/B3 Great Victoria (des.), Austl.
28/F4 Great Wall, China
21/J4 Greece
53/F2 Greeley, Co,US
52/E3 Green (riv.), US
55/F3 Green (mts.), Vt,US
54/B2 Green Bay, Wi,US
57/H2 Greeneville, Tn,US
55/F3 Greenfield, Ma,US
49/R2 Greenland (sea)
49/N2 Greenland, Den.
18/C3 Greenock, Sc,UK
57/J2 Greensboro, NC,US
54/E3 Greensburg, Pa,US
57/F3 Greenville, Ms,US
57/J3 Greenville, NC,US
57/H3 Greenville, SC,US
57/F3 Greenwood, Ms,US
57/H3 Greenwood, SC,US
45/D2 Gregory (range), Austl.
59/J5 Grenada
20/E2 Grenoble, Fr.
57/F4 Gretna, La,US
45/D3 Grey (range), Austl.
57/G3 Griffin, Ga,US
18/D3 Grimsby, Eng,UK
18/F3 Groningen, Neth.
45/C2 Groote Eylandt (isl.), Austl.
21/G2 Grossglockner (mt.), Aus.
23/G5 Groznyy, Rus.
59/F3 Guacanaybo (gulf), Cuba
58/A3 Guadalajara, Mex.
20/C3 Guadalajara, Sp.
46/E6 Guadalcanal (isl.), Sol.
20/B4 Guadalquivir (riv.), Sp.
58/B2 Guadalupe, Mex.
56/B3 Guadalupe (mts.), US
56/B4 Guadalupe Mts. Nat'l Pk., Tx,US
20/B3 Guadarrama (mts.), Sp.
59/J4 Guadeloupe, Fr.
59/J4 Guadeloupe Passage (chan.), West Indies
20/B4 Guadiana (riv.), Eur.
64/B5 Guafo (str.), Chile
62/E3 Guainiá (riv.), Col.
62/D1 Guajira (pen.), SAm.
64/C5 Gualicho (marsh), Arg.
46/D3 Guam
28/F5 Guangyuan, China
30/B3 Guangzhou (Canton), China
59/F3 Guantánamo, Cuba
62/F6 Guaporé (Itényez) (riv.), Braz.
62/E2 Guárico (res.), Ven.
58/C4 Guatemala
58/C5 Guatemala (cap.), Guat.
62/E3 Guaviare (riv.), Col.
62/B4 Guayaquil, Ecu.
62/B4 Guayaquil (gulf), Ecu.
59/M8 Guaymas, Mex.
19/H3 Guben (Wilhelm-Pieck-Stadt), Ger.
54/D3 Guelph, On,Can
18/D4 Guernsey (isl.), Chl.
62/F2 Guiana Highlands (mts.), SAm.
30/B2 Guilin, China
40/C5 Guinea
40/F7 Guinea (gulf), Afr.
40/B5 Guinea-Bissau
35/J2 Guiyang, China
35/K2 Gujranwala, Pak.
33/K2 Gujrāt, Pak.
34/C4 Gulbarga, India
56/D5 Gulf Coastal (plain), Tx,US
57/F4 Gulfport, Ms,US
23/F6 Güneydogu Toroslar (mts.), Turk.
34/D4 Guntur, India
64/F2 Gural (mts.), Braz.
62/F2 Guri (res.), Ven.
63/H4 Gurupá, Grande de (isl.), Braz.
63/J4 Gurupi (mts.), Braz.
63/J4 Gurupi (riv.), Braz.
23/H4 Gur'yev, Kaz.
53/H4 Guthrie, Ok,US
62/G3 Guyana
32/C4 Gwalior, India
42/E4 Gweru, Zim.
24/H2 Gyda (pen.), Rus.
21/H2 Győr, Hun.
23/F5 Gyumri, Arm.

H

18/F3 Haarlem, Neth.
32/E5 Hadhramaut (reg.), Yem.
29/K4 Haeju, NKor.
46/D3 Hagåtña (cap.), Guam
54/E4 Hagerstown, Md,US
18/F3 Hague, The (cap.), Neth.
29/J3 Haicheng, China
32/B2 Haifa, Isr.
30/B3 Haikou, China
30/B4 Hainan (isl.), China
29/J5 Haining, China
35/J3 Haiphong, Viet.
59/G4 Haiti
29/N3 Hakodate, Japan
32/C1 Halab (Aleppo), Syria
45/D2 Halifax (bay), Austl.
55/J2 Halifax (cap.), NS,Can
18/G4 Halle, Ger.
37/G3 Halmahera (isl.), Indo.
37/G4 Halmahera (sea), Indo.
22/E4 Hälsingborg, Swe.
32/E2 Hamadan, Iran
32/C1 Hamāh, Syria
29/M5 Hamamatsu, Japan
18/G3 Hamburg, Ger.
45/A3 Hamersley (range), Austl.
29/K3 Hamgyong (mts.), NKor.
29/K3 Hamhung, NKor.
54/E3 Hamilton, On,Can
45/H6 Hamilton, NZ
54/C4 Hamilton, Oh,US
18/F3 Hamm, Ger.
22/G1 Hammerfest, Nor.
54/C3 Hammond, In,US
57/F4 Hammond, La,US
54/E4 Hampton, Va,US
40/H3 Hamrā, Al Hamādah al (upland), Libya
29/K4 Han (riv.), SKor.
28/G4 Handan, China
52/C3 Hanford, Ca,US
28/D2 Hangayn (mts.), Mong.
30/D1 Hangzhou (Hangchow), China
53/K3 Hannibal, Mo,US
18/G3 Hannover, Ger.
35/J3 Hanoi (cap.), Viet.
55/F3 Hanover, NH,US
28/F5 Hanzhong, China
42/F4 Harare (cap.), Zim.
29/K2 Harbin, China
41/P6 Hargeysa, Som.
56/D5 Harlingen, Tx,US
54/E3 Harrisburg (cap.), Pa,US
54/E4 Harrisonburg, Va,US
54/C4 Harrodsburg, Ky,US
55/F3 Hartford (cap.), Ct,US
18/D3 Hartlepool, Eng,UK
18/G4 Harz (mts.), Ger.
53/H2 Hastings, Ne,US
57/F4 Hattiesburg, Ms,US
41/Q6 Haud (reg.), Eth.
58/E3 Havana (cap.), Cuba
52/D4 Havasu (lake), US
55/G3 Haverhill, Ma,US
50/F3 Havre, Mt,US
47/K2 Hawaii (state), US
47/K3 Hawaii (isl.), Hi,US
47/H2 Hawaiian (isls.), US
32/E3 Hawalli, Kuw.
49/F3 Hay River, NW,Can
53/H3 Hays, Ks,US
50/A2 Hazelton (mts.), BC,Can
54/F3 Hazleton, Pa,US
28/G4 Hebi, China
18/C2 Hebrides, Inner (isls.), Sc,UK
18/B2 Hebrides, Outer (isls.), Sc,UK
29/H5 Hefei, China
29/L2 Hegang, China
18/G4 Heidelberg, Ger.
18/G4 Heilbronn, Ger.
29/J1 Heilong (riv.), China
22/N7 Hekla (mt.), Ice.
28/F4 Helan (mts.), China
50/F4 Helena (cap.), Mt,US
33/H2 Helmand (riv.), Afg.
22/H3 Helsinki (cap.), Fin.
57/G2 Henderson, Ky,US
57/J2 Henderson, NC,US
52/D3 Henderson, Nv,US
35/G2 Hengduan (mts.), China
30/B2 Hengyang, China
33/H2 Herat, Afg.
59/M8 Hermosillo, Mex.
57/H5 Hialeah, Fl,US
51/K4 Hibbing, Mn,US
57/H3 Hickory, NC,US
57/H3 High Point, NC,US
19/K2 Hiiumaa (isl.), Est.
32/C3 Hijāz, Jabal al (mts.), SAr.
50/C4 Hillsboro, Or,US
47/K3 Hilo, Hi,US
27/G6 Himalaya (mts.), Asia
32/C2 Ḩimş, Syria
33/J1 Hindu Kush (mts.), Asia
29/N3 Hirosaki, Japan
29/L5 Hiroshima, Japan
59/G4 Hispaniola (isl.), NAm.
29/N4 Hitachi, Japan
45/D5 Hobart, Austl.
53/G4 Hobbs, NM,US
35/J5 Ho Chi Minh City (Saigon), Viet.
21/F2 Hohe Tauern (range), Aus.
28/G3 Hohhot, China
29/N3 Hokkaidō (isl.), Japan
59/F3 Holguín, Cuba
54/C3 Holland, Mi,US
57/H5 Hollywood, Fl,US
18/C3 Holyhead, Wal,UK
55/F3 Holyoke, Ma,US
57/H5 Homestead, Fl,US
19/M3 Homyel', Bela.
58/D4 Honduras
58/D4 Honduras (gulf), NAm.
30/B3 Hong Kong, China
46/E5 Honiara (cap.), Sol.
47/K2 Honolulu (cap.), Hi,US
29/M5 Honshu (isl.), Japan
50/C4 Hood (mt.), Or,US
52/D3 Hoover (dam), US
56/E3 Hope, Ar,US
54/E4 Hopewell, Va,US
54/B4 Hopkinsville, Ky,US
23/E4 Horlivka, Ukr.
33/G3 Hormuz (str.), Asia
64/C8 Horn (cape), Chile
54/E3 Hornell, NY,US
21/J2 Hortobágyi Nat'l Park, Hun.
56/E3 Hot Springs Nat'l Park, Ar,US
57/F4 Houma, La,US
56/E4 Houston, Tx,US
28/E1 Hövsgöl (lake), Mong.
47/H4 Howland (isl.), PacUS
34/E3 Howrah, India
19/H4 Hradec Králové, Czh.
19/K3 Hrodna, Bela.
30/D3 Hsinchu, Tai.
28/H5 Huaibei, China
30/B2 Huaihua, China
29/H5 Huainan, China
42/C3 Huambo, Ang.
62/C6 Huancayo, Peru
62/E8 Huanchaca (peak), Bol.
29/H4 Huang He (Yellow) (riv.), China
30/C2 Huangshi, China
62/C5 Huascarán (mt.), Peru
62/C5 Huascarán Nat'l Park, Peru
62/E6 Huatunas (lake), Bol.
28/F5 Huaying, China
34/C4 Hubli-Dharwar, India
18/D3 Huddersfield, Eng,UK
49/J3 Hudson (bay), Can.
49/K3 Hudson (str.), Can.
54/F3 Hudson (riv.), US
35/J4 Hue, Viet.
20/B4 Huelva, Sp.
42/B4 Huila (plat.), Ang.
62/C3 Huila (peak), Col.
54/F2 Hull, Qu,Can
18/D3 Hull, Eng,UK
28/H2 Hulun (lake), China
52/E4 Humphreys (peak), Az,US
21/H2 Hungary
29/K4 Hŭngnam, NKor.
29/K3 Hunjiang, China
57/G3 Huntington, In,US
54/D4 Huntington, WV,US
52/C4 Huntington Beach, Ca,US
57/G3 Huntsville, Al,US
56/E4 Huntsville, Tx,US
54/D2 Huron (lake), NAm.
51/J4 Huron, SD,US
53/H3 Hutchinson, Ks,US
29/J5 Huzhou, China
42/E4 Hwange Nat'l Park, Zim.
34/C4 Hyderabad, India
33/J3 Hyderabad, Pak.
20/E3 Hyères (isls.), Fr.

I

21/K2 Iaşi, Rom.
40/F6 Ibadan, Nga.
62/C3 Ibagué, Col.
64/E2 Iberá (marsh), Arg.
20/C3 Iberica, Sistema (range), Sp.
20/D4 Ibiza (isl.), Sp.
62/E4 Iça (riv.), Braz.
22/N7 Iceland
28/G5 Ichang (Yichang), China
50/E5 Idaho (state), US
50/E5 Idaho Falls, Id,US
40/F6 Ife, Nga.
40/F3 Iforas, Ardar des (mts.), Alg., Mali
64/F2 Iguaçu (riv.), Braz.
64/F2 Iguazú (falls), SAm.
64/F2 Iguazu Nat'l Park, Arg.
40/D2 Iguidi, Èrg (des.), Alg.
21/K4 Ikaria (isl.), Gre.
47/X15 Iles du Vent (isls.), FrPol.
40/F6 Ilesha, Nga.
63/H7 Ilha Salteira (res.), Braz.
62/E7 Illimani (mtn.), Bol.
54/B4 Illinois (state), US
54/B3 Illinois (riv.), Il,US
23/D2 Il'men (lake), Rus.
30/D5 Iloilo, Phil.
40/F6 Ilorin, Nga.
63/J5 Imperatriz, Braz.
35/F3 Imphal, India
29/K4 Inch'ŏn, SKor.
53/J3 Independence, Ks,US
53/J3 Independence, Mo,US
27/G7 India
54/C3 Indiana (state), US
54/E3 Indiana, Pa,US
54/C4 Indianapolis (cap.), In,US
15/N6 Indian Ocean
25/Q3 Indigirka (riv.), Rus.
52/C4 Indio, Ca,US
35/C1 Indochina (reg.), Asia
36/E4 Indonesia
34/C3 Indore, India
27/F7 Indus (riv.), Asia
62/C4 Ingapirca (ruins), Ecu.
18/G4 Ingolstadt, Ger.
21/G1 Inn (riv.), Eur.
18/C2 Inner Hebrides (isls.), Sc,UK
28/G3 Inner Mongolia (reg.), China
21/F2 Innsbruck, Aus.
35/G4 Insein, Myanmar
50/B2 Interior (plat.), BC,Can
51/H3 International Peace Garden, NAm.
49/D3 Inuvik, Can.
45/G6 Invercargill, NZ
18/C2 Inverness, Sc,UK
42/B4 Iona Nat'l Park, Ang.
21/H4 Ionian (sea), Eur.
21/H4 Ionian (isls.), Gre.
53/J2 Iowa (state), US
53/K2 Iowa City, Ia,US
63/K7 Ipatinga, Braz.
36/B3 Ipoh, Malay.
18/E3 Ipswich, Eng,UK
49/L3 Iqaluit, Can.
62/D8 Iquique, Chile
62/D4 Iquitos, Peru
21/K5 Iráklion, Gre.
27/E6 Iran
58/A3 Irapuato, Mex.
32/D2 Iraq
32/D1 Irbil, Iraq
18/B3 Ireland
18/C3 Ireland, Northern, UK
37/J4 Irian Jaya (reg.), Indo.
63/H4 Iriri (riv.), Braz.
18/C3 Irish (sea), Eur.
28/E1 Irkutsk, Rus.
21/J2 Iron Gate (gorge), Rom.
54/D4 Ironton, Oh,US
35/F4 Irrawaddy, Mouths of the (delta), Myanmar
24/G4 Irtysh (riv.), Rus.
52/C4 Irvine, Ca,US
53/H4 Irving, Tx,US
42/J11 Isala Massif (mts.), Madg.
18/G4 Isar (riv.), Ger.
20/E2 Isère (riv.), Fr.
40/F6 Iseyin, Nga.
62/E7 Isiboro Securé Nat'l Park, Bol.
23/E6 Iskenderun, Turk.
21/J3 Iskūr (riv.), Bul.
33/K2 Islamabad (cap.), Pak.
64/B5 Isla Magdalena Nat'l Park, Chile
18/C3 Isle of Man, UK
54/B1 Isle Royale (isl.), Mi,US
54/B2 Isle Royale Nat'l Pk., Mi,US
32/B2 Ismailia, Egypt
31/B4 Ismail Samani (peak), Taj.
23/D6 Isparta, Turk.
32/B2 Israel
23/C5 Istanbul, Turk.
21/G2 Istria (pen.), Cro.
63/L6 Itabuna, Braz.
64/E1 Itaipu (res.), Braz., Par.
21/F3 Italy
63/K7 Itambé (peak), Braz.
63/L6 Itapicuru (riv.), Braz.
62/F6 Iténez (Guaporé) (riv.), Bol.
54/E3 Ithaca, NY,US
23/B4 Ivano-Frankivs'k, Ukr.
23/F2 Ivanovo, Rus.
40/D7 Ivory Coast (reg.), C.d'Iv.
29/N4 Iwaki, Japan
46/D2 Iwo Jima (isl.), Japan
23/H2 Izhevsk, Rus.
33/G4 Izkī, Oman
23/C6 Izmir, Turk.
23/C5 Izmit, Turk.

J

34/C3 Jabalpur, India
54/C3 Jackson, Mi,US
57/F3 Jackson (cap.), Ms,US
57/F3 Jackson, Tn,US
56/E3 Jacksonville, Ar,US
57/H4 Jacksonville, Fl,US
54/B4 Jacksonville, Il,US
57/J3 Jacksonville, NC,US
20/C4 Jaén, Sp.
34/C6 Jaffna, SrL.
34/C2 Jaipur, India
36/C5 Jakarta (cap.), Indo.
33/K2 Jalālābād, Afg.
58/B4 Jalapa, Mex.
34/C3 Jalgaon, India
59/F4 Jamaica
59/F4 Jamaica (chan.), Haiti, Jam.
63/G5 Jamanxim (riv.), Braz.
36/B4 Jambi, Indo.
49/J4 James (bay), Can.
54/E4 James (riv.), Va,US
51/J4 Jamestown, ND,US
54/E3 Jamestown, NY,US
33/K2 Jammu, India
34/B3 Jamnagar, India
34/E3 Jamshedpur, India
63/J3 Janaucu (isl.), Braz.
54/B3 Janesville, Wi,US
17/D1 Jan Mayen (isl.), Nor.
29/M4 Japan
29/L3 Japan (sea), Asia
29/M4 Japanese Alps (mts.), Japan
62/E4 Japurá (riv.), Braz.
63/H3 Jari (riv.), Braz.
47/J5 Jarvis (isl.), Pacific
63/H4 Jauaru (mts.), Braz.
62/F3 Jaua Sarisarinama Nat'l Park, Ven.
36/C5 Java (isl.), Indo.
36/D5 Java (sea), Indo.
37/K4 Jayapura, Indo.
53/J3 Jefferson City (cap.), Mo,US
54/C4 Jeffersonville, In,US
36/D5 Jember, Indo.
18/G4 Jena, Ger.
63/K7 Jequitinhonha (riv.), Braz.
20/B4 Jerez de la Frontera, Sp.
18/D4 Jersey (isl.), Chl.
32/D2 Jerusalem (cap.), Isr.
55/N6 Jésus (isl.), Qu,Can
21/H3 Jezerce (mt.), Alb.
33/K2 Jhang Sadar, Pak.
34/C2 Jhansi, India
33/K2 Jhelum, Pak.
29/L2 Jiamusi, China
30/D2 Jiaojiang, China
28/G4 Jiaozuo, China
29/J5 Jiaxing, China
32/C4 Jiddah, SAr.
29/K3 Jilin, China
29/H4 Jinan (Tsinan), China
30/C2 Jingdezhen, China
28/G5 Jingmen, China
30/C2 Jinhua, China
28/G3 Jining, China
29/J3 Jinzhou, China
30/C2 Jiujiang, China
29/L2 Jixi, China
32/D5 Jīzān, SAr.
63/M5 João Pessoa, Braz.
34/B2 Jodhpur, India
42/E6 Johannesburg, SAfr.
50/C4 John Day (riv.), Or,US
57/H2 Johnson City, Tn,US
47/J3 Johnston (atoll), PacUS
54/E3 Johnstown, Pa,US
36/B3 Johor Baharu, Malay.
64/G2 Joinvile, Braz.
54/B3 Joliet, Il,US
57/F3 Jonesboro, Ar,US
22/E4 Jönköping, Swe.
55/G1 Jonquière, Qu,Can
53/J3 Joplin, Mo,US
32/C2 Jordan
32/C2 Jordan (riv.), Asia
40/G6 Jos (plat.), Nga.
45/B2 Joseph Bonaparte (gulf), Austl.
50/B3 Juan de Fuca (str.), NAm.
61/A6 Juan Fernández (isls.), Chile
63/L5 Juazeiro do Norte, Braz.
20/C4 Júcar (riv.), Sp.
63/K8 Juiz de Fora, Braz.
63/G3 Juliana Top (peak), Sur.
33/L2 Jullundur, India
53/H3 Junction City, Ks,US
63/J8 Jundiaí, Braz.
49/D4 Juneau (cap.), Ak,US
20/F2 Jungfrau (mt.), Swi.
20/E2 Jura (mts.), Eur.
62/E4 Juruá (riv.), Braz.
58/E3 Juventud (isl.), Cuba

K

33/L1 K2 (mt.), Asia
41/M7 Kabalega Nat'l Park, Ugan.
33/J2 Kabul (cap.), Afg.
42/E3 Kabwe, Zam.
40/G5 Kaduna, Nga.
29/K4 Kaesŏng, NKor.
42/E4 Kafue (riv.), Zam.
42/E3 Kafue Nat'l Park, Zam.
29/L5 Kagoshima, Japan
23/E6 Kahramanmaras, Turk.
37/H5 Kai (isls.), Indo.
28/G5 Kaifeng, China
18/G4 Kaiserslautern, Ger.
35/H3 Kaiyuan, China
34/D4 Kakinada, India
49/N2 Kalaallit Nunaat (Greenland), Den.
42/D5 Kalahari (des.), Afr.
42/C6 Kalahari-Gemsbok Nat'l Park, Bots.
54/C3 Kalamazoo, Mi,US
41/K2 Kalanshiyū, Sahīr (des.), Libya
28/G3 Kalgan (Zhangjiakou), China
36/D4 Kalimantan (reg.), Indo.
19/K3 Kaliningrad (Königsberg), Rus.
19/J4 Kalisz, Pol.
23/E3 Kaluga, Rus.
25/R4 Kalyma (riv.), Rus.
17/K3 Kama (riv.), Rus.
25/R4 Kamchatka (pen.), Rus.
24/G4 Kamensk-Ural'skiy, Rus.
50/C3 Kamloops, BC,Can
41/M7 Kampala (cap.), Ugan.
23/C4 Kam'yanets'-Podil's'kyy, Ukr.
23/G3 Kamyshin, Rus.
42/D2 Kananga, D.R. Congo
29/M4 Kanazawa, Japan
34/E2 Kanchenjunga (mt.), Asia
34/D6 Kandy, SrL.
45/C4 Kangaroo (isl.), Austl.
35/F2 Kangto (peak), China, India
24/E3 Kanin (pen.), Rus.
54/C3 Kankakee, Il,US
57/H3 Kannapolis, NC,US
41/G5 Kano, Nga.
34/D2 Kānpur, India
52/D2 Kansas (state), US
53/H3 Kansas (riv.), Ks,US
53/J3 Kansas City, Ks,US
53/J3 Kansas City, Mo,US
24/K4 Kansk, Rus.
62/G3 Kanuku (mts.), Guy.
30/D3 Kaohsiung, Tai.
42/B4 Kaokoveld, Namb.
42/B4 Kaokoveld (mts.), Namb.
41/B5 Kaolack, Sen.
36/C4 Kapuas (riv.), Indo.
24/G2 Kara (sea), Rus.
23/D5 Karabük, Turk.
33/J4 Karachi, Pak.
25/S4 Karaginskiy (isl.), Rus.
32/F1 Karaj, Iran
33/K1 Karakoram (mts.), Asia
28/E2 Karakorum (ruins), Mong.
24/F5 Karakumy (des.), Trkm.
25/S4 Karanginskiy (bay), Rus.
42/E4 Kariba (lake), Afr.
36/C4 Karimata (str.), Indo.
41/L8 Karisimbi (vol.), D.R. Congo
41/Q6 Karkaar (mts.), Som.
23/D4 Karkinits'ka Zatoka (gulf), Ukr.
19/H4 Karlovy Vary, Czh.
18/G4 Karlsruhe, Ger.
23/C6 Kárpathos (isl.), Gre.
23/F5 Kars, Turk.
42/C1 Kasai (riv.), D.R. Congo
32/F2 Kashan, Iran
30/C4 Kashi (Kashgar), China
41/N4 Kassala, Sudan
18/G4 Kassel, Ger.
32/E3 Kasūr, Pak.
55/G2 Katahdin (mt.), Me,US
42/D2 Katanga (reg.), D.R. Congo
34/E2 Kathmandu (cap.), Nepal
19/J4 Katowice, Pol.
40/G5 Katsina, Nga.
22/D4 Kattegat (str.), Eur.
47/K2 Kauai (isl.), Hi,US
42/C5 Kaukaveld, Namb.
19/K3 Kaunas, Lith.
29/M4 Kawasaki, Japan
23/E6 Kayseri, Turk.
24/G5 Kazakhstan
23/G2 Kazan', Rus.
53/H2 Kearney, Ne,US
21/J5 Kecskemét, Hun.
36/D5 Kediri, Indo.
30/D2 Keelung, Tai.
55/F3 Keene, NH,US
36/B3 Kelang, Malay.
50/D3 Kelowna, BC,Can
50/C3 Kelso, Wa,US
24/J4 Kemerovo, Rus.
57/H5 Kendall, Fl,US
40/D1 Kenitra, Mor.
57/F4 Kenner, La,US
50/D4 Kennewick, Wa,US
54/C3 Kenosha, Wi,US
54/D3 Kent, Oh,US
54/B4 Kentucky (lake), US
54/C4 Kentucky (state), US
39/F4 Kenya
41/M8 Kenya (Batian) (mt.), Kenya
53/K2 Keokuk, Ia,US
23/E4 Kerch, Ukr.
21/H4 Kérkira (Corfu) (isl.), Gre.
46/G7 Kermadec (isls.), NZ
33/G2 Kerman, Iran
52/D4 Kerrville, Tx,US
24/J4 Ket' (riv.), Rus.
24/K2 Keta (riv.), Rus.
49/D4 Ketchikan, Ak,US
54/C4 Kettering, Oh,US
54/B2 Keweenaw (pen.), Mi,US
54/C2 Keweenaw (pt.), Mi,US
57/H5 Key West, Fl,US
29/M2 Khabarovsk, Rus.
21/J3 Khalkhidhikhi (pen.), Gre.
21/J4 Khalkís, Gre.
32/D5 Khamīs Mushayţ, SAr.
29/L3 Khanka (lake), China, Rus.
24/G3 Khanty-Mansiysk, Rus.
34/E3 Kharagpur, India
23/E3 Kharkiv, Ukr.
41/M4 Khartoum (cap.), Sudan
41/M4 Khartoum North, Sudan
25/L2 Khatanga (gulf), Rus.
25/L2 Khatanga (riv.), Rus.
23/D4 Kherson, Ukr.
21/K4 Khíos (isl.), Gre.
23/C4 Khmel'nytskyy, Ukr.
23/F3 Khopër (riv.), Rus.
32/E2 Khorramabad, Iran
32/E2 Khorramshahr, Iran
35/H4 Kho Sawai (plat.), Thai.
34/E3 Khulna, Bang.
33/J3 Khuzdār, Pak.
23/G6 Khvoy, Iran
33/K2 Khyber (pass), Asia
40/F5 Kianji (lake), Nga.
18/G3 Kiel, Ger.
19/K4 Kielce, Pol.
23/D3 Kiev (cap.), Ukr.
42/F1 Kigali (cap.), Rwa.
42/C2 Kikwit, D.R. Congo

69

Kilgo – Munto

56/E3 Kilgore, Tx,US
42/G1 Kilimanjaro (mt.), Tanz.
18/C3 Kilkenny, Ire.
18/B3 Killarney, Ire.
56/D4 Killeen, Tx,US
45/B2 Kimberley (plat.), Austl.
42/D6 Kimberley, SAfr.
29/K3 Kimch'aek, NKor.
23/F2 Kineshma, Rus.
45/D4 King (isl.), Austl.
45/B2 King (sound), Austl.
45/B2 King Leopold (ranges), Austl.
52/D4 Kingman, Az,US
52/C3 Kings Canyon Nat'l Pk., Ca,US
57/H2 Kingsport, Tn,US
59/F4 Kingston (cap.), Jam.
54/F3 Kingston, NY,US
59/J5 Kingstown (cap.), StV.
56/D5 Kingsville, Tx,US
42/C1 Kinshasa (cap.), D.R. Congo
57/J3 Kinston, NC,US
18/C3 Kintyre (pen.), Sc,UK
46/H5 Kiribati
23/D6 Kırıkkale, Turk.
47/K4 Kiritimati (isl.), Kiri.
53/J2 Kirksville, Mo,US
32/D1 Kirkuk, Iraq
23/D4 Kirovohrad, Ukr.
41/L7 Kisangani, D.R. Congo
41/M8 Kisumu, Kenya
29/L5 Kitakyushu, Japan
54/D3 Kitchener, On,Can
21/J4 Kithira (isl.), Gre.
42/E3 Kitwe, Zam.
42/E1 Kivu (lake), Afr.
23/D5 Kizilirmak (riv.), Turk.
22/E2 Kjølen (Kölen) (mts.), Eur.
21/G2 Klagenfurt, Aus.
19/K3 Klaipeda, Lith.
52/B2 Klamath (mts.), Ca,Or,US
50/C5 Klamath Falls, Or,US
25/S4 Klyuchevskaya Sopka (mtn.), Rus.
57/H3 Knoxville, Tn,US
29/L5 Kobe, Japan
18/F4 Koblenz, Ger.
37/H5 Kobroor (isl.), Indo.
29/L5 Kochi, Japan
49/B4 Kodiak (isl.), Ak,US
19/L2 Kohtla-Järva, Est.
54/C3 Kokomo, In,US
24/G4 Kökshetaū, Kaz.
24/D3 Kola (pen.), Rus.
34/B4 Kolhāpur, India
34/E3 Kolkata (Calcutta), India
18/F4 Köln (Cologne), Ger.
23/E2 Kolomna, Rus.
23/D2 Kolpino, Rus.
42/E3 Kolwezi, D.R. Congo
25/R2 Kolyma (lowland), Rus.
25/R3 Kolyma (range), Rus.
25/S4 Komandorskiye (isls.), Rus.
19/J5 Komárno, Slvk.
37/E5 Komodo (isl.), Indo.
40/E6 Komoé (riv.), C.d'Iv.
25/L1 Komsomolets (isl.), Rus.
25/M1 Komsomol'sk-na-Amure, Rus.
33/J1 Kondūz, Afg.
18/G5 Konstanz, Viet.
35/J5 Kon Tum, Viet.
23/D6 Konya, Turk.
50/D3 Kootenai (riv.), US
21/G2 Koper, Slov.
24/G4 Kopeysk, Rus.
21/H3 Korčula (isl.), Cro.
29/J4 Korea (bay), China, NKor.
29/K5 Korea (str.), Japan, SKor.
29/K3 Korea, North
29/K4 Korea, South
29/N4 Koriyama, Japan
31/E3 Korla, China
46/C4 Koror (cap.), Palau
25/T5 Koryak (range), Rus.
23/C6 Kos (isl.), Gre.
45/D4 Kosciusko (mt.), Austl.
19/K4 Košice, Slvk.
21/J3 Kosovo (reg.), Yugo.
41/D6 Kossou (lake), C.d'Iv.
23/F2 Kostroma, Rus.
19/J3 Koszalin, Pol.
34/C2 Kota, India
36/B2 Kota Baharu, Malay.
37/E2 Kota Kinabalu, Malay.
25/P2 Kotel'nyy (isl.), Rus.
34/C6 Kotte, SrL.
49/A3 Kotzebue, Ak,US
63/H2 Kourou, FrG.
23/F2 Kovrov, Rus.
30/B3 Kowloon, China
34/C5 Kozhikode (Calicut), India
35/G6 Kra (isth.), Thai.
36/C5 Krakatau (isl.), Indon.
19/J4 Kraków, Pol.
23/E4 Kramators'k, Ukr.
23/E4 Krasnodar, Rus.
24/K4 Krasnoyarsk, Rus.
35/H5 Kravanh (mts.), Camb.
23/D4 Kremenchuk, Ukr.
23/D4 Kremenchuts'ke (res.), Ukr.
25/T3 Kresta (gulf), Rus.
22/C4 Kristiansand, Nor.
21/G2 Krk (isl.), Cro.
42/F5 Kruger Nat'l Park, SAfr.
35/H5 Krung Thep (Bangkok), Thai.
23/D4 Kryvyy Rih, Ukr.
36/B3 Kuala Lumpur (cap.), Malay.
36/B2 Kuala Terengganu, Malay.
36/B3 Kuantan, Malay.
23/E4 Kuban (riv.), Rus.
36/D3 Kuching, Malay.
41/K3 Kufrah (oasis), Libya
23/G5 Kuma (riv.), Rus.
29/L5 Kumamoto, Japan
21/J3 Kumanovo, FYROM
40/E6 Kumasi, Gha.
35/G2 Kumon (range), Myanmar
42/E3 Kundelungu Nat'l Park, D.R. Congo
36/C5 Kuningan, Indo.
31/C4 Kunlun (mts.), Asia
35/H3 Kunming, China
29/K4 Kunsan, SKor.
37/F6 Kupang, Indo.
23/G6 Kura (riv.), Asia
32/D1 Kurdistan (reg.), Asia
21/K3 Kurdzhali, Bul.
24/K3 Kureyka (riv.), Rus.
24/G4 Kurgan, Rus.
25/Q5 Kuril (isls.), Rus.
34/C4 Kurnool, India
23/E3 Kursk, Rus.
28/B3 Kuruktag (mts.), China
29/L5 Kurume, Japan
29/N3 Kushiro, Japan
23/F5 K'ut'aisi, Geo.
34/A3 Kutch (gulf), India
34/A3 Kutch (reg.), India
34/A3 Kutch, Rann of (salt marsh), India
32/E3 Kuwait
32/E3 Kuwait (cap.), Kuw.
23/G2 Kuybyshev (res.), Rus.
23/H3 Kuybyshev (Samara), Rus.
46/F4 Kwajalein (atoll), Mrsh.
29/K4 Kwangju, SKor.
42/C1 Kwango (riv.), Ang., D.R. Congo
42/N7 Kyoga (lake), Ugan.
29/K4 Kyŏngju, SKor.
29/M4 Kyoto, Japan
31/B3 Kyrgyzstan
29/L5 Kyushu (isl.), Japan
28/C1 Kyzyl, Rus.

L

58/E6 La Amistad Int'l Park, CR
40/C2 Laayoune, WSah.
49/M4 Labrador (sea), Can.
49/L3 Labrador (reg.), Nf,Can
34/B5 Laccadive (sea), India
34/B5 Laccadive (Cannanore) (isls.), India
58/D4 La Ceiba, Hon.
45/C4 Lacepede (bay), Austl.
55/G3 Laconia, NH,US
20/A3 La Coruña, Sp.
54/B3 La Crosse, Wi,US
33/L2 Ladakh (mts.), Asia
24/D3 Ladoga (lake), Rus.
46/D5 Lae, PNG
54/C3 Lafayette, In,US
56/E4 Lafayette, La,US
64/F2 Lages, Braz.
40/F6 Lagos, Nga.
50/D4 La Grande, Or,US
57/G3 La Grange, Ga,US
33/K2 Lahore, Pak.
56/E4 Lake Charles, La,US
52/D4 Lake Havasu City, Az,US
57/H4 Lakeland, Fl,US
50/D3 Lake Louise, Ab,Can
50/F3 Lakewood, Ca,US
57/H5 Lake Worth, Fl,US
34/B5 Lakshadweep (isls.), India
20/C4 La Mancha (reg.), Sp.
40/H8 Lambaréné, Gabon
21/J4 Lamía, Gre.
47/K2 Lanai (isl.), Hi,US
18/D3 Lancaster, Eng,UK
52/C4 Lancaster, Ca,US
54/D4 Lancaster, Oh,US
54/E3 Lancaster, Pa,US
18/C4 Land's End (prom.), Eng,UK
28/H4 Langfang, China
20/E2 Langres (plat.), Fr.
54/C3 Lansing (cap.), Mi,US
30/C2 Lanxi, China
29/E4 Lanzhou (Lanchow), China
35/C2 Laos
62/E7 La Paz (cap.), Bol.
59/M9 La Paz, Mex.
29/N2 La Pérouse (str.), Asia
22/F1 Lapland (reg.), Eur.
54/C3 La Porte, In,US
25/M2 Laptev (sea), Rus.
50/G5 Laramie (mts.), US
50/G5 Laramie, Wy,US
56/D5 Laredo, Tx,US
57/H5 Largo, Fl,US
21/J4 Lárisa, Gre.
33/J3 Lārkāna, Pak.
20/C2 La Rochelle, Fr.
59/H4 La Romana, DRep.
52/F4 Las Cruces, NM,US
40/B2 Las Palmas de Gran Canaria, Sp.
21/F2 La Spezia, It.
52/B2 Lassen Volcanic Nat'l Pk., Ca,US
53/F4 Las Vegas, NM,US
52/C3 Las Vegas, Nv,US
32/C1 Latakia, Syria
21/G3 Latina, It.
19/L2 Latvia
62/E7 Lauca Nat'l Park, Chile
45/D5 Launceston, Austl.
57/F4 Laurel, Ms,US
54/C1 Laurentian (plat.), Can.
21/E2 Lausanne, Swi.
37/E4 Laut (isl.), Indo.
55/F2 Laval, Qu,Can
53/J3 Lawrence, Ks,US
55/G3 Lawrence, Ma,US
53/H4 Lawton, Ok,US
53/J3 Leavenworth, Ks,US
32/C2 Lebanon
54/E3 Lebanon, Pa,US
21/H4 Lecce, It.
18/D3 Leeds, Eng,UK
18/F3 Leeuwarden, Neth.
59/J4 Leeward (isls.), NAm.
19/J4 Legnica, Pol.
20/D2 Le Havre, Fr.
18/D3 Leicester, Eng,UK
18/F3 Leiden, Neth.
18/C3 Leinster (reg.), Ire.
19/H4 Leipzig, Ger.
30/A3 Leizhou (pen.), China
20/D1 Le Mans, Fr.
25/N3 Lena (riv.), Rus.
63/K4 Lençóis Maranhenses Nat'l Park, Braz.
30/B2 Lengshuijiang, China
30/B2 Lengshuitan, China
31/B4 Lenina (peak), Kyr., Taj.
24/J4 Leninsk-Kuznetskiy, Rus.
20/D1 Lens, Fr.
58/A3 León, Mex.
58/D5 León, Nic.
20/B3 León, Sp.
20/F2 Lepontine Alps (mts.), It., Swi.
20/D3 Lérida (Lleida), Sp.
35/H2 Leshan, China
21/J3 Leskovac, Yugo.
42/E6 Lesotho
59/H4 Lesser Antilles (isls.), NAm.
50/E2 Lesser Slave (lake), Ab,Can
21/K4 Lésvos (isl.), Gre.
37/G5 Leti (isls.), Indo.
18/C2 Lewis (isl.), Sc,UK
50/E3 Lewis (range), Mt,US
18/C2 Lewis, Butt of (prom.), Sc,UK
50/D4 Lewiston, Id,US
55/G2 Lewiston, Me,US
54/C4 Lexington, Ky,US
57/H3 Lexington, NC,US
30/D5 Leyte (isl.), Phil.
31/F6 Lhasa, China
20/D3 L'Hospitalet, Sp.
29/H5 Lianyungang, China
28/H4 Liaocheng, China
29/J3 Liaodong (gulf), China
29/K3 Liaoyuan, China
53/G3 Liberal, Ks,US
19/H4 Liberec, Czh.
40/D6 Liberia
40/G7 Libreville (cap.), Gabon
41/J2 Libya
41/K2 Libyan (des.), Afr.
41/K1 Libyan (plat.), Afr.
29/F5 Lichuan, China
20/D4 Lido di Ostia, It.
21/F2 Liechtenstein
18/F4 Liège, Belg.
19/K2 Liepāja, Lat.
20/F3 Ligurian (sea), It.
42/E3 Likasi, D.R. Congo
20/D1 Lille, Fr.
22/D3 Lillehammer, Nor.
42/F3 Lilongwe (cap.), Malw.
62/C6 Lima (cap.), Peru
54/C3 Lima, Oh,US
32/B2 Limassol, Cyp.
64/C4 Limay (riv.), Arg.
63/J8 Limeira, Braz.
18/B3 Limerick, Ire.
21/K4 Limnos (isl.), Gre.
20/D2 Limoges, Fr.
58/E5 Limón, CR
42/F5 Limpopo (riv.), Afr.
30/C2 Linchuan, China
54/B3 Lincoln, Il,US
53/H2 Lincoln (cap.), Ne,US
47/K4 Line (isls.), Kiri.
38/B3 Lingga (isls.), Indo.
22/E4 Linköping, Swe.
21/G1 Linz, Aus.
20/D3 Lions (gulf), Fr.
29/J5 Lioyang, China
21/G4 Lipari (isls.), It.
23/E3 Lipetsk, Rus.
62/E8 Lípez (mts.), Bol.
20/A4 Lisbon (cap.), Port.
18/C3 Lisburn, NI,UK
19/K3 Lithuania
59/E4 Little Cayman (isl.), Cay.
52/E4 Little Colorado (riv.), US
53/J4 Little Rock (cap.), Ar,US
30/A3 Liuzhou, China
18/D3 Liverpool, Eng,UK
50/E3 Livingstone (range), Ab,Can
42/B2 Livingstone (falls), D.R. Congo
42/E4 Livingstone, Zam.
21/F3 Livorno (Leghorn), It.
21/G2 Ljubljana (cap.), Slov.
56/C3 Llano Estacado (plain), US
62/D3 Llanos (plain), SAm.
20/D3 Lleida (Lérida), Sp.
64/C1 Llullaillaco (vol.), Chile
42/B3 Lobito, Ang.
54/E3 Lockport, NY,US
52/B3 Lodi, Ca,US
19/J4 Łódź, Pol.
22/D2 Lofoten (isls.), Nor.
49/D3 Logan (mt.), ,Can.
52/E2 Logan, Ut,US
54/C3 Logansport, In,US
20/C3 Logroño, Sp.
20/C2 Loire (riv.), Fr.
41/N8 Loita (hills), Kenya
40/C6 Loma (mts.), SLeo.
64/E3 Lomas de Zamora, Arg.
63/H3 Lombarda (mts.), Braz.
37/E5 Lombok (isl.), Indo.
40/F6 Lomé (cap.), Togo
18/C2 Lomond (lake), Sc,UK
52/B4 Lompoc, Ca,US
54/D3 London, On,Can
18/E4 London (cap.), Eng,UK
18/C2 Londonderry, NI,UK
64/F1 Londrina, Braz.
59/F3 Long (isl.), Bahm.
25/T2 Long (str.), Rus.
55/F3 Long (isl.), NY,US
52/C4 Long Beach, Ca,US
54/F3 Long Branch, NJ,US
55/G2 Longfellow (mts.), Me,US
53/F2 Longmont, Co,US
55/K2 Long Range (mts.), Nf,Can
56/E3 Longview, Tx,US
50/C4 Longview, Wa,US
35/J5 Long Xuyen, Viet.
30/C2 Longyan, China
25/R4 Lopatka (cape), Rus.
30/E3 Lop Nur (Lop Nor) (dry lake), China
54/D3 Lorain, Oh,US
46/E8 Lord Howe (isl.), Austl.
20/C2 Lorient, Fr.
20/E1 Lorraine (reg.), Fr.
53/F4 Los Alamos, NM,US
52/C4 Los Angeles, Ca,US
59/N8 Los Mochis, Mex.
62/E1 Los Roques (isls.), Ven.
62/E1 Los Teques, Ven.
35/H4 Louangphrabang, Laos
30/B2 Loudi, China
56/E4 Louisiana (state), US
54/C4 Louisville, Ky,US
20/C3 Lourdes, Fr.
53/F2 Loveland, Co,US
55/G3 Lowell, Ma,US
24/K3 Lower Tunguska (riv.), Rus.
42/E4 Lower Zambezi Nat'l Park, Zam.
47/V12 Loyalty (isls.), NCal.
42/E1 Lualaba (riv.), D.R. Congo
42/B2 Luanda (cap.), Ang.
42/F3 Luangwa (riv.), Moz., Zam.
42/F3 Luangwa Nat'l Park, Zam.
42/E3 Luanshya, Zam.
56/C3 Lubbock, Tx,US
18/G3 Lübeck, Ger.
19/K4 Lublin, Pol.
42/E3 Lubumbashi, D.R. Congo
20/F2 Lucerne (Luzern), Swi.
34/D2 Lucknow, India
29/J4 Lüda (Dalian), China
33/L2 Ludhiana, India
56/E4 Lufkin, Tx,US
21/F2 Lugano, Swi.
42/G3 Lugenda (riv.), Moz.
20/B3 Lugo, Sp.
23/E4 Luhans'k, Ukr.
22/G2 Luleå, Swe.
57/J3 Lumberton, NC,US
18/G3 Lüneburg, Ger.
29/G5 Luoyang, China
42/E2 L'Upemba Nat'l Park, D.R. Congo
42/G3 Lúrio (riv.), Moz.
42/E3 Lusaka (cap.), Zam.
18/D4 Luton, Eng,UK
23/C3 Luts'k, Ukr.
18/F4 Luxembourg
18/F4 Luxembourg (cap.), Lux.
32/B3 Luxor, Egypt
30/D4 Luzon (isl.), Phil.
23/B4 Lviv, Ukr.
18/D4 Lyme (bay), Eng,UK
57/J2 Lynchburg, Va,US
55/G3 Lynn, Ma,US
20/E2 Lyon, Fr.
23/E4 Lysychans'k, Ukr.

M

22/H1 Maanselkä (mts.), Fin.
18/F4 Maas (riv.), Neth.
18/F4 Maastricht, Neth.
64/B6 Maca (mtn.), Chile
63/H3 Macapa, Braz.
30/B3 Macau, China
45/C3 Macdonnell (ranges), Austl.
21/J3 Macedonia, Former Yugoslav Republic of
63/L5 Maceió, Braz.
62/B4 Machala, Ecu.
62/D6 Machu Picchu (ruins), Peru
49/E3 Mackenzie (riv.), NW,Can
54/B3 Macomb, Il,US
20/E2 Mâcon, Fr.
57/H3 Macon, Ga,US
45/D4 Macquarie (riv.), Austl.
32/C2 Ma'daba, Jor.
42/K10 Madagascar
62/F5 Madeira (riv.), Braz.
40/B1 Madeira (isls.), Port.
54/B3 Madison (cap.), Wi,US
36/D5 Madiun, Indo.
62/E6 Madre de Dios (riv.), Bol.
58/A4 Madre del Sur, Sierra (mts.), Mex.
59/N8 Madre Occidental, Sierra (range), Mex.
58/A2 Madre Oriental, Sierra (range), Mex.
20/C3 Madrid (cap.), Sp.
36/D5 Madura (isl.), Indo.
34/C6 Madurai, India
29/M4 Maebashi, Japan
25/R4 Magadan, Rus.
55/J2 Magdalen (isls.), Qu,Can
62/D3 Magdalena (riv.), Col.
18/G3 Magdeburg, Ger.
36/C5 Magelang, Indo.
64/B7 Magellan (str.), SAm.
24/F4 Magnitogorsk, Rus.
19/M3 Mahilyow, Bela.
40/H5 Maiduguri, Nga.
41/L8 Maiko Nat'l Park, D.R. Congo
18/G4 Main (riv.), Ger.
55/G3 Maine (gulf), US
55/G2 Maine (state), US
18/G4 Mainz, Ger.
20/E4 Majorca (isl.), Sp.
46/G4 Majuro (atoll), Mrsh.
34/E2 Makālu (peak), China, Nepal
37/E4 Makassar (str.), Indo.
23/G5 Makhachkala, Rus.
23/E4 Makiyivka, Ukr.
33/H3 Makran (reg.), Iran, Pak.
33/G3 Makran Coast (reg.), Asia
34/B5 Malabar (coast), India
40/G7 Malabo (cap.), EqG.
36/A3 Malacca (str.), Asia
20/B4 Málaga, Sp.
36/D5 Malang, Indo.
42/C2 Malange, Ang.
23/E6 Malatya, Turk.
42/F3 Malawi
36/B2 Malay (pen.), Asia
36/B3 Malaya (reg.), Malay.
32/E2 Malāyer, Iran
36/C2 Malaysia
27/G9 Maldives
27/G9 Male (cap.), Mald.
34/B3 Malegaon, India
40/E4 Mali
22/E5 Malmö, Swe.
62/B3 Malpelo (isl.), Col.
21/G5 Malta
37/J4 Mamberamo (riv.), Indo.
54/C4 Mammoth Cave Nat'l Pk., Ky,US
62/F4 Manacapura, Grande de (lake), Braz.
37/F3 Manado, Indo.
58/D5 Managua (cap.), Nic.
32/F3 Manama (cap.), Bahr.
34/D2 Manaslu (mtn.), Nepal
54/E4 Manassas, Va,US
62/F4 Manaus, Braz.
18/D4 Manchester, Eng,UK
55/G3 Manchester, NH,US
29/J3 Manchuria (reg.), China
35/G3 Mandalay, Myanmar
51/H4 Mandan, ND,US
41/P5 Mandeb, Bab el (str.), Afr., Asia
21/H3 Manfredonia (gulf), It.
63/J6 Mangabeiras (uplands), Braz.
34/B5 Mangalore, India
53/H3 Manhattan, Ks,US
30/D5 Manila (cap.), Phil.
23/C6 Manisa, Turk.
18/C3 Man, Isle of (isl.), UK
51/J2 Manitoba (prov.), Can.
54/D2 Manitoulin (isl.), On,Can
54/C2 Manitowoc, Wi,US
62/C2 Manizales, Col.
51/K5 Mankato, Mn,US
34/C6 Mannar (gulf), India, SrL.
18/G4 Mannheim, Ger.
54/D3 Mansfield, Oh,US
62/B4 Manta, Ecu.
63/K8 Mantiqueira (mts.), Braz.
21/F2 Mantova, It.
62/D6 Manú (riv.), Peru
45/H6 Manukau, NZ
62/D6 Manú Nat'l Park, Peru
59/P10 Manzanillo, Mex.
37/J4 Maoke (mts.), Indo.
30/B3 Maoming, China
42/F6 Maputo (cap.), Moz.
63/J3 Maracá (isl.), Braz.
62/D1 Maracaibo, Ven.
62/D2 Maracaibo (lake), Ven.
63/H7 Maracaju (mts.), Braz.
62/E1 Maracay, Ven.
32/E1 Marāgheh, Iran
63/J4 Marajó (bay), Braz.
63/H4 Marajó (isl.), Braz.
62/C4 Marañón (riv.), Peru
20/B4 Marbella, Sp.
64/D3 Mar Chiquita (lake), Arg.
33/K2 Mardān, Pak.
64/E4 Mar del Plata, Arg.
63/F1 Margarita (isl.), Ven.
41/L7 Margherita (peak), D.R. Congo
58/E3 Marianao, Cuba
21/G2 Maribor, Slov.
43/T Marie Byrd Land (reg.), Ant.
57/G3 Marietta, Ga,US
63/H8 Marília, Braz.
63/H8 Maringá, Braz.
54/C3 Marion, In,US
54/D3 Marion, Oh,US
23/E4 Mariupol', Ukr.
54/E3 Markham, On,Can
23/C5 Marmara (sea), Turk.
20/E1 Marne (riv.), Fr.
63/H3 Maroni (riv.), Braz.
47/M5 Marquesas (isls.), FrPol.
54/C2 Marquette, Mi,US
41/K5 Marrah, Jabal (mts.), Sudan
62/E3 Marrahuaca (mtn.), Ven.
40/D1 Marrakech, Mor.
20/E3 Marseille, Fr.
56/E3 Marshall, Tx,US
46/G3 Marshall Islands
53/J2 Marshalltown, Ia,US
36/D4 Martapura, Indo.
55/G3 Martha's Vineyard (isl.), Ma,US
19/J4 Martin, Slvk.
59/J4 Martinique, Fr.
59/J4 Martinique Passage (chan.), West Indies
24/G6 Mary, Trkm.
54/E4 Maryland (state), US
55/L2 Marystown, Nf,Can
40/H3 Marzūq, Sahrā (des.), Libya
42/G1 Masai Steppe (grsld.), Tanz.
29/K4 Masan, SKor.
30/D5 Masbate (isl.), Phil.
42/E6 Maseru (cap.), Les.
32/G1 Mashhad, Iran
33/H3 Māshkel, Hāmūn-i (lake), Pak.
33/G4 Masira (gulf), Oman
32/E2 Masjed-e Soleymān, Iran
53/J2 Mason City, Ia,US
55/F3 Massachusetts (state), US
20/D2 Massif Central (plat.), Fr.
54/D3 Massillon, Oh,US
42/B2 Matadi, D.R. Congo
56/D4 Matagorda (isl.), Tx,US
58/B2 Matamoros, Mex.
55/H1 Matane, Qu,Can
58/E3 Matanzas, Cuba
37/E5 Mataram, Indo.
46/H6 Mata Utu (cap.), Wall.
63/G6 Mato Grosso (plat.), Braz.
29/L5 Matsuyama, Japan
20/E2 Matterhorn (mt.), Eur.
54/B4 Mattoon, Il,US
62/F2 Maturín, Ven.
47/K2 Maui (isl.), Hi,US
40/C4 Mauritania
15/M7 Mauritius
55/F4 May (cape), NJ,US
59/G3 Mayaguana (isl.), Bah.
59/H4 Mayagüez, PR
23/F5 Maykop, Rus.
39/G6 Mayotte, Fr.
33/J1 Mazar-i-Sharif, Afg.
59/N9 Mazatlán, Mex.
19/K3 Mazury (reg.), Pol.
19/M3 Mazyr, Bela.
42/F6 Mbabane (cap.), Swaz.
41/J7 Mbandaka, D.R. Congo
42/F2 Mbeya, Tanz.
42/F2 Mbeya (range), Tanz.
42/D2 Mbuji-Mayi, D.R. Congo
53/J4 McAlester, Ok,US
56/D5 McAllen, Tx,US
15/N8 McDonald (isls.), Austl.
54/E3 McKeesport, Pa,US
49/B3 McKinley (mt.), Ak,US
49/G2 M'Clintock (chan.), Can.
52/D3 Mead (lake), US
63/J5 Mearim (riv.), Braz.
32/C4 Mecca, SAr.
18/G3 Mecklenburger Bucht (bay), Ger.
19/J5 Mecsek (mts.), Hun.
36/A3 Medan, Indo.
62/C2 Medellín, Col.
50/C5 Medford, Or,US
52/F2 Medicine Bow (range), Wy,US
50/F3 Medicine Hat, Ab,Can
32/C4 Medina, SAr.
15/K4 Mediterranean (sea)
34/C2 Meerut, India
40/D1 Meknès, Mor.
35/J5 Mekong (riv.), Asia
35/J6 Mekong, Mouths of the (riv.), Viet.
36/B3 Melaka (Malacca), Malay.
46/E5 Melanesia (reg.), Pacific
45/D4 Melbourne, Austl.
57/H4 Melbourne, Fl,US
20/C5 Melilla, Sp.
23/E4 Melitopol', Ukr.
45/C2 Melville (isl.), Austl.
49/F2 Melville (isl.), Can.
49/J3 Melville (pen.), Can.
18/G5 Memmingen, Ger.
57/F3 Memphis, Tn,US
64/C3 Mendoza, Arg.
54/B3 Menominee Falls, Wi,US
36/A4 Mentawai (isls.), Indo.
54/D3 Mentor, Oh,US
20/E2 Mercantour Nat'l Park, Fr.
52/B3 Merced, Ca,US
64/C3 Mercedario (mtn.), Arg.
35/G5 Mergui (arch.), Myanmar
58/D3 Mérida, Mex.
20/B4 Mérida, Sp.
62/D2 Mérida, Ven.
62/E2 Mérida (mts.), Ven.
57/F3 Meridian, Ms,US
64/E3 Merlo, Arg.
41/M4 Meroe (ruins), Sudan
23/D6 Mersin, Turk.
52/E4 Mesa, Az,US
52/E3 Mesa Verde Nat'l Pk., Co,US
64/E3 Mesopotamia (reg.), Arg.
32/D2 Mesopotamia (reg.), Iraq
56/D3 Mesquite, Tx,US
21/G4 Messina, It.
21/J4 Messini (gulf), Gre.
21/G2 Mestre, It.
62/D2 Meta (riv.), Ven.
57/F4 Metairie, La,US
20/E1 Metz, Fr.
20/E1 Meuse (riv.), Eur.
59/L7 Mexicali, Mex.
63/J3 Mexicana (isl.), Braz.
58/A3 Mexico
58/C3 Mexico (gulf), NAm.
58/B4 Mexico (cap.), Mex.
33/H1 Meymaneh, Afg.
57/H5 Miami, Fl,US
57/H5 Miami Beach, Fl,US
28/E5 Mianyang, China
24/F4 Miass, Rus.
54/C2 Michigan (lake), US
54/C2 Michigan (state), US
54/C3 Michigan City, In,US
54/C2 Michipicoten (isl.), On,Can
23/F3 Michurinsk, Rus.
46/E3 Micronesia (reg.), Pacific
46/D4 Micronesia, Fed. States of
55/F3 Middlebury, Vt,US
18/D3 Middlesbrough, Eng,UK
54/E2 Midland, On,Can
54/C3 Midland, Mi,US
56/C4 Midland, Tx,US
46/H2 Midway Islands, PacUS
53/H4 Midwest City, Ok,US
21/K4 Mikonos (isl.), Gre.
62/C4 Milagro, Ecu.
21/F2 Milan, It.
51/K4 Mille Lacs (lake), Mn,US
54/C3 Milwaukee, Wi,US
37/F3 Minahasa (pen.), Indo.
18/C2 Minch, The (sound), Sc,UK
30/D6 Mindanao (isl.), Phil.
30/D5 Mindoro (isl.), Phil.
23/G5 Mingäçevir, Azer.
33/K2 Mingāora, Pak.
51/K4 Minneapolis, Mn,US
51/K4 Minnesota (state), US
20/B3 Miño (riv.), Sp.
20/E3 Minorca (Menorca) (isl.), Sp.
51/H3 Minot, ND,US
19/L3 Minsk (cap.), Bela.
36/D3 Miri, Malay.
64/F3 Mirim (lake), Braz.
33/L1 Mīrpur, Pak.
21/J4 Mirtóön (sea), Gre.
54/C3 Mishawaka, In,US
64/F2 Misiones (mts.), Arg.
21/J1 Miskolc, Hun.
37/H4 Misool (isl.), Indo.
40/J1 Mişrātah, Libya
56/D5 Mission, Tx,US
52/C4 Mission Viejo, Ca,US
57/F4 Mississippi (riv.), US
57/F3 Mississippi (state), US
50/E4 Missoula, Mt,US
53/J3 Missouri (riv.), US
53/J3 Missouri (state), US
62/D7 Misti, El (mt.), Peru
41/L8 Mitimbu (mts.), D.R. Congo
58/B4 Mitla (ruin), Mex.
29/M4 Mito, Japan
64/C7 Mitre (pen.), Arg.
42/E2 Mitumba (mts.), D.R. Congo
29/L5 Miyazaki, Japan
57/F4 Mobile, Al,US
21/F2 Modena, It.
52/B3 Modesto, Ca,US
41/Q7 Mogadishu (cap.), Som.
31/A3 Moinkum (des.), Kaz.
52/C4 Mojave (des.), Ca,US
62/E6 Mojos (plain), Bol.
29/K5 Mokp'o, SKor.
19/M5 Moldova
21/K2 Moldoveanu (peak), Eur.
54/B3 Moline, Il,US
47/K2 Molokai (isl.), Hi,US
37/G4 Molucca (sea), Indo.
37/G3 Moluccas (isls.), Indo.
42/G1 Mombasa, Kenya
62/E6 Momoré (riv.), Bol.
49/H4 Mona (passage), NAm.
20/E3 Monaco
50/D3 Monashee (mts.), BC,Can
55/H2 Moncton, NB,Can
28/D2 Mongolia
56/E3 Monroe, La,US
54/D3 Monroe, Mi,US
40/C6 Monrovia (cap.), Libr.
18/E4 Mons, Belg.
50/F4 Montana (state), US
62/D6 Montaña, La (reg.), Peru
21/F3 Montecristo (isl.), It.
59/F4 Montego Bay, Jam.
21/H3 Montenegro (rep.), Yugo.
63/L7 Monte Pascoal Nat'l Park, Braz.
52/B3 Monterey, Ca,US
62/C2 Montería, Col.
58/A2 Monterrey, Mex.
63/K7 Montes Claros, Braz.
64/E3 Montevideo (cap.), Uru.
57/G3 Montgomery (cap.), Al,US
54/F2 Mont-Laurier, Qu,Can
55/G2 Montmagny, Qu,Can
55/F2 Montpelier (cap.), Vt,US
20/D3 Montpellier, Fr.
54/F2 Montréal, Qu,Can
55/N6 Mont-Royal, Qu,Can
59/J4 Montserrat, UK
20/D3 Montserrat (mt.), Sp.
35/F3 Monywa, Myanmar
21/F2 Monza, It.
53/H4 Moore, Ok,US
47/K6 Moorea (isl.), FrPol.
51/J4 Moorhead, Mn,US
55/G2 Moosehead (lake), Me,US
50/G3 Moose Jaw, Sk,Can
34/C1 Moradabad, India
19/J4 Morava (riv.), Eur.
21/J3 Morava (riv.), Yugo.
19/J4 Moravia (reg.), Czh.
18/D2 Moray (firth), Sc,UK
58/A4 Morelia, Mex.
20/B4 Morena, Sierra (range), Sp.
52/C4 Moreno Valley, Ca,US
57/F4 Morgan City, La,US
54/E4 Morgantown, WV,US
29/N4 Morioka, Japan
30/D6 Moro (gulf), Phil.
40/C1 Morocco
64/E3 Morón, Arg.
39/G6 Moroni (cap.), Com.
37/G3 Morotai (str.), Indo.
57/H2 Morristown, Tn,US
63/J6 Morro Alto (peak), Braz.
63/H6 Mortes (riv.), Braz.
23/E2 Moscow (cap.), Rus.
50/D4 Moscow, Id,US
18/F4 Mosel (riv.), Ger.
20/E1 Moselle (riv.), Fr.
50/D4 Moses Lake, Wa,US
58/E5 Mosquito Coast (reg.), Nic.
58/E6 Mosquitos (gulf), Pan.
63/L5 Mossoró, Braz.
57/F4 Moss Point, Ms,US
19/H4 Most, Czh.
40/E1 Mostaganem, Alg.
21/H3 Mostar, Bosn.
32/D1 Mosul, Iraq
58/D5 Motagua (riv.), Guat.
18/D3 Motherwell, Sc,UK
35/G4 Moulmein, Myanmar
55/L2 Mount Pearl, Nf,Can
50/C4 Mount Rainier Nat'l Pk., Wa,US
54/B4 Mount Vernon, Il,US
54/D3 Mount Vernon, Oh,US
50/C3 Mount Vernon, Wa,US
42/G4 Mozambique
39/G6 Mozambique (chan.), Afr.
42/F3 Muchinga (mts.), Zam.
29/K3 Mudanjiang, China
42/E3 Mufulira, Zam.
42/E2 Muhila (mts.), D.R. Congo
19/K4 Mukacheve, Ukr.
19/H4 Mulde (riv.), Ger.
20/C4 Mulhacén (mt.), Sp.
20/E2 Mulhouse, Fr.
32/K2 Multan, Pak.
34/B4 Mumbai (Bombay), India
54/C3 Muncie, In,US
18/G4 Munich (München), Ger.
64/B7 Muñoz Gamero (pen.), Chile
18/F4 Münster, Ger.
36/C4 Muntok, Indo.

Mupa - Queen

71

Queim – Tangs

63/H4 **Queimada** (isl.), Braz.
58/A3 **Querétaro**, Mex.
50/C2 **Quesnel**, BC,Can
33/J2 **Quetta**, Pak.
58/C5 **Quezaltenango**, Guat.
30/D5 **Quezon City**, Phil.
29/H4 **Qufu**, China
42/B2 **Quiçama Nat'l Park**, Ang.
64/B5 **Quilán** (cape), Chile
20/B1 **Quimper**, Fr.
54/B4 **Quincy**, Il,US
55/G3 **Quincy**, Ma,US
35/J5 **Qui Nhon**, Viet.
62/C4 **Quito** (cap.), Ecu.
30/C2 **Quzhou**, China
24/G5 **Qyzylordä**, Kaz.

R

40/D1 **Rabat** (cap.), Mor.
46/E5 **Rabaul**, PNG
41/K3 **Rabyanāh, Sahra'** (des.), Libya
49/M5 **Race** (cape), Nf,Can
54/C3 **Racine**, Wi,US
19/K4 **Radom**, Pol.
21/H4 **Ragusa**, It.
33/K3 **Rahīmyār Khān**, Pak.
50/C4 **Rainier** (mt.), Wa,US
51/K3 **Rainy** (lake), NAm.
34/D3 **Raipur**, India
34/D4 **Rajahmundry**, India
36/D3 **Rajang** (riv.), Malay.
34/B3 **Rajkot**, India
34/E3 **Rājshāhi**, Bang.
33/K1 **Rakaposhi** (mtn.), Pak.
57/J3 **Raleigh** (cap.), NC,US
63/K6 **Ramalho** (mts.), Braz.
18/E4 **Ramsgate**, Eng,UK
34/E3 **Ranchi**, India
54/B3 **Rantoul**, Il,US
47/L7 **Rapa** (isl.), FrPol.
51/H4 **Rapid City**, SD,US
54/E4 **Rappahannock** (riv.), Va,US
47/J7 **Rarotonga** (isl.), Cook Is.
64/D5 **Rasa** (pt.), Arg.
41/N5 **Ras Dashen Terara** (mt.), Eth.
32/E1 **Rasht**, Iran
32/F3 **Ra's Tannūrah** (cape), SAr.
45/H6 **Raupehu** (mtn.), NZ
34/D3 **Raurkela**, India
21/G2 **Ravenna**, It.
21/F2 **Ravensburg**, Ger.
33/K2 **Ravi** (riv.), Asia
33/K2 **Rawalpindi**, Pak.
50/G5 **Rawlins**, Wy,US
55/K2 **Ray** (cape), Nf,Can
21/K3 **Razgrad**, Bul.
18/D4 **Reading**, Eng,UK
54/F3 **Reading**, Pa,US
62/E7 **Real** (mts.), Bol.
63/M5 **Recife**, Braz.
32/C4 **Red** (sea)
27/K7 **Red** (riv.), Asia
53/J5 **Red** (riv.), US
50/E2 **Red Deer**, Ab,Can
50/F3 **Red Deer** (riv.), Ab,Can
52/B2 **Redding**, Ca,US
51/J4 **Red River of the North** (riv.), US
41/N3 **Red Sea** (hills), Sudan
52/A2 **Redwood Nat'l Pk.**, Ca,US
18/C3 **Ree** (lake), Ire.
18/G4 **Regensburg**, Ger.
21/G4 **Reggio di Calabria**, It.
21/F2 **Reggio nell'Emilia**, It.
51/G3 **Regina** (cap.), Sk,Can
20/E1 **Reims**, Fr.
64/A7 **Reina Adelaida** (arch.), Chile
49/G4 **Reindeer** (lake), Can.
54/E2 **Renfrew**, On,Can
20/C1 **Rennes**, Fr.
52/C3 **Reno**, Nv,US
28/H4 **Renqiu**, China
53/H2 **Republican** (riv.), US
64/E2 **Resistencia**, Arg.
21/J2 **Reşita**, Rom.
21/J2 **Retrezap Nat'l Park**, Rom.
15/M7 **Réunion**, Fr.
18/G4 **Reutlingen**, Ger.
50/D3 **Revelstoke**, BC,Can
49/F8 **Revillagigedo** (isls.), Mex.
50/F5 **Rexburg**, Id,US
22/N7 **Reykjavík** (cap.), Ice.
58/B2 **Reynosa**, Mex.
18/F3 **Rhine** (riv.), Eur.
55/G3 **Rhode Island** (state), US
23/C6 **Rhodes** (isl.), Gre.
23/C6 **Rhodes** (Ródhos), Gre.
18/D4 **Rhondda**, Wal,UK
20/E2 **Rhône** (riv.), Eur.
18/C2 **Rhum** (isl.), Sc,UK
36/B3 **Riau** (arch.), Indo.
63/J8 **Ribeirão Preto**, Braz.
19/M5 **Rîbniţa**, Mol.
50/D4 **Richland**, Wa,US
54/C4 **Richmond**, In,US
54/C4 **Richmond**, Ky,US
54/E4 **Richmond** (cap.), Va,US
51/H3 **Riding Mtn. Nat'l Pk.**, Mb,Can
40/E1 **Rif, Er** (mts.), Mor.
19/L2 **Riga** (cap.), Lat.
19/K2 **Riga** (gulf), Lat.
33/H2 **Rīgestan** (des.), Afg.
21/G2 **Rijeka**, Cro.
21/K2 **Rîmnicu Vîlcea**, Rom.
21/G2 **Rimini**, It.
55/G1 **Rimouski**, Qu,Can
62/C5 **Río Abiseo Nat'l Park**, Peru
62/E5 **Rio Branco**, Braz.
63/J8 **Rio Claro**, Braz.
64/D3 **Río Cuarto**, Arg.
63/K8 **Rio de Janeiro**, Braz.
56/C4 **Rio Grande** (riv.), NAm.
62/F4 **Rio Jaú Nat'l Park**, Braz.
64/E3 **Río Negro** (res.), Uru.
62/D2 **Ritacuba** (mtn.), Col.
45/D4 **Riverina** (reg.), Austl.
52/C4 **Riverside**, Ca,US
57/H5 **Riviera Beach**, Fl,US
55/G2 **Rivière-du-Loup**, Qu,Can
23/C3 **Rivne**, Ukr.
32/E4 **Riyadh** (cap.), SAr.
23/F5 **Rize**, Turk.
28/F4 **Rizhao**, China
59/J4 **Road Town** (cap.), BVI
54/E4 **Roanoke**, Va,US
57/J2 **Roanoke Rapids**, NC,US
55/F1 **Roberval**, Qu,Can
45/A3 **Robinson** (ranges), Austl.
51/K4 **Rochester**, Mn,US
55/G3 **Rochester**, NH,US
54/E3 **Rochester**, NY,US
54/B3 **Rockford**, Il,US
45/E2 **Rockhampton**, Austl.
57/H3 **Rock Hill**, SC,US
54/B3 **Rock Island**, Il,US
50/F5 **Rock Springs**, Wy,US
49/E4 **Rocky** (mts.), NAm.
57/J3 **Rocky Mount**, NC,US
50/E2 **Rocky Mountain House**, Ab,Can
53/F2 **Rocky Mountain Nat'l Pk.**, Co,US
53/J3 **Rogers**, Ar,US
21/J2 **Romania**
21/G3 **Rome** (cap.), It.
57/G3 **Rome**, Ga,US
54/F3 **Rome**, NY,US
63/H6 **Roncador** (mts.), Braz.
43/W **Ronne Ice Shelf**, Ant.
63/H6 **Ronuro** (riv.), Braz.
43/N **Roosevelt** (isl.), Ant.
62/F6 **Roosevelt** (riv.), Braz.
62/F2 **Roraima** (mtn.), Guy.
64/D3 **Rosario**, Arg.
59/J4 **Roseau** (cap.), Dom.
50/C5 **Roseburg**, Or,US
18/H5 **Rosenheim**, Ger.
43/P **Ross** (sea), Ant.
43/P **Ross Ice Shelf**, Ant.
18/H3 **Rostock**, Ger.
23/E4 **Rostov**, Rus.
53/F4 **Roswell**, NM,US
18/D3 **Rotherham**, Eng,UK
18/F4 **Rotterdam**, Neth.
46/G6 **Rotuma** (isl.), Fiji
20/D1 **Rouen**, Fr.
54/E1 **Rouyn-Noranda**, Qu,Can
52/D2 **Roy**, Ut,US
42/F2 **Ruaha Nat'l Park**, Tanz.
32/E5 **Rub' al Khali** (des.), Asia
24/G4 **Rūdnyy**, Kaz.
42/G2 **Rufiji** (riv.), Tanz.
19/H3 **Rügen** (isl.), Ger.
42/F2 **Rukwa** (lake), Tanz.
59/G3 **Rum** (cay), Bahm.
51/F1 **Rupert** (riv.), Qu,Can
21/K3 **Ruse**, Bulg.
24/H3 **Russia**
23/G5 **Rust'avi**, Geo.
56/E3 **Ruston**, La,US
55/F3 **Rutland**, Vt,US
42/G3 **Ruvuma** (riv.), Tanz.
42/E1 **Rwanda**
23/E3 **Ryazan'**, Rus.
23/E2 **Rybinsk**, Rus.
23/E2 **Rybinsk** (res.), Rus.
23/G4 **Ryn-Peski** (des.), Kaz.
46/B2 **Ryukyu** (isls.), Japan
19/K4 **Rzeszów**, Pol.

S

50/C3 **Saanich**, BC,Can
18/F4 **Saarbrücken**, Ger.
19/K2 **Saaremaa** (isl.), Est.
21/H2 **Šabac**, Yugo.
20/D3 **Sabadell**, Sp.
37/E2 **Sabah** (reg.), Malay.
56/E4 **Sabine** (riv.), US
55/H3 **Sable** (cape), NS,Can
55/J3 **Sable** (isl.), NS,Can
33/G1 **Sabzevar**, Iran
55/H2 **Sackville**, NB,Can
52/B3 **Sacramento** (cap.), Ca,US
52/B2 **Sacramento** (riv.), Ca,US
53/F4 **Sacramento** (mts.), NM,US
40/H1 **Safāqis** (Sfax), Tun.
40/D1 **Safi**, Mor.
33/H2 **Safid** (mts.), Afg.
29/L5 **Saga**, Japan
54/D3 **Saginaw**, Mi,US
55/G1 **Saguenay** (riv.), Qu,Can
40/G3 **Sahara** (des.), Afr.
33/L3 **Saharanpur**, India
33/K2 **Sāhīwāl**, Pak.
35/J5 **Saigon** (Ho Chi Minh City), Viet.
50/E2 **St. Albert**, Ab,Can
57/H4 **St. Augustine**, Fl,US
54/E3 **St. Catharines**, On,Can
53/K3 **St. Charles**, Mo,US
51/K4 **St. Cloud**, Mn,US
51/K4 **St. Croix** (riv.), US
59/H4 **St. Croix** (isl.), USVI
54/F2 **Ste-Agathe-des-Monts**, Qu,Can
55/G2 **Ste-Foy**, Qu,Can
20/E2 **St-Étienne**, Fr.
55/K1 **St. George** (cape), Nf,Can
18/C4 **St. George's** (chan.), Eur.
59/J5 **St. George's** (cap.), Gren.
42/C7 **St. Helena** (bay), SAfr.
14/J6 **St. Helena & Dependencies**, UK
50/C4 **St. Helens** (mt.), Wa,US
18/D4 **St. Helier** (cap.), Jersey, Chl.,UK
55/F2 **St-Hyacinthe**, Qu,Can
55/F1 **St-Jean** (lake), Qu,Can
55/F2 **St-Jérôme**, Qu,Can
55/H2 **St. John**, NB,Can
55/H2 **St. John** (riv.), NAm.
59/J4 **St. Johns** (cap.), Anti.
55/L2 **St. John's** (cap.), Nf,Can
53/J3 **St. Joseph**, Mo,US
59/J4 **St. Kitts** (isl.), StK.
59/J4 **St. Kitts & Nevis**
63/H2 **Saint-Laurent-du-Maroni**, FrG.
55/J1 **St. Lawrence** (gulf), Can.
55/G1 **St. Lawrence** (riv.), NAm.
49/A3 **St. Lawrence** (isl.), Ak,US
53/K3 **St. Louis**, Mo,US
59/J5 **St. Lucia**
20/C1 **Saint-Malo**, Fr.
20/C1 **Saint-Malo** (gulf), Fr.
59/J4 **Saint Martin** (isl.), Fr.
55/F2 **St-Maurice** (riv.), Qu,Can
20/C2 **St-Nazaire**, Fr.
51/K4 **St. Paul** (cap.), Mn,US
18/D4 **St. Peter Port** (cap.), Guernsey, Chl.,UK
19/M2 **St. Petersburg**, Rus.
57/H5 **St. Petersburg**, Fl,US
55/K2 **St. Pierre & Miquelon**, Fr.
57/H4 **St. Simons** (isl.), Ga,US
55/H2 **St. Stephen**, NB,Can
54/D3 **St. Thomas**, On,Can
59/H4 **St. Thomas** (isl.), USVI
59/J5 **St. Vincent & the Grenadines**
46/D3 **Saipan** (isl.), NMar.
29/M5 **Sakai**, Japan
51/H4 **Sakakawea** (lake), ND,US
23/D5 **Sakarya** (riv.), Turk.
25/Q4 **Sakhalin** (gulf), Rus.
25/Q4 **Sakhalin** (isl.), Rus.
30/D3 **Sakishima** (isls.), Japan
64/D2 **Salado** (riv.), Arg.
20/B3 **Salamanca**, Sp.
14/D7 **Sala y Gómez** (isl.), Chile
40/D1 **Salé**, Mor.
24/G3 **Salekhard**, Rus.
34/C5 **Salem**, India
55/G3 **Salem**, NH,US
50/C4 **Salem** (cap.), Or,US
54/D4 **Salem**, Va,US
21/G3 **Salerno**, It.
53/H3 **Salina**, Ks,US
52/B3 **Salinas**, Ca,US
18/D4 **Salisbury**, Eng,UK
54/F4 **Salisbury**, Md,US
50/E4 **Salmon** (riv.), Id,US
50/E4 **Salmon River** (mts.), Id,US
41/K8 **Salonga Nat'l Park**, D.R. Congo
64/C1 **Salta**, Arg.
58/A2 **Saltillo**, Mex.
52/E2 **Salt Lake City** (cap.), Ut,US
64/E3 **Salto Grande** (res.), Arg., Uru.
52/C4 **Salton Sea** (lake), Ca,US
57/H3 **Saluda** (riv.), SC,US
63/H2 **Salut** (isls.), FrG.
63/L6 **Salvador**, Braz.
27/J8 **Salween** (riv.), Asia
21/G2 **Salzburg**, Aus.
18/G3 **Salzgitter**, Ger.
30/E5 **Samar** (isl.), Phil.
23/H3 **Samara**, Rus.
37/E4 **Samarinda**, Indo.
24/G6 **Samarqand**, Uzb.
36/C3 **Sambas**, Indo.
47/H6 **Samoa**
23/C5 **Sámos** (isl.), Gre.
21/K3 **Samothráki** (isl.), Gre.
23/E5 **Samsun**, Turk.
32/D5 **Sanaa** (San'a) (cap.), Yem.
58/E5 **San Andrés** (isl.), Col.
56/C4 **San Angelo**, Tx,US
56/D4 **San Antonio**, Tx,US
52/C4 **San Bernardino**, Ca,US
64/B3 **San Bernardo**, Chile
52/C4 **San Clemente** (isl.), Ca,US
46/F6 **San Cristobal** (isl.), Sol.
62/D2 **San Cristóbal**, Ven.
52/C4 **San Diego**, Ca,US
54/D3 **Sandusky**, Oh,US
52/E2 **Sandy**, Ut,US
57/G3 **Sandy Springs**, Ga,US
57/H4 **Sanford**, Fl,US
55/G3 **Sanford**, Me,US
57/J3 **Sanford**, NC,US
52/B3 **San Francisco**, Ca,US
62/C4 **Sangay Nat'l Park**, Ecu.
34/B4 **Sāngli**, India
53/F3 **Sangre de Cristo** (mts.), US
52/B3 **San Joaquin** (val.), Ca,US
64/C6 **San Jorge** (gulf), Arg.
58/E6 **San José** (cap.), CR
52/B3 **San Jose**, Ca,US
62/J8 **San José dos Campos**, Braz.
64/C3 **San Juan**, Arg.
59/H4 **San Juan** (cap.), PR
52/E3 **San Juan** (riv.), US
21/F2 **Sankt Gallen**, Swi.
62/B4 **San Lorenzo** (cape), Ecu.
59/N9 **San Lucas** (cape), Mex.
52/B4 **San Luis Obispo**, Ca,US
58/A3 **San Luis Potosí**, Mex.
56/D4 **San Marcos**, Tx,US
21/G3 **San Marino**
52/B3 **San Mateo**, Ca,US
64/D5 **San Matías** (gulf), Arg.
62/F6 **San Miguel** (riv.), Bol.
58/D5 **San Miguel**, ESal.
64/C2 **San Miguel de Tucumán**, Arg.
52/C4 **San Nicolas** (isl.), Ca,US
58/A2 **San Nicolás de los Garzas**, Mex.
25/P2 **Sannikova** (str.), Rus.
64/C1 **San Pedro** (vol.), Chile
58/D4 **San Pedro Sula**, Hon.
62/C3 **Sanquianga Nat'l Park**, Col.
20/E3 **San Remo**, It.
59/G3 **San Salvador** (isl.), Bahm.
58/D5 **San Salvador** (cap.), ESal.
64/C1 **San Salvador de Jujuy**, Arg.
20/C3 **San Sebastián**, Sp.
58/D5 **Santa Ana**, ESal.
52/C4 **Santa Ana**, Ca,US
52/C4 **Santa Barbara**, Ca,US
52/C4 **Santa Catalina** (isl.), Ca,US
64/G2 **Santa Catarina** (isl.), Braz.
59/E3 **Santa Clara**, Cuba
62/F7 **Santa Cruz**, Bol.
40/B2 **Santa Cruz** (isls.), Sol.
52/B3 **Santa Cruz**, Ca,US
40/B2 **Santa Cruz de Tenerife**, Sp.
64/D3 **Santa Fe**, Arg.
53/F4 **Santa Fe** (cap.), NM,US
64/B7 **Santa Inés** (isl.), Chile
64/F2 **Santa Maria**, Braz.
52/B4 **Santa Maria**, Ca,US
62/D1 **Santa Marta**, Col.
20/C3 **Santander**, Sp.
20/F3 **Sant'Antioco** (isl.), It.
63/H4 **Santarém**, Braz.
52/B3 **Santa Rosa**, Ca,US
57/J3 **Santee** (riv.), SC,US
64/B3 **Santiago** (cap.), Chile
59/G4 **Santiago**, DRep.
56/C4 **Santiago** (mts.), Tx,US
20/A3 **Santiago de Compostela**, Sp.
59/F4 **Santiago de Cuba**, Cuba
64/D2 **Santiago del Estero**, Arg.
64/G1 **Santo Andre**, Braz.
59/H4 **Santo Domingo** (cap.), DRep.
62/B3 **Santo Domingo de los Colorados**, Ecu.
64/G1 **Santos**, Braz.
64/B6 **San Valentín** (mtn.), Chile
63/J8 **São Carlos**, Braz.
64/G2 **São Francisco** (isl.), Braz.
63/L5 **São Francisco** (riv.), Braz.
63/K4 **São João** (isls.), Braz.
62/F5 **São João** (mts.), Braz.
63/K8 **São João del Rei**, Braz.
63/J8 **São José do Rio Preto**, Braz.
63/J8 **São José dos Campos**, Braz.
63/G7 **São Lourenço** (riv.), Braz.
63/K4 **São Luis**, Braz.
63/K4 **São Marcos** (bay), Braz.
20/E2 **Saône** (riv.), Fr.
64/G1 **São Paulo**, Braz.
63/M5 **São Roque** (cape), Braz.
63/K8 **São Tomé** (cape), Braz.
40/G7 **São Tomé** (cap.), SaoT.
40/F7 **São Tomé and Principe**
20/A4 **São Vincent** (cape), Port.
29/N3 **Sapporo**, Japan
20/C3 **Saragossa**, Sp.
21/H3 **Sarajevo** (cap.), Bosn.
23/G3 **Saransk**, Rus.
23/H2 **Sarapul**, Rus.
57/H5 **Sarasota**, Fl,US
54/F3 **Saratoga Springs**, NY,US
23/G3 **Saratov**, Rus.
36/D3 **Sarawak** (reg.), Malay.
21/F3 **Sardinia** (isl.), It.
33/K2 **Sargodha**, Pak.
32/F1 **Sārī**, Iran
54/D3 **Sarnia**, On,Can
29/K5 **Sasebo**, Japan
50/G2 **Saskatchewan** (prov.), Can.
51/G2 **Saskatchewan** (riv.), Can.
50/G3 **Saskatoon**, Sk,Can
20/F3 **Sassari**, It.
34/C3 **Satpura** (range), India
21/J2 **Satu Mare**, Rom.
32/D4 **Saudi Arabia**
54/C2 **Sault Ste. Marie**, On,Can
54/C2 **Sault Ste. Marie**, Mi,US
21/H2 **Sava** (riv.), Eur.
47/R9 **Savai'i** (isl.), Sam.
57/H3 **Savannah** (riv.), US
57/H3 **Savannah**, Ga,US
35/H4 **Savannaket**, Laos
42/F5 **Save** (riv.), Moz.
20/F2 **Savona**, It.
37/F5 **Savu** (sea), Indo.
52/F3 **Sawateh** (range), Co,US
41/M2 **Sawhāj**, Egypt
52/D1 **Sawtooth** (mts.), Id,US
18/D3 **Scarborough**, Eng,UK
21/F2 **Schaffhausen**, Swi.
54/F3 **Schenectady**, NY,US
18/G4 **Schwäbische Alb** (range), Ger.
18/G4 **Schweinfurt**, Ger.
18/G3 **Schwerin**, Ger.
18/C4 **Scilly** (isls.), Eng,UK
54/D4 **Scioto** (riv.), Oh,US
43/W **Scotia** (sea), Ant.
18/C2 **Scotland**, UK
52/G2 **Scottsbluff**, Ne,US
57/G3 **Scottsboro**, Al,US
52/E4 **Scottsdale**, Az,US
54/F3 **Scranton**, Pa,US
21/H3 **Scutari** (lake), Eur.
50/C4 **Seattle**, Wa,US
62/B5 **Sechura** (bay), Peru
62/B5 **Sechura** (des.), Peru
53/J3 **Sedalia**, Mo,US
20/B3 **Segovia**, Sp.
20/D1 **Seine** (riv.), Fr.
40/E7 **Sekondi**, Gha.
50/D3 **Selkirk** (mts.), BC,Can
51/J3 **Selkirk**, Mb,Can
57/G3 **Selma**, Al,US
62/E5 **Selvas** (for.), Braz.
36/D5 **Semarang**, Indo.
31/D1 **Semey**, Kaz.
40/B5 **Senegal**
40/B4 **Senegal** (riv.), Afr.
29/K4 **Seoul** (cap.), SKor.
55/H1 **Sept-Îles**, Qu,Can
52/C3 **Sequoia Nat'l Pk.**, Ca,US
36/C3 **Serasan** (str.), Malay.
42/F1 **Serengeti** (plain), Tanz.
42/F1 **Serengeti Nat'l Park**, Kenya, Tanz.
63/H5 **Seringa** (mts.), Braz.
24/G4 **Serov**, Rus.
23/E3 **Serpukhov**, Rus.
63/K5 **Serra da Capivara Nat'l Park**, Braz.
62/E3 **Serranía de la Neblina Nat'l Park**, Ven.
40/G1 **Sétif**, Alg.
20/A4 **Setúbal**, Port.
20/A4 **Setúbal** (bay), Port.
23/G5 **Sevan** (lake), Arm.
23/E5 **Sevastopol'**, Ukr.
21/J2 **Severnaya Zemlya** (isls.), Rus.
17/H2 **Severodvinsk**, Rus.
52/D3 **Sevier** (riv.), Ut,US
20/B4 **Seville**, Sp.
49/C3 **Seward**, Ak,US
15/M6 **Seychelles**
23/E6 **Seyhan** (riv.), Turk.
18/F3 **'s Gravenhage** (The Hague) (cap.), Neth.
34/C2 **Shahjahanpur**, India
35/G3 **Shan** (plat.), Myanmar
29/J4 **Shandong** (pen.), China
29/J5 **Shanghai**, China
30/C2 **Shangrao**, China
18/B3 **Shannon** (riv.), Ire.
25/P4 **Shantar** (isls.), Rus.
30/B3 **Shaoguan**, China
30/D2 **Shaoxing**, China
30/B2 **Shaoyang**, China
54/D3 **Sharon**, Pa,US
52/B2 **Shasta** (lake), Ca,US
52/B2 **Shasta** (mt.), Ca,US
32/E2 **Shatt-al-'Arab** (riv.), Asia
40/G1 **Shaţţ al Jarīd** (depr.), Tun.
55/F2 **Shawinigan**, Qu,Can
53/H4 **Shawnee**, Ok,US
54/C3 **Sheboygan**, Wi,US
18/D3 **Sheffield**, Eng,UK
33/K2 **Shekhūpura**, Pak.
25/S2 **Shelagskiy** (cape), Rus.
57/H3 **Shelby**, NC,US
25/R3 **Shelekhov** (gulf), Rus.
54/E4 **Shenandoah Nat'l Pk.**, Va,US
29/J3 **Shenyang** (Mukden), China
55/G2 **Sherbrooke**, Qu,Can
50/G4 **Sheridan**, Wy,US
56/D3 **Sherman**, Tx,US
18/F3 **'s Hertogenbosch**, Neth.
50/E2 **Sherwood Park**, Ab,Can
18/D1 **Shetland** (isls.), Sc,UK
51/J4 **Sheyenne** (riv.), ND,US
31/E3 **Shihezi**, China
28/G4 **Shijiazhuang**, China
29/L5 **Shikoku** (isl.), Japan
35/F2 **Shillong**, India
29/M5 **Shimizu**, Japan
29/L5 **Shimonoseki**, Japan
32/F3 **Shiraz**, Iran
30/B2 **Shishou**, China
28/G5 **Shiyan**, China
28/F4 **Shizuishan**, China
29/M5 **Shizuoka**, Japan
21/H3 **Shkodër**, Alb.
34/C4 **Sholapur**, India
56/E3 **Shreveport**, La,US
29/L2 **Shuangyashan**, China
32/B2 **Shubrā al Khaymah**, Egypt
21/K3 **Shumen**, Bul.
31/A3 **Shymkent**, Kaz.
33/H2 **Siāh** (mts.), Afg.
33/K2 **Sialkot**, Pak.
19/K3 **Šiauliai**, Lith.
24/K3 **Siberia** (reg.), Rus.
21/K2 **Sibiu**, Rom.
30/D5 **Sibuyan** (sea), Phil.
21/G4 **Sicily** (isl.), It.
40/E1 **Sidi Bel-Abbès**, Alg.
40/K1 **Sidra** (gulf), Libya
18/G4 **Siegen**, Ger.
62/D3 **Sierra de la Macarena Nat'l Park**, Col.
40/C6 **Sierra Leone**
52/C3 **Sierra Nevada** (mts.), US
62/D2 **Sierra Nevada Nat'l Park**, Ven.
52/E5 **Sierra Vista**, Az,US
29/M2 **Sikhote-Alin'** (mts.), Rus.
34/E2 **Sikkim** (state), India
19/H4 **Silesia** (reg.), Pol.
34/E2 **Silīguri**, India
54/D3 **Simcoe**, On,Can
54/E2 **Simcoe** (lake), On,Can
41/N5 **Simēn** (mts.), Eth.
23/D5 **Simferopol'**, Ukr.
45/C3 **Simpson** (des.), Austl.
32/B3 **Sinai** (pen.), Egypt
36/B3 **Singapore**
36/B3 **Singapore** (cap.), Sing.
36/C3 **Singkawang**, Indo.
23/E5 **Sinop**, Turk.
59/J4 **Sint Maarten** (isl.), NAnt.
29/J3 **Sinŭiju**, NKor.
42/D4 **Sioma Ngwezi Nat'l Park**, Zam.
53/H2 **Sioux City**, Ia,US
51/J5 **Sioux Falls**, SD,US
29/J3 **Siping**, China
21/G4 **Siracusa** (Syracuse), It.
21/K2 **Siret** (riv.), Rom.
35/F3 **Sitākunda**, Bang.
49/D4 **Sitka**, Ak,US
23/E6 **Sivas**, Turk.
41/L2 **Siwah** (oasis), Egypt
34/D2 **Siwalik** (range), India, Nepal
22/D4 **Skagerrak** (str.), Eur.
41/G1 **Skikda**, Alg.
21/K4 **Skiros** (isl.), Gre.
21/J3 **Skopje** (cap.), FYROM
18/C2 **Skye** (isl.), Sc,UK
49/F4 **Slave** (riv.), Can.
21/H2 **Slavonski Brod**, Cro.
57/F4 **Slidell**, La,US
18/B3 **Sligo**, Ire.
21/K3 **Sliven**, Bul.
19/J4 **Slovakia**
21/G2 **Slovenia**
19/J3 **Słupsk**, Pol.
21/J2 **Smederevo**, Yugo.
50/B2 **Smithers**, BC,Can
54/E2 **Smiths Falls**, On,Can
53/G3 **Smoky Hill** (riv.), Ks,US
23/D3 **Smolensk**, Rus.
57/G3 **Smyrna**, Ga,US
50/D5 **Snake** (riv.), US
18/C3 **Snowdon** (mt.), Wal,UK
63/K6 **Sobradinho** (res.), Braz.
23/E5 **Sochi**, Rus.
37/K6 **Society** (isls.), FrPol.
27/E8 **Socotra** (isl.), Yem.
21/J3 **Sofia** (cap.), Bulg.
23/F5 **Sokhumi**, Geo.
62/C1 **Soledad**, Col.
62/E4 **Solimões** (Amazon) (riv.), Braz.
46/E5 **Solomon** (sea)
46/E6 **Solomon Islands**
18/C3 **Solway** (firth), UK
41/Q6 **Somalia**
49/H2 **Somerset** (isl.), NW,Can
20/D1 **Somme** (riv.), Fr.
29/K2 **Songhua** (riv.), China
35/H6 **Songkhla**, Thai.
55/F2 **Sorel**, Qu,Can
63/K8 **Sorocaba**, Braz.
37/H4 **Sorong**, Indo.
19/J4 **Sosnowiec**, Pol.
55/J2 **Souris**, PE,Can
51/H3 **Souris** (riv.), NAm.
45/H7 **South** (isl.), NZ
42/D6 **South Africa**
61/* **South America**
49/J3 **Southampton** (isl.), NW,Can
18/D4 **Southampton**, Eng,UK
45/C3 **South Australia** (state), Austl.
54/C3 **South Bend**, In,US
55/F2 **South Burlington**, Vt,US
57/H3 **South Carolina** (state), US
27/L8 **South China** (sea), Asia
51/H4 **South Dakota** (state), US
45/G7 **Southern Alps** (mts.), NZ
45/B2 **Southesk Tablelands** (plat.), Austl.
43/X **South Georgia** (isl.), Ant.
29/K4 **South Korea**
52/C3 **South Lake Tahoe**, Ca,US
43/W **South Orkney** (isls.), Ant.
24/E5 **South Ossetia** (reg.), Geo.
53/G2 **South Platte** (riv.), US
43/A **South Pole**
43/Y **South Sandwich** (isl.), Ant.
50/F3 **South Saskatchewan** (riv.), Can.
34/E3 **South Suburban**, India
42/E6 **Soweto**, SAfr.
20/B3 **Spain**
59/F4 **Spanish Town**, Jam.
52/C3 **Sparks**, Nv,US
57/H3 **Spartanburg**, SC,US
21/J4 **Sparta** (Spárti), Gre.
45/C4 **Spencer** (gulf), Austl.
24/B2 **Spitsbergen** (isl.), Nor.
21/H3 **Split**, Cro.
50/D4 **Spokane**, Wa,US
30/B5 **Spratly** (isls.)
19/H4 **Spree** (riv.), Ger.
53/J3 **Springdale**, Ar,US
54/B4 **Springfield** (cap.), Il,US
54/F3 **Springfield**, Ma,US
53/J3 **Springfield**, Mo,US
54/D4 **Springfield**, Oh,US
50/C4 **Springfield**, Or,US
54/F3 **Springfield**, Vt,US
55/H2 **Springhill**, NS,Can
50/C3 **Squamish**, BC,Can
33/K3 **Sri Gangānagar**, India
34/D6 **Sri Lanka**
33/K2 **Srinagar**, India
23/E4 **Stakhanov**, Ukr.
54/F3 **Stamford**, Ct,US
64/E7 **Stanley** (cap.), Falk.
41/L8 **Stanley** (falls), D.R. Congo
25/N4 **Stanovoy** (range), Rus.
21/K3 **Stara Zagora**, Bulg.
57/F3 **Starkville**, Ms,US
23/E3 **Staryy Oskol**, Rus.
54/E3 **State College**, Pa,US
57/H3 **Statesboro**, Ga,US
57/H3 **Statesville**, NC,US
54/E4 **Staunton**, Va,US
22/C4 **Stavanger**, Nor.
23/F5 **Stavropol'**, Rus.
53/G2 **Sterling**, Co,US
24/F4 **Sterlitamak**, Rus.
54/D3 **Steubenville**, Oh,US
54/B2 **Stevens Point**, Wi,US
45/G7 **Stewart** (isl.), NZ
53/H3 **Stillwater**, Ok,US
18/D2 **Stirling**, Sc,UK
22/F4 **Stockholm** (cap.), Swe.
18/D3 **Stockport**, Eng,UK
52/B3 **Stockton**, Ca,US
56/C4 **Stockton** (plat.), Tx,US
18/D3 **Stoke-on-Trent**, Eng,UK
25/P2 **Stolbovoy** (isl.), Rus.
55/Q9 **Stoney Creek**, On,Can
19/H3 **Stralsund**, Ger.
20/E1 **Strasbourg**, Fr.
54/D3 **Stratford**, On,Can
21/G4 **Stromboli** (isl.), It.
21/K3 **Sturma** (riv.), Bul.
45/D3 **Sturt** (des.), Austl.
18/G4 **Stuttgart**, Ger.
53/K4 **Stuttgart**, Ar,US
21/H2 **Subotica**, Yugo.
62/E7 **Sucre** (cap.), Bol.
62/G5 **Sucunduri** (riv.), Braz.
63/H7 **Sucuriú** (riv.), Braz.
41/L5 **Sudan**
40/H5 **Sudan** (reg.), Afr.
54/D2 **Sudbury**, On,Can
19/H4 **Sudeten** (mts.), Eur.
32/B3 **Suez**, Egypt
32/B2 **Suez** (canal), Egypt
32/B3 **Suez** (gulf), Egypt
54/E4 **Suffolk**, Va,US
28/F1 **Sühbaatar**, Mong.
36/C5 **Sukabumi**, Indo.
33/J3 **Sukkur**, Pak.
37/G4 **Sula** (isls.), Indo.
33/J3 **Sulaimān** (range), Pak.
37/E4 **Sulawesi** (Celebes) (isl.), Indo.
53/J5 **Sulphur**, La,US
37/E2 **Sulu** (sea), Asia
37/F3 **Sulu** (arch.), Phil.
36/B4 **Sumatra** (isl.), Indo.
37/E5 **Sumba** (isl.), Indo.
37/E5 **Sumba** (str.), Indo.
37/E5 **Sumbawa** (isl.), Indo.
55/J2 **Summerside**, PE,Can
23/K5 **Sumqayıt**, Azer.
57/H3 **Sumter**, SC,US
23/D3 **Sumy**, Ukr.
36/D4 **Sunda** (isls.), Indo.
36/B5 **Sunda** (str.), Indo.
18/D3 **Sunderland**, Eng,UK
25/P3 **Suntar-Khayata** (mts.), Rus.
54/C2 **Superior** (lake), NAm.
54/A2 **Superior**, Wi,US
23/G3 **Sura** (riv.), Rus.
36/D5 **Surabaya**, Indo.
36/D5 **Surakarta**, Indo.
34/B3 **Surat**, India
24/H3 **Surgut**, Rus.
63/G3 **Suriname**
50/C3 **Surrey**, BC,Can
40/H1 **Sūsah**, Tun.
54/E4 **Susquehanna** (riv.), US
46/G6 **Suva** (cap.), Fiji
57/H4 **Suwannee** (riv.), US
29/J5 **Suzhou**, China
24/B2 **Svalbard** (isls.), Nor.
49/G2 **Sverdrup** (isls.), NW,Can
25/P2 **Svyatyy Nos** (cape), Rus.
58/E4 **Swan** (Santanilla) (isls.), Hon.
18/C4 **Swansea**, Wal,UK
42/F6 **Swaziland**
22/E3 **Sweden**
56/C3 **Sweetwater**, Tx,US
50/F5 **Sweetwater** (riv.), Wy,US
50/G3 **Swift Current**, Sk,Can
18/D4 **Swindon**, Eng,UK
20/E2 **Switzerland**
45/E4 **Sydney**, Austl.
55/J2 **Sydney**, NS,Can
54/E3 **Syracuse**, NY,US
24/G5 **Syrdarīya** (riv.), Kaz.
32/C1 **Syria**
32/C2 **Syrian** (des.), Asia
24/G3 **Syzran'**, Rus.
19/H3 **Szczecin**, Pol.
21/J2 **Szeged**, Hun.
21/H2 **Székesfehérvár**, Hun.
21/H2 **Szombathely**, Hun.

T

63/K6 **Tabatinga** (mts.), Braz.
50/E3 **Taber**, Ab,Can
42/F2 **Tabora**, Tanz.
23/G6 **Tabrīz**, Iran
47/K4 **Tabuaeran** (isl.), Kiri.
32/C3 **Tabūk**, SAr.
50/C4 **Tacoma**, Wa,US
62/D7 **Tacora** (vol.), Chile
40/H2 **Tadrart** (mts.), Afr.
29/K4 **T'aebaek** (mts.), NKor., SKor.
29/K4 **Taegu**, SKor.
29/K4 **Taejŏn**, SKor.
40/G3 **Tafassasset, Ténéré du** (reg.), Niger
23/E4 **Taganrog**, Rus.
63/J7 **Taguatinga**, Braz.
20/B4 **Tagus** (riv.), Eur.
47/L6 **Tahiti** (isl.), FrPol.
52/C3 **Tahoe** (lake), US
29/H4 **Tai'an**, China
30/D3 **T'aichung**, Tai.
30/D3 **T'ainan**, Tai.
21/J4 **Tainaron, Akra** (cape), Gre.
30/D2 **T'aipei** (cap.), Tai.
36/B3 **Taiping**, Malay.
30/D3 **Taiwan** (Rep. of China)
30/C3 **Taiwan** (str.), China, Tai.
28/G4 **Taiyuan**, China
32/D6 **Ta'izz**, Yem.
24/H6 **Tajikistan**
32/F1 **Tajrīsh**, Iran
58/C4 **Tajumulco** (vol.), Guat.
29/L5 **Takamatsu**, Japan
29/M4 **Takaoka**, Japan
45/H6 **Takapuna**, NZ
31/D4 **Takla Makan** (des.), China
40/E6 **Takoradi**, Gha.
37/G3 **Taland** (isls.), Indo.
64/B4 **Talca**, Chile
64/B4 **Talcahuano**, Chile
57/G3 **Talladega**, Al,US
57/G4 **Tallahassee** (cap.), Fl,US
19/L2 **Tallinn** (cap.), Est.
33/J1 **Tāloqān**, Afg.
40/E6 **Tamale**, Gha.
23/F3 **Tambov**, Rus.
57/H5 **Tampa**, Fl,US
22/G3 **Tampere**, Fin.
58/B3 **Tampico**, Mex.
41/N5 **Tana** (lake), Eth.
45/C2 **Tanami** (des.), Austl.
64/E4 **Tandil**, Arg.
35/G4 **Tanem** (range), Thai.
40/E3 **Tanezrouft** (des.), Afr.
42/G2 **Tanga**, Tanz.
42/F2 **Tanganyika** (lake), Afr.
31/E5 **Tanggula** (mts.), China
40/D1 **Tangier**, Mor.
29/H4 **Tangshan**, China